THE CONQUEST
OF THE NIGER
BY LAND AND SEA

PRINTED IN GREAT BRITAIN

THE CONQUEST
OF THE NIGER
BY LAND AND SEA

From the Early Explorers and Pioneer Steamships
to Elder Dempster and Company

by

David Hollett

P.M. Heaton Publishing
Abergavenny, Gwent
Great Britain
1995

ISBN 1 872006 04 3

© First Edition April, 1995: D. Hollett

Published by P.M. Heaton Publishing, Abergavenny, Gwent, NP7 9UH
Printed by The Amadeus Press Ltd, Huddersfield, West Yorkshire HD2 1YJ
Typesetting by Highlight Type Bureau Ltd, Shipley, West Yorkshire BD17 7EG

THE AUTHOR

David Hollett has researched the " Conquest of the Niger by Land and Sea" thoroughly. He is uniquely qualified to do so, as he has lived all his life on Merseyside and has his roots deeply embedded in the maritime history of the area. Married, and with two daughters, his forbears include seven master mariners who served in famous Liverpool and Cumbrian sailing vessels, engaged in the Cape Horn South Pacific Trade, the West Indies Trade - and as commanders in the celebrated fleet of Brocklebank Indiamen.

His published books include "From Cumberland to Cape Horn" - the history of the Sailing Fleet of Thomas & John Brocklebank of Whitehaven and Liverpool 1770 1900, and the early history of their associated Company Robert & Henry Jefferson of Whitehaven, Plantation Owners, Merchants and Shipowners - established 1734; "Fast Passage to Australia - the history of the Black Ball, Eagle, and White Star Lines of Australian packets; " Merseyside & the 19th Century Emigrant Trade to Australia; and "Men of Iron" the history of the world-famous shipbuilding yard of Cammell Laird & Company. His last book, published in 1993, was "The Alabama Affair" which dealt with the involvement of Britain in the American Civil War. It was in fact while David Hollett was researching the history of Cammell Laird & Company that he resolved to write this book - which covers the story of the most controversial vessels built by the firm: the Confederate raider *Alabama*, the infamous "Laird Rams" - and various other vessels, built by the firm to serve the Confederacy - a regime which was constitutionally committed to perpetuating and extending slavery.

His interest in the Niger was also stirred to active research when writing the history of Cammell Laird & Company, for it was Macgregor Laird, younger brother of John Laird the shipbuilder, and an outspoken opponent of slavery, who was the first to establish steamship navigation on this great African river- his African Steamship Company eventually evolving into the world-famous Elder Dempster shipping enterprise.

ACKNOWLEDGEMENTS

The Author wishes to thank:

Mr A.J. Worthington, Director of Leisure Services and Tourism, Metropolitan Borough of Wirral, and Mr Howard Mortimer of this Department.

Mr David Hillhouse, Senior Museums Officer, Metropolitan Borough of Wirral.

Mr Colin Simpson, Curator of the Williamson Art Gallery and Museum, Birkenhead.

Miss Carol Bidston and staff, at Birkenhead Central Reference Library.

Liverpool Central Library and Record Office.

Liverpool University Library.

Colindale Newspaper Library, London.

Mrs Mary Garston of Pantymwyn, North Wales, for proof reading.

Mr John Maude, for details of the Briggs/Maude family.

My wife, Vera, who gave assistance whilst I was producing this book

My daughter, Tina Hollett, for the drawing of Dr. William Balfour Baikie

By the same author:

From Cumberland to Cape Horn - The Complete History of the Sailing Fleet of Thomas and John Brocklebank of Whitehaven and Liverpool, and the early history of their associated Company Robert and Henry Jefferson of Whitehaven. Published by Fairplay Publications Limited, 1984.

Fast Passage to Australia - The History of the Black Ball, Eagle, and White Star Lines of Australian Packets, also published by Fairplay Publications. 1986

Birkenhead and the Nineteenth Century Emigrant Trade to Australia. Published in conjunction with the Australian Bicentennial Exhibition 1988, at the Williamson Art Gallery & Museum, Birkenhead, and published by the Metropolitan Borough of Wirral.

Men of Iron - The Story of Cammel Laird Shipbuilders, 1828 - 1829 Published by Countyvise Limited, and the Metropolitan Borough of Wirral, 1992

The Alabama Affair - The British Shipyards Conspiracy in the American Civil War. Published by Sigma Leisure, 1993

LIST OF ILLUSTRATIONS

7

8

CONTENTS

PREFACE

For countless thousands of years the people of Africa have lived alongside the great River Niger, but until the early years of the last century the source, direction, and outlet of this great stream remained a mystery to the outside world. The Niger actually runs for over 2,000 miles, passing through a land of humid tropical heat, dense forests of cotton-trees, then endless wastes of mangrove swamps, where it finally reaches the Atlantic in the Bight of Benin. For centuries rumours of the fertility and wealth of the area attracted travellers and adventurers, from Arab and European nations, south across the barren wastes of the Sahara, and then along the west coast of Africa in sailing ships. Many did not return, for the Niger was guarded by a deadly insect, the malaria carrying mosquito, to which disease white men had little resistance. Due to this factor the Bight of Benin, and the Niger Country, soon became known as the "White Man's Grave." Undeterred, the travellers persisted.

British interest in the Niger region goes back a long way, but was greatly increased by the sight of gold that reached the coast after the Moorish conquest of Timbuctoo. Participation in the notorious Slave Trade, emanating from this area, was soon to follow, but this activity was confined to the coast. Travellers' tales continued to tell of the great waterway far in the interior, but of its course and outlet none knew. Finally, in 1788, the African Association was formed, with the express purpose of tracing the Niger. Mungo Park, after much suffering, eventually reached the river, only to lose his life later - in 1805 - at hostile hands, when trying to pass through the great gorge at Bussa. Others, including Clapperton and Denham, took up the quest, crossed the Sahara, and discovered Kano and Sokoto, and also proved that the Niger was not, as had been supposed, a tributary of the Nile.

Finally, Richard Lemon Lander, a domestic servant from Cornwall, with his brother John, undertook a further expedition to explore the course and termination of the Niger, this being in 1830. They soon reached Bussa, where Mungo Park had met his fate, and then commenced the descent of the great river in canoes. Eventually they penetrated the forest clad delta, arriving in the Nun branch of the Niger, in the Bight of Benin. At last, they had set at rest the question of the course and outlet of the great and mysterious river Quorra - the Arabic name for the Niger - the Nile of the Negroes.

There was one man in particular who saw in the Landers' discovery an event of far reaching importance, this being Macgregor Laird, merchant, and outspoken opponent of slavery. To him a great highway into the interior of Africa was now opened up, a highway for legitimate trade, which would rapidly develop until it replaced the slave trade. Son of William Laird, and brother of John Laird, the shipbuilders, Macgregor Laird soon joined forces with other merchants from Liverpool, who formed an association with the objective of sending an expedition, under the guidance of Richard Lander, to ascend the Niger. Macgregor Laird, then just twenty three years old, organising the construction of the required steamships.

In 1832 preparations for the expedition were completed. Two steamships, the Quorra and the Alburka, and a small brig, the Columbine, with a total crew of 49, leaving England that year. At the last moment Macgregor Laird decided to join the expedition. The loss of life on this historic voyage was enormous - Lander was to die in Africa - and Laird was to be among the few survivors. In fact he returned to England more dead than alive, his health permanently undermined by fever, but he never lost his interest in Africa - or his love and respect for the Africans; and his firm conviction that the development of legitimate trade was the only realistic way to end the trade in slaves. From this point on the history of the Niger was to be inextricably linked with the development of the steamship.

Other steamship expeditions soon followed, a fully equipped government backed expedition leaving for the Niger in 1841; with the blessing of Queen Victoria, and the active support of the Prince Consort, in ships built by John Laird. This was joined by a young African teacher - afterwards to become the famous Bishop Crowther, of the Niger. Once again though many were to die on this expedition, but the river had been proved navigable for hundreds of miles, although by and large the expedition - which Macgregor Laird had opposed - was considered a failure. However, undaunted, Macgregor Laird, with others, then established the African Steamship Company in 1852.

Two years later he founded another steamship enterprise trading to Africa, the Central Africa Company. and related to this organised another expedition to the Niger, for which his brother John built the exploration vessel Pleiad. Doctor William Balfour Baikie was given command of this expedition, but the risk, main expense and administration were to rest on Macgregor Laird. The injunction being to send a small steamer up the Niger, to its confluence with the Chadda, and then explore the latter stream. In 1857, yet another Laird built exploration vessel, the Dayspring was sent up the great river. This expedition though was to end in disaster, for whilst trying to force a passage through the gorge near Rabba, the ship was wrecked, leaving the crew stranded for many months in the interior.

Macgregor Laird died in 1861, but his memory lives on, notably because the shipping enterprises he established later evolved into the famous firm of Elder, Dempster & Company. In part, this is the story of this merchant, and his early steamships, and the many expeditions and developments he was associated with. It is though, much more than this, as it is also the story of the great Niger River itself, and West Africa, the early explorers, merchants and missionaries, slave traders, and opponents of this trade, brutality and compassion, in the long and bitter scramble for wealth, religious influence and political domination on the continent of Africa.

David Hollett
April, 1995

12

CHAPTER ONE   THE NIGER COUNTRY

Until the 1830's the source, direction and mouth of the River Niger - 'The Nile of the Negroes' - remained a mystery to mankind. Solving this mystery though was no easy task, for the Niger Country was protected by a lethal climate, and a malaria carrying insect - the mosquito! To the north there was the great physical barrier of the Sahara Desert, whilst to the south lay almost impenetrable rain forests. On the coast itself, in the great geographical indentation known as the Gulf of Guinea, there was no visible signs of one large river - that could be positively identified as the Niger - discharging into the Atlantic. The reason for this is that the great river divides here into scores of creeks, in a vast mangrove delta. Which, if any, of these creeks was the Niger?

African people have lived in the Niger region for countless centuries, and travellers who made their way south across the Sahara, or east from the west African coast, eventually came across a great river, but this did not provide a solution to the aforementioned mystery. So far as the source is concerned, we now know that the Niger rises on the eastern slopes of the Fouta Djallon Mountains, less than 200 miles from the Atlantic Ocean, and then flows away from the sea, traversing the southern edge of the Sahara Desert, finally looping southwards, to eventually arrive at the Gulf of Guinea, after a journey of some 2,600 miles. The strange course of the Niger is explained by the fact that the present day river is the result of a union between two ancient rivers, the Upper Niger, once known as the Djoliba, which once continued far northward into the Sahara, and then emptied into a great salt lake, the Djouf, which dried up centuries ago. The Lower Niger, on the other hand, known for hundreds of years by the Arabic name of Quorra, once had its source in the now arid Ahaggar Mountains, in the heart of the great desert. All of this does much to explain why the ancients had such difficulty in resolving matters concerning the Niger. Amongst the first great historians to offer information on the river was the celebrated Greek traveller and writer, Herodotus.

Herodotus was born at Cappadocia in 484 B.C. He was to become generally known as "the Father of History," for it was he who tried to give a history of the world, so far as it was then known. His main work was in nine books, written in the Ionic dialect. It dealt with the early history of Persia, Lydia and Egypt, but its main theme is the struggle between the Greeks and Persians. At the time he wrote, the "civilised world" was almost entirely gathered in those countries which lie around the Eastern end of the Mediterranean. However, despite his strong reservations about nations that were any distance from the sea that touched the coast of Greece, he travelled extensively.

Of interest to students of the Niger is the fact that in his famous 'Geography of Africa' Herodotus stated that some young Nasamonians, a people who then dwelt in the north of Africa, on the borders of the Mediterranean, travelled in a westerly direction from a part of Egypt, until they came to a large river full of crocodiles, and flowing towards the rising sun, and they were then taken by the local people to a large city, situated on its banks. Had these early adventurers reached the legendary river Niger? A Roman was the next in line to offer his views on the issue - to the civilised world bordering the Mediterranean.

The Roman writer Gaius Plinius Secundus, better known as Pliny, who was born in A.D. 23 had some interesting , and imaginative, theories on the Niger. After conducting it from its source in lower Mauretania, through sandy deserts, sometimes flowing over them, and sometimes beneath them, he brought it to the Nile of Egypt, concluding, with complete confidence, that the Niger and the Nile were one and the same river! This view, incidentally, coinciding with the original opinion of Herodotus. However, these fanciful notions were refuted by a more reasonable geographer of his time, Mela , who, while almost agreeing with the aforementioned experts, as to the source of the Niger, after making it flow from west to east, acknowledged his own ignorance, with becoming candour. No one, he stated, really knew what became of the great river, once it reached the centre of Africa. Mela justly depreciated the fabulous notion of the Niger flowing beneath the Sahara, then becoming the Nile, correctly attributing such opinions to the want of any real knowledge.

The Egyptian astronomer and Geographer, Claudius Ptolemaeus, better known as Ptolemy, A.D. 127 - 51 also had some remarkable opinions on the great river. Interestingly, in the light of modern knowledge about the Niger, he stated that the river flowed past the centre of the continent, losing itself in a great central reservoir, like the Caspian Sea, called Wangara. Could this have been the aforementioned lake Djouf ? And was Ptolemy merely repeating an earlier, and correct, opinion about the original destination of the upper Niger?

It was to be about the year 900 A.D. that the Arab followers of Mahommed first reached the Niger. They introduced Islam, at first on a voluntary basis, then forced their religion on the negroes of the area. Trading caravans and the slave trade were then introduced. From this start the great Moslem empire of Songay was to be founded, with its dominions extending westward all the way from Sokoto to Bojador. The extent of this trans-Sahara slave trade could later be gauged from one fact. During the 19th Century great caravans of up to 10,000 camels would leave Morrocco each year, bound for Timbuctoo. Each beast would carry out a load valued at £50 - but the bulk of the return 'cargo' would be slaves, suffering under horrific conditions. Those who fell from exhaustion, as many did, were promptly shot.

Despite the establishment of this empire on the Niger, the mystery surrounding the river's source, route and ultimate destination remained. El Adrisi, circa 1153, was next in line to add to the confusion, by stating, with great confidence, but little supporting evidence, that the great river, which he called the 'Nile of the Negroes,' rose at a place close to the source of the Nile, then flowed west across Africa into the Atlantic. The great Arab traveller, Ibn Batuta was soon to reach the Niger, and offer his views on the route of the river. Born in Tangiers in 1304, this remarkable Arab traveller covered an estimated distance of more than 75,000 miles during his 28 years of travelling. After visiting China and many other places, in 1349 the Moor was back in his native land. Like Marco Polo, he had been absent for twenty -four years. But one more great adventure lay ahead of him, he was to traverse the Sahara to the River Niger, which he called the Nile, down which he sailed to Timbuctoo, stating, correctly, that it flowed to the east!

On his return, his travels were soon brought to the attention of the Sultan of Morocco, who promptly ordered Batuta to dictate an account of his adventures to his secretary. Some centuries later this document was obtained by the French, and then this saga became common knowledge internationally. One can only admire the courage and stamina of these early travellers, who undertook their long and difficult journeys with little support, and no hope of rescue, should things go wrong.

Soon the Portuguese were to venture close to the Niger and the Slave Coast, but by sea, not by the overland route. The prospect of obtaining gold being the main attraction. This desirable commodity was reaching the European market, well before the 15th century, and it was coming from Africa! Apparently it was coming from the hinterland of the Magreb, where Arab travellers were obtaining it from Negro traders. Not surprisingly the Portuguese hit on the idea of trying to find the source of supply, and cutting out the Arab middlemen. Added to this, Spanish and Portuguese merchants were also most anxious to discover a direct sea route to India, which would likewise also enable them to avoid Arab intermediaries. By 1471 the gold trade had been opened up at Mina and trade expeditions were sent out each winter. It was to be during the winter of 1472 - 3 that Fernao do Po and Pero de Cintra first explored the Bights of Biafra and Benin.

Of the European peoples the Portuguese were to have the honour of leading the way in discovering many new lands. By the middle of the 15th century they had reached Cape Verd, and seen men with skins as black as ebony. It was then that it occurred to the sagacious mind of Prince Henry of Portugal that India could perhaps be reached by following the African coast. Henry, Prince of Portugal, called the Navigator, was the son of John 1. and, through his mother, a grandson of John of Gaunt, Duke of Lancaster. He was born in Oporto, March 4, 1394. Most of his life was to be spent at Sagres. There he built an observatory, and in many other ways began to aid the infant science of navigation. Most importantly though, he organised the funding of a succession of voyages of exploration to the Asian and African coasts.

In 1486 Prince Henry sent out Bartholomew Diaz on a voyage which took him almost to the mouth of the Orange River of South Africa, which rises in the Drakensberg range, and then flows 1300 miles to the coast, reaching the Atlantic at a point 45 miles north of Port Nolloth. On resuming his voyage Diaz encountered a violent storm, which drove him round the Cape of Good Hope, and he anchored in Algoa Bay. It was at this point that his crew decided that enough was enough, and refused to go any further! He returned home, and then had the vexation of seeing command of the next expedition given to Vasco Da Gama.

Da Gama, the greatest of all the Portuguese navigators, set out in July, 1497. Despite adverse weather, and a mutinous crew, he rounded the Cape by the end of the year. He hugged the coast as far as Melinda, then sailed straight across the Indian Ocean, landing at Calicut in May, 1498. He was subsequently employed several times by the King of Portugal to establish colonies on the coast of Africa and India.

It was though by 1480 that the Portuguese had virtually completed their exploration of the west coast of Africa, and gold from Mina and peppers from Benin began to flow north to Europe. To strengthen their monopoly in this new trading development the Portuguese had also, previous to this, had the commendable foresight to call on the services of religion and the Pope . Obligingly, he had given them Papal Bulls about their 'rights' on the coast in 1451, 1455 and 1456. These official decrees of the Pope were primarily obtained to keep down the Castilians who, between 1450 and 1475 had also made regular trading voyages to the coast of Africa.

In 1483, John 11 modestly declared himself to be the "Lord of Guinea" but in reality this very impressive title meant very little. His actual control over these lands extended no further than the coastal forts his nation had established, in particular "San Jorge da Mina" which they had built to provision their ships on the long voyage to the East. Both Spain and Portugal were strongly Catholic countries, and apart from commercial reasons their desire to spread their religion throughout the world was to play a dominant role in future developments in Africa. Spain had recently expelled Moslems, and both Spain and Portugal still feared counter-attacks for this from Morocco. The establishment of Christianity in Africa, as an ideological force, would therefore strengthen their position enormously, against their religious and trading adversaries.

In 1481 the Gold Coast was eventually reached by the Portuguese, who extended their discoveries east until they reached the swamps of the great

Above: A 'CARAVEL' OF THE
GENOESE STYLE
The type of sailing vessel of the 15th
and 16th centuries in which the early
Portuguese and English voyages were
made to the coast of West Africa

Left: VASCO DA GAMA
The Portuguese navigator who first
sailed round the Cape of Good Hope
to East Africa and India

delta of the Niger. There they traded, totally unaware that this mass of creeks constituted the many mouths of the legendary river, whose fabled wealth had fired the imagination of the adventurous men of many nations for centuries. It was also in this year that Edward 1V. of England prohibited the fitting out of an expedition to Guinea organised by John Tintam and William Fabian at Bristol. This expedition was doubtless inspired by the Duke Medina Sidonia as an unfriendly act against Portugal, and Jao 11 of Portugal sent over his ambassador, Ruy de Sousa to explain to his cousin, Edward 1V. of England that sending expeditions to the coast of Africa was against the orders of the Pope, whereupon Edward commanded his Bristol men to desist. But when the reformation came, and England had no goodwill of the Pope's to lose, expeditions were to set off to the West Coast, as a prelude to Britain extending her influence over the entire African continent.

The Slave Coast, so called from the great number of slaves that were to be exported from this part of Africa, extended from the River Volta, on the west, to the Niger Delta, in the Gulf of Benin, in the east. Between these two rivers, the Atlantic Ocean on the south, and the area then known as the "Kong Mountains" on the north, were included the three kingdoms of Dehomi, Yoruba, and Benin. These states though were soon to be broken up into many small independent communities, having little or no traditional knowledge of the more extended organisations which once existed among their forefathers. Above all other factors, the Slave Trade was soon to be responsible for this rapid deterioration in the social structure of Africa. The brutal measures which were to be employed in carrying on this trade, on a very extensive scale, were, in themselves, quite sufficient to undermine the foundations of any nation in the world.

For many years slaves were to be procurred by the more powerful chiefs by waging war on their less powerful neighbours, for this express purpose. As soon as these external supplies began to fail, the larger communities began to prey on their own people. Those convicted of crimes found their sentences commuted into a Bill of Sale, and loaded onto the slaving vessels. If the supply of genuine criminals began to slow down, false accusations were rapidly brought forward, the charge of witchcraft being a convenient, and much used accusation. Not surprisingly, distrust and suspicion grew, soon making it impossible for these communities to live together in harmony. All of this contributed to the downfall of existing African governments. From the time that the white men first appeared on these shores, bringing with them the products of a more advanced society, those in a powerful position in African Society courted their favour, all in order to secure for themselves a share of these treasures.

Portuguese influence now began to spread along the coast of Africa, Benin, the most easterly of the Niger provinces, being discovered by the

Portuguese explorer Alfonso de Aviro in 1485. At this point in time it was at the height of its power. and was probably the ultimate destination of caravans from the north. It had a highly developed art, in the form of bronzes, a large standing army, and a sophisticated administration.. The Portuguese began by buying natural products such as pepper, but almost at once slaves were to become the main object of trade - with Benin and all along the coast to its east.

When Alfonso de Aviro at last made his way back to his native land, he was accompanied by an Ambassador from the King of Benin to the Court of Portugal, with the request that Christian Missionaries should be sent out to instruct the people of Benin in the principles of the Christian faith. Portugal wasted no time in responding to this request, Fernao do Po being dispatched immediately to the Gulf of Benin. Here he discovered the beautiful island that was to bear his name, and then he made his way up the Benin River. At a place called Gaton he founded a small settlement, built a church, and rapidly converted a thousand people to the Catholic faith.

The slave trade from Africa really has its origins with the Spanish, who, on taking possession of many islands in the West Indies, forced the native Caribs to work the mines of Hispaniola. The labour was cruel, dangerous and exhausting, and the Caribs suffered, died, and almost became extinct. The Portuguese moved in, and as early as 1503 a few slaves were sent by them to the Spanish colonies. In 1511 Ferdinand V. of Spain, is said to have permitted an importation of negroes into the colonies, but Cardinal Ximes, who held the reins of government was opposed to the trade. Things were soon to change though, after the accession of Charles V. of Spain, who, it should be added, was also sovereign of Germany and the Netherlands. He promptly granted an exclusive patent to several members of the Flemish nobility, to import four thousand Africans annually, into Hispaniola, Cuba, Jamaica, and Porto Rico. Ironically though, it was an eminent Spanish divine, Bartholomew Las Casas, who was to be the prime mover in this sad development.

Las Casas was born at Seville, in the year 1474; and at the age of nineteen, accompanied his father to the West Indies. At this time Rodrigo Albuquerque ruled in Hispaniola, which the Spanish still regarded as their principal colony. Albuquerque was a violent and greedy man, under whose rule the native Indians led a miserable life. Worked to the point of exhaustion, and subjected to brutal treatment, they were almost exterminated. To their eternal credit the missionaries stood in opposition to the whole system of splitting up the Indians and placing them at the disposal of the Spanish settlers, by which means they became the slaves of the conquerors. The Dominicans, in particular, had strongly protested against the "repartimientos" (or sharing) as it was termed; denouncing those involved both in private, and from the pulpit. Bartholomew Las Casas soon became a leading light in this campaign. With great courage he remonstrated with Albuquerque upon his conduct; but found this tyrant was not the least bit sympathetic to humanitarian considerations. His attention seemed to be focused on one thing - the acquiring of as much gold as possible! Faced with this impossible situation Las Casas decided to go back to Spain in order to lay his complaint at the feet of Ferdinand.

After a long and difficult voyage Las Casas eventually arrived in Cadiz, and quickly obtained an interview with his sovereign, whom he found to be in a very poor state of health. Ferdinand listened carefully to all that Las Casas had to say about the sufferings endured by the natives of the West Indies under his rule, assured Las Casas that he felt very guilty about his own role in these developments; and finally, he promised to take steps which would put matters right. Unfortunately though Ferdinand then died, and he was succeeded by Charles V. of Germany, who appointed Cardinal Ximenes his regent. Las Casas wasted no time, promptly obtaining an interview with Ximenes.

He put his case so well that Ximenes appointed a commission of monks from St. Jerome to go to the West Indies, directing Las Casas to go with them, holding the title of "Protector of the Indians." Upon their arrival they proceeded with caution to investigate the matter, eventually coming to the conclusion that the Spanish had two options. The first being to give up their American conquests, or be satisfied with very little gain. The second being to tolerate the system of slavery, but try to ensure that the Indians were not treated so brutally. All were satisfied with these proceedings - except Las Casas - who continued to campaign for total exemption. This stance upset the planters, to the extent that he had to retire into a convent to preserve his life. Eventually he made his way back to Spain, once more putting his case to the highest in the land, who agreed to appoint a further commission, but Las Casas knew that they would meet with great opposition, and fail. It was at this point that he hit on another idea which would help save the natives of the West Indies, the introduction of stronger labourers into the islands in lieu of the Indians!

This plan was put before the Council in Spain, and although strongly resisted by Cardinal Ximenes, who rightly considered it wrong that an innocent people should be condemned to perpetual slavery to save another, the measure was carried by a majority of voices, and Charles granted a patent to a favourite courtier, empowering him to purchase slaves in West Africa, and ship them to the West Indies. This patent was then purchased by some Genoese merchants, who immediately put it into execution, and thus began the detestable "Slave Trade." It was in this way that men calling themselves *Christians*, and professing to follow the doctrines of their divine Master, conveniently set on one side his great humanitarian precept - " Do unto others as you would have others do unto you."

The reasoning by which Las Casas defended his position was to argue, arithmetically, that as one strong negro would perform the labour of four weaker Indians, the substitution would effect a four-fold diminution of human suffering! His concern for the Indians was clearly obscuring his judgement. So impressed with the miseries he had seen in the West Indies, he was completely overlooking the tremendous miseries his "remedy" would, inevitably, cause.

At first the number of Africans allowed to be imported was limited to four thousand per annum, but they proved to be so strong, and worked so well, that this limitation was soon put on one side; and in the course of another century all the European Colonies in the New World were engaged in enslaving the peoples of Africa. Thus the notorious slave trade was originated from the best of motives by Bartholomew de Las Casas, Bishop of Chiapa, a tender and devout man, attempting to mitigate the sufferings of the Indians, who were sinking by the thousands under the unwonted toil imposed upon them in the gold mines of the New World. This sad development was to have the most profound impact on the history of Africa in general, and on the Niger Region and the Slave Coast in particular.

So far as the actual exploration of the Niger region is concerned, the next person of historical note to reach the great river was Al-Hassan Ibn-Mohammed Al-Wezaz Al-Fazi, a Moor, baptised as Giovanni Leone, but better known as Leo Africanus. His written works on Africa being "Done into English in the year 1600." A native of Grenada, the last Moslem stronghold in Spain, he was born , according to Doctor Robert Brown, of the Hakluyt Society, c 1494-95. Other historians give a different date. However, what is clear is, that after the surrender of the Moors to Ferdinand and Isabella, Leo Africanus moved to Fez with his parents. Who his father was we are not told, except that he owned land. Leo's uncle was obviously a person of great consequence, for he was sent as an Ambassador from the King of Fez, to the King of Timbuctoo, and had a wide reputation for being "an excellent Oratour and a most wittie Poet."

In Fez Leo studied, and then began to travel, financing his expeditions with legal work. In 1518 he was on board an Arab galley, off the coast of Tunisia, when it was captured by Christian Corsairs. His captors were so impressed with his learning that they presented him to the Pope, Leo X, son of Lorenzo the Magnificent. The Pope decided to free the young Moor, and then persuaded him to become a Christian. His conversion completed, the Medici Pope baptized him Giovanni Leone, giving him his own name. Under the influence of the Pope, Leo mastered Italian and agreed to write the aforementioned account of his travels - for he had made two notable trips into Africa, south of the Sahara, between 1510 and 1518. So far as the Niger is concerned, Leo Africanus only managed to add to the confusion, assigning a westerly course to the great river - thus confirming the mistake made four centuries earlier by Al-Idrisi.

However, his published account of Africa gave Europeans the first eyewitness account of the interior of "The Dark Continent." His graphic observations on the legendary city of Timbuctoo, and many other places, make fascinating reading, but in the context of this work on the Niger his comments regarding the great river are worth quoting:-

" This lande of the Negros hath a mightie riuer, which taking his name of the region, is called Niger: this riuer taketh his originall from the east out of a certain desert called by the foresaide Negros Sen. Others will haue this riuer to spring out of a certaine lake, and so to run westward till it exonerateth it selfe into the Ocean sea. Our Cosmographers affirme that the said riuer of Niger is deriued out of Nilus, which they imagine for some certaine space to be swallowed vp of the earth, and yet at last to burst forth into such a lake as is before mentioned. "

It was not until Mungo Park eventually saw the current of the Niger flowing east that this error was, at long last, corrected. But all of this lay far ahead in the future. In the meantime, in the face of such solid evidence, most European maps of Africa, published after 1600, showed the Niger flowing to the west.

The deliberate and conscious exploration of Africa by Europeans started in the fifteenth century. Many were involved, but the lead given by Henry the Navigator, made the Portuguese role the dominant one. The lust for gold, which was said to exist beyond the Sahara, providing the main motivation for all this effort and risk. However, it has to be said, Henry had other, less mercenary motives. He was fascinated by tales of a lost Kingdom. All of this being based on Prester John, legendary 12th century figure, who, it was said, had established a kingdom in the Far East. He is referred to in many medieval traveller's tales, and attempts have been made to show that Prester John was the ruler of a state in Abyssinia. Eventually the Portuguese navigators completed their exploration of the West Coast, pushed round the Cape of Good Hope, and found in Abyssinia, what satisfied them - evidence of Prester John. The Portuguese then fought to stop a violent Moslem attack on the Abyssinian Kingdom, but the resulting friendly feelings of the Abyssinians towards these Europeans was soon lost due to the over-enthusiastic crusading zeal of the Jesuits. The Abyssinians, backed by the Coptic Church, closed the country to Europeans. By 1530 the first drive to the interior was over.

Meanwhile, the flow of negro slaves, from Africa, to Hispaniola, Cuba, Jamaica, and Porto Rico, continued unabated. In Spain Charles V. still ruled, perhaps at first, still unaware of the suffering attending this traffic. At last though it dawned on him just how bad things were, and to his eternal credit he acted.   In 1542 he made a code of laws for his Indian subjects, and he liberated all the negro slaves, at one fell swoop putting an end to slavery. Unfortunately though, he then made the mistake of resigning his crown, and retiring into a monastery. His Minister of Mercy, Pedro de la Gasca, then returned to Spain, leaving the brutal colonial oppressors free to enslave the freed negroes once more.

Soon after this sad development the first English ships reached the Benin river on the West Coast of Africa, this being in 1553, and the long British connection with the Niger region was begun.

These ships were under the command of Captain Thomas Wyndham, but were piloted by a Portuguese navigator, Anes Pinteado, who, by all accounts, was very badly treated by Wyndham and all the other Englishmen. Pinteado guided the ships into the mouth of the Benin river, the anchors were dropped and the vessels remained there.   With the squadron was a small group of English merchants, anxious to establish trade links.   Pinteado and these men took a small boat, and made their way up-river for a distance of about 150 miles, before leaving the river and making their way across country to the city of Benin.   The king gave them a warm welcome, after which they settled down to trade for the next month, obtaining during this period about 80 tons of pepper.   Meanwhile, back at the mouth of the river the men of Wyndham's Squadron were dying at an alarming rate, sometimes as many as three or four a day. The cause being put down to agues and fever , although malaria was probably the main killer, for which the Europeans had no natural resistance. In something of a panic Wyndham sent a further party up-river to recall Pinteado and the merchants.

When this party eventually reached Benin they discovered that the merchants were most reluctant to make a rapid departure, as more pepper was arriving for them every day. Faced with this difficult situation Anes Pinteado decided to go back to the ships to prevail on Wyndham to wait a little longer, but when he arrived he discovered he was already dead.   The survivors were in no mood to wait. Pinteado pleaded with them to let him return to Benin, explain the situation to the merchants, and bring them back to the ships. This was refused, so Pinteado wrote them a note, promising to come back and rescue them, within a week though he was dead. The ships then made their way back to England, crewed by the forty survivors, 100 out of 140 who sailed having died.   This high rate of mortality for Europeans who came to the West Coast was to continue for centuries, a total lack of resistance to tropical diseases, in particular malaria, being the problem. It was this factor that was to make the Bight of Benin infamous, the whole area soon becoming known as the "White Man's Grave."   Fortunes were soon to be made here by Europeans, firstly from the notorious slave trade, and then from legitimate trade - but the risks were enormous, and the chances of surviving a long stay on "The Coast" extremely limited.

However, the disasters of this particular voyage were mainly attributed to Wyndham, so next year another group of merchants - Sir George Barnes, Sir John Yorke, Thomas Lok, Antony Hickman, and Edward Castelin - associated themselves and sent out another expedition to the West Coast. On the 11th October, 1554, they sailed from the Thames, the ships being the *John Evangelist, Bartholomew* and *Trinity.* This expedition was far more successful than Wyndham's. It brought home over 400lb of gold, 250 elephants teeth, (tusks) of various sizes, and 36 butts of Guinea pepper. In addition to these desirable treasures Mr Lok also brought back the complete head of an elephant, which proved to be an exciting curiosity throughout England. Encouraged by this successful expedition to the Coast, others were soon organised. The prime mover in the next three in fact being Towrson. The first of these being made in 1555 from Newport, in the Isle of Wight, with two ships, the *Hind* and the *Art*, their destination being the River Sestos, in Guinea. This was a very successful voyage. The second voyage was in 1556, made in the *Tyger*, of London, 120 tons, commanded by Towrson; the *Hart*, of London, Captain John Skirl; and a small pinnace of just 16 tons, Captain John Davies. A notable feature of this expedition being the fact that Towrson took back with him on this expedition the Africans that he had brought home to England on his former voyage.

The third voyage of Towrson was made in 1557, the four ships being the *Minion, Christopher, Tyger*, and *Unicorn.* The passage out was interesting, for on the way they fell in with two large vessels from Hamburg, which Mr Towrson seized and looted! He then fell foul of five Portuguese ships, but survived. No doubt encouraged by this, he then went in search of four French ships he had heard were on the Coast, his intention being to drive them from the trade. Continuing what was clearly becoming his own private war with other European powers, he found three, two escaped; but the third, the *Mulet*, he captured. She proved to be a valuable prize, Towrson and his companions finding on board 50lbs of gold. He then began trading on the Coast, with a good measure of success, after which he set sail for England. Further adventures lay ahead of them, for when they were off the Cape Verde islands the *Tyger* began to leak badly. The cargo was put on board the remaining ships and she was abandoned. This loss was perhaps not to be regretted, for their stay on the Coast had reduced the number of fit survivors to just thirty men, leaving just ten per ship to bring the vessels back. The *Christopher* and *Minion* parted off Vigo, the *Minion* eventually reaching the Isle of Wight with just six mariners and six merchants able to work the ship. Despite the loss of life, the voyages of Towrson's were financially encouraging. Other merchants soon began to fit further trading ships, but apart from an odd reference, little detail remains about their adventures.

It is though from these voyages that the British slave Trade began, for John Lok, who had brought the five negroes mentioned above, back from Africa, had actually tried to sell them in London! This, however, had shocked the English people, and it was public pressure that had obliged Towrson to take the captured men back to their native land. Five years later though the English conscience had grown less sensitive, when John Hawkins, that man of many contradictory qualities sailed for the coast of Africa, with three ships, and purchased 300 negroes, selling them into slavery in the West Indies at a great profit. It was undoubtedly Hawkins, slaver, buccaneer, hero - and fervent Christian, who inaugurated the iniquitous commerce in human flesh which was to lead to the exploitation of Africa by England.

John Hawkins was born at Plymouth in 1532, he was the son of a sailor and went to sea when he was a boy. It was in 1562 that he obtained command of the ship that took the aforementioned slaves to the West Indies. In 1567 he led a small fleet of ships on the same mission, that other great British naval hero, Drake, being one of his officers. On this voyage he managed to do a great deal of looting and plundering, but lost these ill-gotten gains in a fight with the Spaniards, and narrowly escaped with his life. He later became an M.P. for Plymouth in 1572, and served as comptroller of the navy whilst at the same time carrying on a shipbuilding business at Deptford. He commanded his own ship, the *Victory* against the Spanish in 1588, and was knighted. Hawkins then joined various looting expeditions, and he was with Drake when he died off Porto Rico in November, 1595.

It is interesting to note here though, that in 1592, just three years before he died, Sir John Hawkins was so ashamed of what he had done by introducing the slave trade to his countrymen, who had eagerly pursued it, that he decided to build a hospital at Rochester, to atone, in some very small measure, for his violation of the laws of humanity.

Queen Elizabeth though had been most impressed with Hawkin's first venture, this to the extent that she had invested funds in one of his later slaving expeditions, on which John Hawkins had sold 500 negroes into slavery. In the same year that Sir John built his hospital Queen Elizabeth issued another patent for the West African trade to Thomas Gregory and others of Taunton, for traffic between the rivers Nunez and Sierra Leone. These patents ran only for a period of ten years and were revokable by the Queen or Privy Council on six months' notice. However, this seal of approval having been put on the trade it was not long before Bristol merchants began to fit out ships, and the commerce extended to an alarming extent.

The increasing value of this trade now began to be recognised in England, and in 1618 a Royal Charter was granted by King James 1. to " The Company of the Adventurers of London trading into Africa." Sir Robert Rich being the leading light in this company to adventure "The Golden

Trade." Their Charter gave them exclusive rights to trade in the Guinea, but little else, other than to warn other Englishmen off, leaving the "Adventurers" to fight their own battles with the French, Dutch and Portuguese, who were already trading on the Coast. Not one of these European nations already trading on the West Coast welcomed the arrival of the English, and in fact battles between all of them were numerous and bloody. Despite all of these problems the "Merchant Adventurers" pushed their way into the trade, becoming the first to establish trading posts ashore. This company also built 'Fort James' on a small island in the River Gambia, not far from the present site of Bathurst.

It was also in 1616 that Thompson set out for the Gambia. He left his ship and some of his men, in order to trade up river, but whilst he was away some Portuguese murdered the men left with the ship. News eventually got back to London about this tragedy, and a rescue ship was sent out. Contact was made with Thompson, but he refused to come back, his aim being to establish contact with an African merchant by the name of Buckor Sano, through whom he hoped to obtain gold. Alas, the thought of all this gold seems to have turned his brain, he became arrogant and overbearing, this to the extent that one of his men killed him.

Two years later, in October, 1620, Richard Jobson sailed for the Gambia, in a ship of 200 tons called the *Lyon*. Jobson also made his way up river, eventually making contact with the merchant Thompson had failed to reach, Buckor Sano. Jobson left a written account of his adventures, from which we gather that he and Sano got on very well together, the latter being particularly fond of Jobson's alcohol. Sano was a man of great wealth and influence, an indication of which can be gained from the fact that he kept 300 horses to carry salt. He also bought and sold slaves, but to his eternal credit Jobson refused to buy slaves from him, stating, not altogether truthfully, " We were a people who did not deal in such commodities."

Despite much effort on the part of the Company of Merchant Adventurers, their enterprise did not do very well financially. The unhealthiness of the West Coast took an enormous toll on those involved, and cost the lives of many men. Another problem was the "interlopers," namely, freelance English mariners and traders who went to the West Coast on their own account, conveniently ignoring the exclusive rights given to the Company by the king. The main problem though was the fierce competition presented by the French, Portuguese and Dutch, who were already well established in the trade. Just a few short years after Jobson's voyage the traders of London decided enough was enough, and withdrew their stock and capital. This development meant that England was not to be represented on the Coast for some time - at least not by an authorised company.

It was during this period that the Dutch took full advantage of the

26

Timbuktoo

Market at Sokota

situation, the Netherlands West India Company being established on the Coast in 1621. This organisation operated under the patronage of the States General, and it soon developed into a very powerful enterprise, it becoming abundantly clear to the rest of Europe that the Dutch, through this company, intended to dominate the West Africa trade. The French though also had their foot in the door, continuing to trade on the Coast through an association of merchants from Rouen and Dieppe.

The English merchants began to get worried about the situation, for they realised that despite the problems encountered by the "Adventurers," money was to be made on the Coast. The growing power of the Dutch in general also disturbed them. King Charles was now on the throne and he was asked to intervene on their behalf. Taking his lead from his father, King James, he granted then another Charter, this being in 1638. This impressive piece of paper was merely intended to encourage them to look after their own affairs, which, in fact, it did. The African Company was established, Humprey Sladen, Nicholas Crisp, and various other London merchants, being the prime movers behind this venture.

The English though did not become involved in the notorious slave trade from the West Coast, at least to any significant extent, until Antigua and Barbados were colonised (1623-5). They then started trading as enthusiastically as their Dutch, French, Portuguese and Spanish rivals had long been doing in the interests of their colonies in the New World. The West Indies proprietors included many of the most aristocratic and 'respectable' families in England, but in profiting from the Slave Trade they were only following earlier and still more exalted forerunners, notably Admiral Sir John Hawkins and Queen Elizabeth! But the Royal Family had then, and was to have in the future, members who used their considerable influence to stand for Abolition and Emancipation. Of these the most constant was to be the Duke of Gloucester, one of the sons of George III, at whose house Abolitionist meetings were frequently held, who became the first President of the African Society and who spoke courageously for Abolition in the House of Lords. At a much later date Prince Albert was also to become an outspoken supporter of the Abolitionists.

Large numbers of slaves were to be required to feed this growing trade, but, significantly, it was not found necessary to establish formal colonies on the Coast to ensure a constant supply. In Africa slavery was a well established system, and the African rulers were not only prepared to trade with the Europeans, but insisted that all commerce with the interior had to pass through their hands. Their main concern being to ensure that they received a cut from the profits obtained from selling their fellow Africans down the proverbial river.

In 1672 a new chartered company was set up, this being the Royal African

Company. Not only was the Duke of York interested in this company, but the king himself. This was a powerful enterprise, for the bounds of the company concession ran from South Barbary to the Cape of Good Hope. It started business with a capital fund of just £110,000, out of which it had to pay another charter company, the Royal Adventurers, £34,000 for Cape Coast Castle, Fort James and Bence's Island at Sierra Leone. The Royal African prospered, and soon built new ports at Accra,, Secundee, and Kommenda, and it also bought Fredericksborg, at Cape Coast, from the Danes.

This company was soon exporting annually manufactured goods to Africa to the value of £70,000.   From Africa it brought home ivory, red wood, and other valuable items. The most significant direct import though being gold dust, this to the extent that the company was frequently coining up to 50,000 guineas at a time, which were all known by the elephant sign, and maintained a value of 21s.   It also shipped great numbers of slaves to our American colonies, at a moderate rate, which in its day was considered virtuous conduct. However, opposition to the Slave Trade also began to grow.

Between 1670 and 1680, Godwyn, a clergyman of the Established Church, described with great eloquence, the brutality of slavery, as he had seen it practiced in Barbados. Richard Baxter, the celebrated non-conformist also spoke out against this traffic, denouncing those engaged in it as pirates and robbers. These preachers and writers were soon to be followed by Southern, Hutcheson, Foster, Atkins, Wallis, and others. Bishop Warburton, in 1676, preached a very strong sermon, in which he condemned those who "talk, as of herds of cattle, of property in rational creatures!"

Trade with Africa continued to develop, but all of this activity was confined to the coast, our knowledge of the Niger in particular, and the interior of Africa in general remained virtually static. Nothing perhaps illustrates this better than William 111's attempts to have geography taught to William, Duke of Gloucester - the only surviving son of Princess Anne - when a series of extremely imaginative maps were drawn for this purpose. These maps indicated that the Niger rose in a great lake close to the Nile, then ran in a straight line across Africa to the Atlantic. Interestingly, the same map also showed that the Nile itself rose from two great inland oceans, near the Zambesi. The centre of Africa remained empty; this disguised, to an extent, by the geographer, who filled the wide open spaces with little brown mountains, and the occasional large town, which, needless to say, did not exist. Three beautifully printed names, Abisina, Negroland and Nubia occupying the remaining blanks on this informative production. In essence, this map was the same as the one that Leo Africanus had proudly presented to Pope Leo X in the 16th century, apart from the fact that the coast was more accurately described. Little had been learned in 200 years, and more than a century was to pass before the veil was to be completely lifted.

Meanwhile, the slave trade continued. The English Company that succeeded the Company of Royal Adventurers was to become known as "The Assiento Company," from its having secured - by the Peace of Utrecht - the right to supply slaves to the Spanish colonies in America, as well as all English possessions. Prior to this the Assiento had been held by the French, securing it for England in 1713 being considered something of a triumph. The terms of the contract specified that they could import 4,800 slaves per annum into the Spanish colonies in America, for the 30 year term of the contract, and as many more negroes as they could sell in areas not controlled by the Spanish. It was anticipated that this contract would yield large profits, but this was not the case. The actual terms of the agreement were not designed to favour the contract holder! Firstly the company had to pay a large sum of money - in advance - to the King of Spain, who also demanded a royalty on each slave sold. Not satisfied with this cut the Spanish Crown also demanded one-quarter of the net company profits. Further strains were put on the company budget by the English King, who also demanded a quarter of the remaining profits. By 1739 The Assiento Company owed a considerable sum of money to the King of Spain, who threatened to cancel the bargain. Relations grew somewhat strained between England and Spain - mainly due to this problem - and war broke out shortly afterwards.

The Assiento was suspended, and though the peace of 1748 renewed it for four more years, it was finally ended after just two years. A convention signed in 1750 obliging the Spanish government to pay £100,000 to England by way of compensation. The Assiento was ended, and the actual exploration of Africa was at a standstill, but the slave trade continued, this despite the curious fact that there was no English statute actually authorising the holding of slaves, either in England, or in the American colonies. Another inconvenient fact, that was conveniently ignored by Englishmen participating in the slave trade, was that the common law of England was incompatible with slavery, and neither recognised nor permitted its existence! This being brought home to the public at large by Lord Mansfield, who, when presiding at the Court of King's Bench, in 1772, affirmed these legal facts, deciding that there neither was, nor ever had been any *legal* slavery in England.

Legal or not, London, Bristol and Liverpool merchants, in particular, continued to grow fat on the profits of the slave trade, London being the first to be involved. The merchants from the capital though working in accordance with the "legitimate" way of accredited corporations, approved by Parliament - despite the aforementioned contradiction with basic English law, noted by Mansfield. Bristol was the next to be involved, their enterprising merchants trading to the West Coast, uninhibited by regard for any regulations. Liverpool was the last of the big ports to enter the trade, but in the end came to dominate it.

At first the Liverpool men were unable to equip vessels for the Africa trade, as the capital requirements were very high, and the risks considerable. But early in the 18th century Spain made it possible for the Liverpool men to enter the trade, via an unexpected route! Spain shipped to her American colonists goods subjected to a duty of no less than three hundred percent. The temptation that this level of duty presented to Spanish and English smugglers alike was too great to resist. Liverpool ships began to ship to the West Indies goods manufactured in Manchester, such as coarse checks and silk handkerchiefs, and a variety of other goods. These goods, carried in Liverpool ships, soon ousted from the West Indies Trade the continental goods carried in the Bristol ships. The three hundred per cent duty, imposed by the Spanish on their West Indies islands was being expertly evaded by local smugglers, who took their schooners down from Carthagena, Havannah and Portobello to the English colony of Jamaica. Here the goods were speedily moved from one vessel to another, to be sold at a great profit by the smugglers - provided they evaded the Spanish patrol vessels! Also favouring these adventurers was the fact that these smuggled items, imported from Manchester, were of much better quality than those imported legally from the continent.

Understandably, the Spanish Government objected very strongly to this trade being allowed to continue, making continual representations to London about the issue. At the same time they put their Guarda Costa under increasing pressure to stamp out this wholesale smuggling, but with little success, for it continued to earn fortunes for those involved locally for a period of about twenty years. Back in England, when this trade was at its zenith, it was estimated that the annual returns to Manchester were over £500,000, whilst the Liverpool shippers managed to pocket £273,000 - in a good year. It was these profits which were to enable the Liverpool Merchants to enter, then dominate the Slave Trade. Their main source of supply for slaves being the West Coast of Africa, but in particular the area adjacent to the Niger in the Bight of Benin.

Whilst profits obtained from the slave trade increased, religious and political opposition to this trade also increased - on an international scale. The anti-slavery movement began to develop in England. In 1776 a motion was put to the House of Commons that the Slave Trade was contrary to the laws of God and the rights of man, which, alas, was defeated. But a small, though very influential group of men, were now on the move, notably, William Wilberforce, Granville Sharp and Thomas Clarkson who were soon to become known as the Abolitionists. In 1787 they established the 'Society for the Abolition of the Slave Trade'. Wilberforce soon gained the support of William Pitt, then Prime Minister, and that of other influential members of Parliament, but another two decades were to pass before Wilberforce was to secure a successful vote for abolition.

On the International scene profound political developments, notably in France and America, were influencing long-standing British attitudes to slavery, making it clear that the sale of one human being to another was not acceptable, and could not be treated as just another form of legitimate trade. On June 26th,1775, George Washington of Virginia arrived in Boston and assumed command of the Continental Army, the American War of Independence was underway. On the 4th July, 1776, the thirteen North American British Colonies issued their Declaration of Independence, which embraced concepts incompatible with the continuation of the slave system. The American colonies had broken away from British rule in search of liberty, justice and equality, proclaiming that ' We hold these truths to be self-evident that all men are created equal, that they are endowed by their Creator with certain unalienable rights, that among these are life, liberty, and the pursuit of happiness.'

The great upheaval in the social fabric of France occurred in 1789, when the people rose up against an unjust code of laws, an oppressive system of taxation and a corrupt Court. France was ruthlessly divided by a rigid caste system. A Frenchman who was not of noble birth could not rise to high office in the state, the church or the army. Taxes were enormous and very unjustly levied. The land tax, one of the heaviest, was actually paid by only a third of those who held land, the nobles, the clergy, and those in government service, being exempt from payment. Crowds of courtiers, worthless and dissolute men, hung about the palaces, living in a most extravagant style - which stood in stark contrast to the miserable life style of the majority of Frenchmen - and in particular the peasantry - who actually worked the land. The storming of the Bastille by the peasants and workers on the 14th July, 1789, ushered in a spirit of fraternity towards the oppressed and enslaved that was to have its repercussions on the Slave Trade, the Niger and West Africa. The impact of this revolution also surfaced dramatically in the West Indies, notably on the island of Grenada in 1795.

The island of Grenada, in the Windward Islands, was discovered by Columbus in 1498, settled by the French, and finally became a British colony in 1762, French influence therefore remaining strong in 1795. French forces landed on the island, at Grenville Bay, on 3 March, 1795, and then began to march across the island towards the capitol, St. George, carrying with them a flag on which were inscribed the words ' Liberte, Egalite, ou la Mort.' The ideals of the French Revolution, 'Liberty, Equality and Fraternity,' thus reaching this outpost of empire in a most memorable manner. The invaders lost no time in joining forces with the discontented and enslaved negro population on the island, and so what had begun as a French invasion of Grenada quickly developed in to a combined invasion and insurrection.

32

Other insurrections in the West Indies were to follow. Humanity was on the move, and in this atmosphere the idea that Negroes were an integral part of the human race, and just as entitled to freedom as other men, began to take root. Almost a century though was still to pass before the export of slaves from West Africa was finally ended.

It was against this social, historical and political background that the mystery of the source, direction and final outlet of the River Niger remained unsolved at the close of the 18th century. This though did not in any way inhibit numerous 'Armchair Explorers' from advancing imaginative theories to fill the gap. Some suggested that the Niger terminated in the White Nile, which D'Anville had then traced to the south-west of Senaar. Outdoing them all though was a Mr Jackson Grey, who published the interesting fact that, in 1780, seventeen native travellers from Timbuctoo had reached Cairo by water the whole way in eighteen months, passing no less that 1,200 towns and cities on the way!

The truth about Africa in general, and the Niger in particular, was to be finally established under the guidance of a remarkable London based institution - the 'Association for Promoting the Discovery of the Interior Parts of Africa', commonly known as 'The African Association'. Formed in 1788, its president was Sir Joseph Banks, an outstanding individual who had accompanied Captain Cook on his voyage to the South Pacific. Many years were still to pass though before the efforts of the Association were to be crowned with success.

Cape Coast Castle, 1682

CHAPTER TWO   THE AFRICAN ASSOCIATION

Sir Joseph Banks, leading light of the African Association, was born in London on the 13th February, 1743. He received his early education under a private tutor, before going to Harrow, then Oxford. Apart from his academic achievements, he was also a very wealthy man, having taken possession of his paternal fortune in 1764. His liking for botany increased, which led to him being elected a fellow of the Royal Society, and then to accompanying Captain Cook, discoverer of Australia, on his voyage to the South Pacific (1768-71). Banks though is perhaps best remembered for his work with The African Association.

In 1788 Banks, with eleven other wealthy and influential men, was a member of an informal eating club, which met each Saturday evening at St. Albans Tavern, in Pall Mall. On 9th June, nine of these men turned up for the usual gathering, but this meeting was to be an historic one, for 'The Dark Continent' was the subject of their discussion, and they were to pass a resolution that was to change the history of Africa:

" That no species of information is more ardently desired, or more generally useful, than that which improves the science of Geography; and as the vast continent of Africa, notwithstanding the efforts of the Ancients, and the wishes of the Moderns, is still in a great measure unexplored, the Members of this Club do form themselves into an Association for Promoting the Discovery of the Inland Parts of that Quarter of the World."

This Association was subsequently to receive a charter, and finally to be incorporated in the Geographical Society of London. The changing of this informal Saturday evening eating club into the African Association being hardly noticed at the time. The first committee consisted of Lord Rawdon, afterwards Marquis of Hastings; Sir Joseph Banks, then President of the Royal Society; the Bishop of Llandaff, Mr. Beaufoy, and Mr Stuart. Each of the members agreed to subscribe five guineas a year for three years, which was far from being an intolerable burden, for they were all extremely wealthy men. This modest levy though did not give them a capital fund commensurate with the ambitions of their Association. In fact it was soon to prove insufficient to meet the out-of-pocket expenses of any man who would agree to explore Africa for them. The members themselves clearly having no desires whatsoever to actually leave their armchairs, and make their own way to darkest Africa.

Soon after the Association was formed the committee agreed not to disclose, except to fellow members, any information that they would, no doubt, from time to time, receive from their hired explorers. This group of landed gentry, Lords, and members of Parliament, these wealthy dilettantes, were, at long last, to be instrumental in solving the mystery of the River Niger. Many explorers were now to be sent to their deaths in the search for the elusive Niger - the river no one could trace.

The first man who volunteered for this extremely heavy task, on notably light pay, was an individual already well known to Sir Joseph Banks, Mr J. Ledyard, an American by birth, who appears to have been burdened with an insatiable desire to keep moving. By 1788 Ledyard had already been round the world, with Captain Cook - and Banks.

John Ledyard , a friend of Thomas Jefferson was, by all accounts, a somewhat reckless character. He began his travels when little more that a child, this he achieved by persuading Captain Cook to take him on his third expedition. He then spent a considerable number of years with the American Indians. After this he set himself the modest task of walking round the world. He started on this adventure by going from Stockholm, round the Gulf of Bothnia, before heading for Asiatic Russia. True to character though, he was too impatient to wait for permission from Catherine the Great's officials before embarking on this ramble. However, he did manage to reach Yakutsk in Siberia before the enraged Russians caught up with him, and returned him to their borders with Europe.

Ledyard then made his way back to London, undaunted, but apparently little the richer for his excursion to the frozen north. He then called on his old fellow-voyager, Sir Joseph Banks, who, by coincidence, was then earnestly seeking someone to send out to the Niger. Banks received Ledyard with open arms, and promptly introduced him to a fellow member of the Association, Mr Beaufoy, who was, by all accounts, deeply impressed by the seasoned traveller, and asked him when he would be ready to set out for Africa. Ledyard said "Tomorrow" !

The Association were not as ready as that, for one obstacle to the rapid departure of their first Geographical Missionary still remained, this being the meagre funds available. At this point in time the Association had only been in existence for about two months, and their membership was still restricted to a few individuals. Also,being gentlemen, they naturally considered it was beneath their dignity to canvas for subscriptions. Faced with this dilemma the committee were driven to the conclusion that there was no alternative, other than to dip into their own pockets, to obtain the required capital. This they did, raising £430, which enabled them to provide equipment for their traveller, and letters of credit. Upon the conclusion of these tiresome formalities the eager Mr Ledyard was unleashed on Africa.

To Ledyard they assigned - at his own request - an ambitious enterprise, which stood absolutely no chance of success, this being to traverse, from east to west, in the latitude attributed to the Niger, the widest part of the continent of Africa. The injunction being to strike in from Cairo, in search of the

Niger, and also to obtain as much information as possible about the uncharted interior of the Dark Continent.

He reached Cairo in August, 1788, immediately sending back to the Association a depressing account of the general state of Egypt. From his communications one can see that he was a somewhat nervous and irritable man, who was constantly upset by the inevitable delays in getting things started in Africa. He then fell ill with a stomach complaint, overdosed himself with medicine, and died!

At about the same time that the Association had engaged Ledyard it also engaged a Mr Lucas, this in consideration of the knowledge he possessed of the language and manners of the Arabs. He had obtained this knowledge the hard way, for when he was young he had been captured by a Sallee Rover and kept for three years as a slave in Morocco. This episode, in his varied career, does not seem to have disturbed him unduly, or left him with a burning desire to leave Morocco, for after his liberation he stayed on there for sixteen years acting as a Vice-Consul, when he added considerably to his knowledge of the language, manners and customs of the Arabs. On his return to England he became an interpreter at the Court of St. James. Suitably impressed with this record, the Association engaged him, then proposed a plan of action.

Lucas was to set out from Tripoli and make his way south across the great desert until he arrived at Fezzan; where "he should collect and transmit by the way of Tripoli, whatever intelligence, respecting the Inland Regions of the Continent, the people of Fezzan, or the traders who might visit the country, might be able to afford; and that he should afterwards return by way of the Gambia, or by that of the coast of Guinea."

Armed with these instructions Lucas made his way to North Africa, arriving in Tripoli early in 1789. The scheme was that he should join the caravan that went from Tripoli to the Niger. He managed to obtain the support of the Bey, and then made his arrangements with two Shereefs, who are sacred persons, being descendants of the Prophet, it being agreed that he could join the next caravan.

Early on Sunday morning, 1st of February, 1789, the Shereefs, Lucas and his companions, took their departure from the suburbs of Tripoli, where they had all spent the previous night camping in the garden of a local merchant, who was travelling to Fezzan with them. Their small, but heavily armed caravan, left Tripoli, heading off in an East-South-Easterly. direction. They soon passed through the town of Tajarah, a miserable collection of clay-walled huts, and then, at 5 p.m. camped for the night on a sandy eminence. The following day they continued along the coast until they reached Mesurata. There they found the tribes in a state of open rebellion against the Pasha of Tripoli, and no supplies procurable, so the entire caravan turned

Kru Town, near Cape Palmas

Cape Coast Castle. 19th century

back to Tripoli, thus bringing Lucas's expedition to a rather ignominious conclusion.

The next emissary was Major Daniel Houghton, an Irishman, who had formerly served as a Captain in the 69th regiment, and in 1779 had served under General Rooke, as a fort major, on the island of Goree. He had also served as a consul in Morocco, which position gave him an excellent understanding of the Arab language and customs. Now middle-aged, and retired without a pension, he was most anxious to find suitable employment. Houghton heard that the Association had formed a plan of penetrating to the Niger by way of Gambia. He offered his services, which were accepted, and he left England on the 16th of October, 1790.

Houghton arrived at the entrance to the Gambia on the 10th of November, and was well received by the King of Barra, who remembered him from his days at Goree, when the Major had paid him a visit. He offered him assistance and protection, so far as his dominion or influence extended. An offer from the Captain of an English ship, trading on the coast, enabled him to reach Junkiconda, where he purchased a horse, five asses, and supplies. He then headed towards Medina, capital of the small Kingdom of Wooli. A few words, accidentally dropped in the Mundingo language, which Houghton understood, forewarned the Major that plans were being hatched to kill him. His lack of popularity being due to the fact that local traders feared that his expedition portended the ruin of their commerce. Armed with this valuable information he took his horse and asses across the river, thus avoiding the thugs who had been sent out to murder him. Houghton then passed through Medina and Bambouk, until he finally reached Ferbanna, where again he was well received by the King, who provided him with a guide and money for his expenses.

The next news of Major Houghton came from Simbing in a letter running: " Major Houghton's compliments to Dr. Laidley; is in good health, on his way to Timbuctoo; robbed of all his goods by Fenda Bucar's son." News of his death soon followed; but before he was murdered, he had sent back sufficient information to establish that almost certainly the Niger flowed to the east and that, in this respect, Leo Africanus was wrong. Details of his death were not known until Mungo Park entered the country, when he heard that the Moors had lured him to a place in the desert called Tisheet, then stripped him of everything. He wandered about in the desert until he sank from thirst and exhaustion, and Park was shown the place where he died. All of which brings us to Mungo Park himself, one of the most outstanding figures of African exploration.

Mungo Park was born on 10th September, 1771. He was the son of a poor lowland farmer, but his sister married James Dickson, the gardener and botanist who was known to Sir Joseph Banks. Educated at home and then at

Mungo Park

Selkirk grammar school , at the age of fifteen he was apprenticed to Thomas Anderson, surgeon at Selkirk. In October 1789 he went to Edinburgh University, where he obtained his surgical diploma, and also distinguished himself by his application to botanical science. After qualifying he made his way to London, where he made contact with his brother-in-law, James Dickson, then working as a gardener in the city. Dickson had also established a considerable reputation in London as a botanist, through which activity he came to know Sir Joseph Banks. Dickson introduced Park to Banks, and through the latter's intervention, Park was appointed assistant medical officer on the East Indiaman *Worcester*. In February, 1792 Park sailed for the island of Sumatra, where he continued his botanical studies, and wisely brought home many rare plants for his patron, Sir Joseph Banks, in whose estimation he rapidly grew. In May, 1794, Banks made it clear to Park that if he wished to travel he could do so on behalf of the African Association. After the formalities of his engagement were concluded he received his instructions, which were very clear and concise, these being that on his arrival in Africa he was....

" to pass on to the river Niger, either by way of Bambouk, or by such other route as should be found most convenient. That I should ascertain the course, and, if possible, the rise and termination of that river. That I should use my utmost exertions to visit the principal towns or cities in its neighbourhood, particularly Tombuctoo and Houssa; and that I should afterwards be at liberty to return to Europe, either by way of the Gambia, or by such other route, as, under all the then existing circumstances of my situation and prospects should appear to me most advisable."

On the 22nd May, 1795 Mungo Park eventually set sail from Portsmouth in the brig *Endeavour*, a small vessel trading to the Gambia for ivory and beeswax. On July 5th he arrived at Pisania, a British factory two hundred miles up the Gambia. Here he was stricken with fever, but was nursed back to health by Doctor Laidley. Whilst recuperating he studied hard to acquire a knowledge of the Mandingo language, a knowledge that was to be of great use to him later. In all five months passed by before he was fit to travel, but on the 2nd of December,1795, he decided to start for the interior accompanied by a few negro servants, rather than leave with a caravan.

On his long journey he was to meet with much kindness, but also a great deal of treachery. One notable incident occurring on the 7th March, 1796, when he was captured by a party of horsemen and taken to Benown, because the wife of the local Moorish King wanted to see what a Christian looked like. Here he was teased, and generally abused, before being robbed of almost all his possessions by Ali, one of the King's sons. Fortunately though he was able to retain one his most valuable possessions, this being his compass. Generally speaking, Park got on very well with the local negro people, but grew to dislike and distrust the Moors.

After escaping from Ali he continued on his way until he arrived at a negro settlement called Wawra, where he was well received.   Here he rested for a few days before setting out for Dingyee, where, much to his surprise, he found that he was regarded as a sacred being !   He pressed on relentlessly, now through heavily populated areas, until he reached a prosperous town called Moorja, a place which he described as being full of gaiety and abundance. He remained here for a while before heading for the city of Sego.

Leaving Moorja, Park now began to pass through country that had been totally devastated by a local war. Villages and crops had been destroyed, trees cut down, and wells filled in, making progress very difficult. Totally exhausted, he struggled on, until at length he neared the great town of Sego, where he soon began to mingle with the crowds making their way to the market. From these people he learned that the next day he would see the great water - the Niger Jolliba. Excited, and unable to sleep Mungo Park was up before daybreak on this fateful day - 20th July, 1796, then, soon after 8 a.m. he arrived opposite Sego, the capital of Bambara, when some fellow travellers called out to him "Geo affili" (see the water); and looking " I saw," says Park, "with infinite pleasure the great object of my mission, the long-sought-for majestic Niger glittering in the morning sun, as broad as the Thames at Westminster and flowing slowly *to the eastwards"*. Unless he had been forestalled three or four hundred years ago by a Spanish monk or a Portuguese adventurer, Park was the first European to actually set eyes on the Niger River, in the far interior of West Africa - and finally establish, from first hand observation, that it did indeed flow towards the east.

From Sego Park proceeded down river as far as Silla, but here, most reluctantly he was forced to return, owing to the total exhaustion of his horse and his lack of means to purchase food.   He left Silla on his return journey on the 3rd of August,1796, making for the Gambia by another route further south, through the Mandingo country; most of the journey, as far as Kamali, he performed on foot. At this place he fell dangerously ill with fever, and his life was only saved through the care of a local slave trader, Kaarfa Taura, in whose house he stayed for seven months.   Although a slave trader, as were most Africans of position of that day, Taura was, according to Park, a really good-hearted man. It is not actually on record that his slaves concurred with this view, nevertheless, but for his intervention it is likely that Mungo Park would have shared the fate of Major Houghton, thus many years may have elapsed before any firm knowledge of the Niger was brought back to Europe.

Leaving Kamalia on the 19th April, 1797, Mungo Park again reached his fellow countrymen on the Upper Gambia on 10th June, 1797. His great adventure though was not concluded, for he still had to get back to England, and regular direct links between the Gambia, and any place in Europe, were few and far between. Park therefore considered himself lucky when an American sailing-ship, the *Charleston*, came to the mouth of the Gambia, for a cargo of slaves, which were to be transported to South Carolina. With Park, and many reluctant emigrants on board, the ship soon set sail for America, but the vessel took a long time to reach the island of Goree, where Major Houghton had once served, and during this short leg of the passage the surgeon of the ship, four American sailors and three of the slaves died of fever. The ship remained at Goree, waiting for provisions, until the beginning of October, when at last they started for America. On her passage across the Western Ocean she sprang a leak, which obliged her to head for the island of Antigua in the West Indies. Here Park left the *Charleston* and obtained a passage on a mail-ship, reaching England in another twenty eight days, arriving at Falmouth on the 22nd of December, 1797, and London on the morning of Christmas Day , just before daylight.

More dead than alive, Mungo Park wandered about the streets of Bloomsbury, as it was still too early to visit his brother-in-law, James Dickson, who was employed at the British Museum, and also had the responsibility of managing the gardens that then surrounded the building. At last Park entered the gardens, and began looking at the shrubs, in the early daylight of the Christmas morning, when his brother-in-law came out for an early inspection. To his utter amazement Dickson then found himself looking at his brother-in-law, the great explorer, Mungo Park, looking more like a ghost than a living creature.   Park had been away for two years and seven months, and Sir Joseph Banks, the African Association, and his relatives and friends had all given him up for lost.

Mungo Park was welcomed back as a hero, which he undoubtedly was, for he had brought back to England firm and conclusive evidence that the Niger flowed to the east. He then speculated, without any real evidence whatsoever, that the Niger, after some considerable distance, flowed to the south, concluded its long journey to the ocean as the River Congo. Despite the hardships he had just endured he was most anxious to be allowed to return, as leader of a properly equipped expedition, and descend the Niger in a boat till it came to its outlet into the ocean. But it was not until nearly eight years later, in 1805, that his wish was to be granted.   After his return Park at first remained in London. He then set about writing an account of his travels, the complete works being published in the spring of 1799.

Following the publication of his travels Park went back to Scotland, then, on the 2nd of August, 1799, he married the eldest daughter of his old Master, Anderson of Selkirk.   For the next two years he and his wife appear to have lived with his family at Fowlshiels. He established himself as a medical practitioner, but he was now a famous man, and clearly had some difficulty in settling down to the hum-drum life of a Scottish country doctor. Riding over the moors, to treat poor lowlands farmers, was certainly not going to add much to his fame - or his fortune, and his frustration began to show. In a letter written to Sir Joseph Banks, dated 31 July 1800, in which he stated that he 'hopes that his exertions in some station or other may be of use to his country' it is clear that he was longing to serve once more as an explorer. His opportunity to act in this capacity was to come in five years time, but in the meantime others were attempting to serve the interests of Empire - and the African Association.

The indefatigable armchair explorers of the African Association continued to send their men out to Africa, clearly undeterred by the failure of Lucas, and the death of Mr Ledyard and Major Houghton. Two years after Park's departure for Africa, on his first voyage, namely in 1797, the Association sent out yet another emissary, this being a German - Frederick Horneman. He was a fit and intelligent young man, who had studied to be a minister at the University of Gottingen, under a famous scholar, Professor Blumenbach, and it was on his recommendation to Sir Joseph Banks that the Association had agreed to engage him. After the formalities were concluded Horneman remained at Gottingen - studying Arabic, but at the expense of the Association.

Horneman left London, bound for Egypt, in July, 1797, his intention being to follow Ledyard's plan, this being to explore Africa westward from Cairo. On his arrival in this city he was considerably delayed by the plague, that is until the arrival of the French army. Napoleon was on the march, and in 1797 had succeeded brilliantly at Lodi and Rivoli, whilst the year of 1789 found him mounting his expeditions to the east, when he occupied Egypt, and won the famous battle of the Pyramids. Horneman was presented to Napoleon, who promised him all the funds and supplies he required for his proposed expedition. He made arrangements to join a caravan of merchants travelling to Fezzan and set out with them on the 5th September, 1798. On the morning of September 8th they entered the desert, which was considered as the boundary of Egypt; and after travelling thirteen hours, encamped on a tract of land known as Muhabag. At long last Horneman was on the way.

He reached Fezzan, then made his way with the caravan to Mourzouk, from which place he wrote his last letter, dated 6 April, 1800. His plan was to go with the caravan into Bornu, and it appears that he probably did reach the Niger, and follow the river downstream to Nupe, where he died. Had a further communication been received from Horneman, before he died, he would, no doubt have revised his views on the Niger contained in this letter: " Some days past I spoke to a man who had seen Mr Brown in Darfoor; he gave me some information respecting the countries he travelled through, and told me, that the communication of the Niger with the Nile was not to be doubted, but that this communication before the rainy season was very little

44

in those parts; the Niger being at the dry period reposing, or *non fluens*."

Another German explorer sent out by the African Association, and destined not to return, was Roentgen. His instructions were to start for the interior from Mogadore, and make his way to Timbuctoo. It was his intention to have accompanied the caravan to this city from Marocco; unfortunately he made the fatal mistake of ignoring much good advise, by hiring a decidedly shady character as his personal servant. Without much delay, and just as predicted, this man murdered Roentgen, thus ending the life of yet another enthusiastic emissary of the African Association.

The travels of Buckhardt, also sent out by the African Association, threw no additional light on the course of the Niger, so, in 1804, at the time when Mungo Park was preparing for his second expedition, the Association recruited yet another explorer, this one being Henry Nicholls, his injunction being to make his way to one of the trading stations on the Gulf of Guinea, spend a year there obtaining information about the area, and then to head north in the hope of finding the Niger. A short cruise along the coast would in fact have brought him to the mouth of the great river, without striking out for the interior, but Henry Nicholls was not to know that, as it was still not suspected that the Niger emptied into the Atlantic at this point on the west coast. Nicholls left Liverpool in November, 1804, in a ship bound for Calabar, a slave trading establishment at the mouth of the Cross River, some distance to the east of the vast delta of the Niger. He arrived on the coast in January, 1805, wrote the first of his reports for the Association, in which he described conditions at the trading station, then caught fever, and died in April. The torch of African exploration was now to be passed back to the great explorer - Mungo Park.

In September,1803, there appeared to be some superficial signs that Park was settling down to life in Scotland, for he wrote to his brother on the death of Doctor Reid, who held the best practice in Peebles: ' There will probably be another surgeon or two here in a week, but I shall have the best part of the practice, come who will.' During this period he was becoming acquainted with Doctor Adam Ferguson, Dugald Stewart, and Walter (afterwards Sir Walter) Scott, his acquaintance with the latter rapidly developing into a very close friendship. However, although he kept silent on the subject, it was strongly suspected, by Scott, that he still entertained hopes of being called upon to undertake another mission to the Niger. In October, 1803, these hopes were realised when Lord Hobart, then secretary of state to the colonies, asked him if he would be interested in organising another - government backed - expedition to the Niger. Park promptly accepted the offer, but a change of administration caused some delays during which period Park studied Arabic. In a memoir which he presented to the colonial office in September, 1804, he stated the objective of the expedition. 'the extension of

British commerce and the enlargement of our geographical knowledge.'

The brevet commission of a Captain in Africa was promptly conferred on Park, and £5,000 placed at his disposal, together with his instructions which were, to pursue the course of the Niger to the utmost possible distance that it can be traced. Park was also empowered to enlist a large party of up to forty-five soldiers to accompany him on his journey. On the 30th January, 1805, Captain Park, accompanied by his brother-in-law, Alexander Anderson, a surgeon, and George Scott, a draughtsman from Selkirk, sailed from Portsmouth on the *Crescent*, bound for Goree.

Goree, at this point in time, was an English garrison, where troops belonging to the Royal African Corps were stationed; their main function being to protect British settlements on the coast from the French. The transport ship *Crescent* arrived on the 28th March, where Park and his colleagues were joined by Lieutenant Martyn R.A., and about thirty-five soldiers, and two sailors under his command. The West coast garrison of Goree, at the time of the Napoleonic war, tended to contain the dregs of the British military establishment, Lieutenant Martyn himself being a cheerful, brutal lunatic, whose favourite sport was shooting negroes! As Park himself was a man who had much respect for negroes, it was a somewhat bizarre turn of events that now obliged him to work closely with such a man.

This large heterogeneous party of white men soon made their departure from Goree, and on the 29th April they reached Pisania, where Park engaged a Mandingo priest named Isaaco to accompany them as guide. Isaaco was the only African on the expedition, and it was because he was a man of such exceptional intelligence, fortitude and devotion that we have any record of Park's second famous expedition. This ill-assorted caravan, dressed in full military or naval uniform, despite the terrible heat and humidity, set out from the coast just two weeks before the rains began. Only Isaaco survived.

A few weeks after setting out the expedition was nearly wrecked by the attack of a large swarm of bees. Nearly all the people with Park were severely stung; seven of the beasts of burden died from the stings, or bolted into the bush and were never recovered. The rains set in with violence, and soon men began to die like flies, from dysentery, fever, and other ills. When they reached the mountains in Upper Senegal their troubles increased, for the ascent was steep and rocky, the asses of the expedition were heavily laden, and most of the surviving soldiers were too sick to walk. Undaunted by all these disasters Park pressed on relentlessly. Crossing one of the many rivers they encountered Isaaco was seized by a crocodile, but survived by having the wonderful presence of mind to thrust his fingers into its eyes, which obliged the brute to release him. Park then patched him up somehow with sticking plaster, and by way of a minor miracle Isaaco survived.

Mungo Parks own efforts can only be described as heroic. He purchased as much food and milk as he could to help his suffering men, and also made efforts to aid the sick by boiling cinchona bark, which produced a quinine type mixture for those that were fever stricken. On reaching one of the many rivers they were obliged to swim or wade across, Park crossed *sixteen times*; on one trip carrying his brother-in-law, Doctor Anderson, who was by then close to death. Despite his great efforts, men still fell by the wayside, where they were attacked by hyenas, or simply disappeared. As they neared the Niger they were constantly under attack by lions, which had to be driven off by firing guns and blowing whistles. By the time Park reached the Niger at Bamaku he had lost most of his men, only about six soldiers, Lieutenant Martyn, Isaaco and himself having survived. Park himself then fell ill with dysentery, but managed to cure himself with a massive dose of calomel, so large in fact that it prevented him from speaking or sleeping for six days.

The country that Park was now in was ruled by King Mansong, who, hearing about the expedition, sent a musician to the white men - with friendly messages, and six large canoes; these enabled what remained of the expedition to reach Sego. Moving down the Niger on this leg of their journey Park later recorded his impressions of the scene in his journal :-

" Nothing could be more beautiful than the views of this immense river - sometimes as smooth as a mirror, at others ruffled with a gentle breeze, but at all times wafting us along at the rate of 6 or 7 miles an hour."

The great King of Bambara refused to see Mungo Park, but through his envoys informed Park that he had no objections to him exploring the Niger. Park in turn sent word back that it would be in the mutual interests of the Europeans and negroes to trade directly with each other - rather than through the Moors, who were bitterly opposed to the arrival of the Europeans, as they had a monopoly on local trade.

Park selected the large town of Sansanding for his task of building a boat with which he was to attempt to descend the Niger, until he reached the ocean. This place was a typical town on the Muhammadan Niger, with a population at that time of about 11,000 inhabitants. The place had a large market square, which was crowded with people from morning to night. Most of the mosques and main buildings being built of dried mud on a wooden frame, which, from a distance looked like European buildings made of masonry.

The vessel that Park put together for this venture was a flat bottomed one based on two large canoes, which he named H.M. schooner *Joliba*, (i.e ' the great water'), he started on his descent, leaving Sansanding on 19th November., accompanied by Lieutenant Martyn, and three soldiers, the remnants of his ill-fated expedition. On the eve of his departure he wrote a memorable letter to Lord Camden.

' I have changed a large canoe into a tolerably good schooner, on board of which I this day hoisted the British flag, and I shall set sail to the east with the fixed resolution to discover the termination of the Niger or perish in the attempt. I have heard nothing I can depend on respecting the course of this mighty stream, but I am more inclined to think it can end nowhere but in the sea. My dear friends, Mr Anderson and likewise Mr Scott, are both dead; but though all Europeans who are with me should die, and though I were myself half dead, I would still persevere; and if I should not succeed in the object of my journey, I would at least die on the Niger.'

This letter, together with some others addressed to his family, and his journal, were given by Park to Isaaco, by whom they were taken to the Gambia, and thus survived. They were to be the last communications to be received from Park. Rumours of his death reached the coast the following year, but no definite account of his fate was obtained until 1812. Isaaco later being sent back by the Governor of the Congo to obtain the facts. These details being subsequently confirmed , by Bowditch, Denham, Clapperton , Lander - and later travellers.

Park and his companions apparently sailed down the stream, until they reached the town of Boussa, some 800 miles beyond Timbuctoo, at which place the great mass of the Niger is forced through a narrow rocky gorge. Here, where the river is most difficult to navigate, a party of raiders were waiting for them. A fight resulted, in which the whole party, except one slave rower lost their lives.

Mungo Park's wife and four children survived him, who received the sum of £4,000 by way of compensation from the government. Speculation though about his fate continued for years, motivating his second son, Thomas, a midshipman in the Royal Navy, to obtain leave so that he could mount an expedition to Boussa, from the coast, in the hope of obtaining some further information about his father's fate. He struck out for the interior, but after covering a distance of two hundred miles he caught fever and died on the ' 31st October, 1827.

Twelve years later, in 1839, when the mystery of the Niger had been solved - and in no small measure due to the courage and dedication of Mungo Park - a huge monument was erected in the centre of Selkirk, to the memory of the explorer. Park is represented standing, with a sextant in his right hand, in his left a scroll, on which is inscribed one of the main sentences from his last letter to Lord Camden - a fitting memorial to a truly remarkable man.

The year of 1805, when Park had mounted his expedition to the Niger, had been a notable one in British history, when Nelson had destroyed the fleets of France and Spain off Cape Trafalgar; but the intensification of the Napoleonic wars prevented further attempts to solve the mystery of the Niger until Wellington had defeated Napolean at the Battle of Waterloo, thus bringing to a close the Napoleonic wars.

However, neither the disastrous conclusion to Park's second Niger

The Busa rapids on the Lower Niger, where Mungo Park and
Lieutenant Martyn were drowned in 1806

The Mungo Park memorial at
Selkirk

49

expedition, or the Napoleon wars, managed to damp down English interest in the great river, or hinder the country from pushing on with the work of exploration at the conclusion of the great European upheaval. The central mystery remained unsolved, Mungo Park had established that the river continued to flow to the east past Timbuctoo, but where did the Niger meet the Atlantic, or did it, as some continued to speculate, fall into the Nile. Park himself had been inclined to the view that the Niger and the Congo were the same river, but this was mere speculation. The issue would clearly only be decided by an intrepid explorer joining the river in the interior, and remaining with it until it met the ocean - or the Nile - or the Congo! The government, naturally influenced by Park's views, decided to send out two simultaneous expeditions, one to ascend the Congo, (or Zaire) the other to descend the Niger. The over-confident assumption, based on this speculation, being that the two rivers *were* one and the same stream, therefore the expeditions *would* meet, and return to England in triumph , having settled the issue of both rivers at one fell swoop.

The expedition to the Congo, sent out in 1816, was commanded by Captain Tuckey, a valiant explorer of the arctic seas, whilst two army officers, Peddie and Campbell, sent out at the same time, were selected to make the descent of the Niger. Both expeditions were large, well funded, and properly equipped. Both were disastrous.

Captain Tuckey, R.N., was accompanied by Lieutenant Hawkins, Mr Fitzmaurice, master and surveyor, Doctor McKerrow, with petty Officers and marines, besides supernumeraries; Professor Smith, botanist; Mr Cranch, zoologist; Mr Tudor, anatomist; and Mr Lockhart, a gardener from Kew. The expedition sailed from Deptford on the 18th February, 1816, sailed 150 miles up the Congo, as far as it is navigable, that is to the Yella rapids, and then came to a halt. They had in fact merely reached the cataract which the Jesuits had discovered in the seventeenth century. A party of thirty men was then sent ashore to explore the Paraballa mountains, but of these only nine returned. Demoralised, Captain Tuckey decided to head for home, but before the vessel had left the Congo he had died, together with Messrs Smith, Galwey, Cranch, Tudor, and many artisans and seamen. The vessel and survivors only just managing to reach the island of Fernando Po.

The army expedition, commanded by Major Peddie, which was to descend the Niger was an equally tragic affair. They managed to reach Kakondi *via* the Nunez River, but failed to reach the main Niger at all. Tragically, the mortality was so great that they were forced to turn back to the coast; over one hundred soldiers died. Once again the west coast had proved a deadly route into the interior of Africa. These horrendous losses, on officially backed, large-scale expeditions, upset the government. A tactical retreat was thought prudent, and the days of the lone wanderer returned.

In 1817 M. Bandia managed to reach Panjikot *via* Egypt, and in the same year P. Rouzie ventured far into the interior. The following year M. Mollieu reached Timbo *via* St. Louis, and later in the same year Captain Gray, of the Royal Africa Corps, struck out for the interior and managed to get as far as Bulibani, the capital of Bondu. In 1818 attention was also turned to the shores of the Mediterranean again, when an expedition was sent to the south from Tripoli, under the command of Mr Ritchie and Lieutenant. Lyon, which got to the south-west border of Fezzan, but just beyond Murzak Ritchie died, and Lyons returned - yet another failure. Three men were now waiting in the wings though - eager to grasp the torch of African exploration - Major Dixon Denham, Captain Hugh Clapperton, and the son of a Cornish Innkeeper, Richard Lemon Lander. Failure, at long last, was about to turn to success, due to the efforts of this trio, and in particular the latter.

CHAPTER THREE DENHAM, CLAPPERTON AND LANDER

Captain Hugh Clapperton, like Mungo Park, was a Lowland Scot, the son of a surgeon from Annan. Unlike Park though, who was apprenticed to a surgeon, then went on to Edinburgh University to obtain his surgical diploma, Clapperton, the son of a surgeon, had a very poor education. No doubt because of this, and whilst still very young, he went to sea, serving as a cabin boy on a merchant ship. When ashore though he managed to be in the wrong place, at the wrong time, and was grabbed by a press-gang, ending up in the Royal Navy. For a period of about five years he served on the East India Station. He then served on the Great Lakes in Canada, obtained promotion, then returned to England on half-pay, this being in 1817.

About the year 1820 Hugh Clapperton was introduced to Walter Oudney, an ex-naval surgeon who was then working as a doctor in Edinburgh. Oudney was, by all accounts, a pleasant young man, with a great interest in nature, but, unfortunately, not very strong. Nevertheless, the Colonial Office decided to send Oudney out to Tripoli, where he was to be responsible for mounting an expedition that was to head south towards Lake Chad, then turn to the west, and make for Kano and the Niger. A prospect that presented a tremendous feat of endurance, even for the strongest of men, making it obvious - to all but the mandarins of the Colonial Office - that Oudney should never have been selected for this task. On the credit side though, they did allow him to select a companion, and he chose an exceptionally fit young man, Lieutenant Hugh Clapperton - recently returned from duty in Canada, and now most anxious to find suitable employment.

Oudney and Clapperton got on well together, but, before formalities were concluded a Major Dixon Denham, then teaching at Sandhurst, volunteered to join them. The Colonial Office then revised their plans, which required Oudney, on arrival at Bornu, to act as the British Consul. Oudney was not keen on the idea, and the somewhat arrogant and ambitious Major Denham took an instant dislike to both Clapperton and Oudney. The final plan was that Oudney would be in charge of the expedition until they arrived at Bornu, then Dixon would be in charge. Needless to say, Clapperton was far from happy about these arrangements.

On the 5 March, 1822 the expedition left for Murzuk. The ultimate object of their mission being the Niger. They ran into trouble when the Sultan of Fezzan refused to let them proceed to Bornu. Presented with this problem it was agreed that Denham would return to Tripoli and take a strong stand with the Basha. He succeeded, not only managing to get the required permission to proceed, but also a welcome agreement that they would have an

Captain Hugh Clapperton, R.N.

armed escort placed at their disposal, under the command of an Arab Merchant. They headed south across the great desert until they reached Lake Chad, being the first Europeans to see this large sheet of water in central Africa. Not surprisingly, there had been some friction between the three travellers en-route, so that when they reached Kuka, near Lake Chad, it was agreed that they should part company. Denham deciding to join a slave-trading group of Arabs, whilst Clapperton and Oudney opted to explore the area to the south of Lake Chad.

Oudney and Clapperton decided to leave Kuku on 14th December, 1823, accordingly they sent off for their camels and servants on that morning, and went in person to take leave of the Sheikh. They informed him that they hoped to return, if possible before the rains set in, and assured him that they were very grateful for his hospitality and kindness. He bade the travellers farewell in a very affectionate manner. Their party consisted of Clapperton, Oudney, two servants, three men from Fezzan, and Jacob, a Jew, who acted as a sort of major domo; also in the Kafila were twenty-seven Arab merchants, and about fifty people from Bornou. As they left, Clapperton noted that Oudney appeared to be in a very poor state of health.

They pressed on, but on the morning of 2nd January the travellers saw that Oudney was in a very weak state. Oudney seemed to think that keeping on the move would help him get better, but the heat of the day, and the very low temperatures at night, apart from the travelling, only seemed to make him worse. On the 10th January they left Katagum, the governor himself staying with the caravan until it was four miles out of town, and then providing them with a guide. By the 11th it was clear that Oudney could not last much longer. He died the following day, Clapperton stating:-

" Doctor Oudney drank a cup of coffee at day-break, and, by his desire, I ordered the camels to be loaded. I then assisted him to dress, and, with the support of his servant, he came out of the tent; but, before he could be lifted on the camel, I observed the ghastliness of death in his countenance, and I had him immediately replaced in the tent, I sat down by his side, and with unspeakable grief, witnessed his last breath, which was without a struggle or groan."

Clapperton, now very depressed, continued alone. On the morning of the 20th January, on the advice of El Wordee, he prepared himself to enter Kano, dressing himself in his full naval uniform, in order to impress the locals. The place itself, at the time, being a town of about 30,000 inhabitants, about half of them being slaves. The place was - and in fact still is - the commercial centre for a very large area between the Niger and Lake Chad. Once he had made his presence known to the Emir he received a warm welcome.

He received an even warmer welcome from the Sultan Bello at Sokoto, who was kind enough to draw him a map of the Niger, and made the point that it would be very easy to reach his country from the sea. Clapperton then

Major Dixon Denham

pointed out to Bello that trade and friendship between his country and Great Britain could only develop on the basis of legitimate trade, and he required an undertaking from the ruler that he would stop the traffic in slaves to the coast. Surprisingly, Bello agreed to all this! From conversations that Clapperton had with Bello, he became certain that the Niger did flow south from this point, and empty into the Bight of Benin.

From Sokoto Clapperton made his way back to Kukawa, where he teamed up with Denham again; the two travellers now managing to establish a somewhat better working relationship. They now headed north across the great desert until they arrived at Tripoli, this being on 26 January, 1825. With him Clapperton carried a letter from Bello to George 1V, holding out the prospect of friendship and legitimate trade

Although Clapperton had been just five days march from the Niger, the Sultan had not allowed him to proceed westward.   However, on this great expedition the three travellers had learned much about Africa, and had seen at first hand the horrors of the slave-trade. Crossing the terrible Tebu Desert on the way out they had been horrified to see that the route was strewn with the bodies of hundreds of black slaves who had perished on their way down from the interior. Now Clapperton had to get back - across endless miles of similar harsh territory. On the 4th May, 1824, he started on his return journey, being rejoined by Denham at Kuka. They then set out together, heading north across the great desert, managing to reach Tripoli, after much suffering, in January, 1825.

Denham and Clapperton arrived in England on 1st June, 1825, where they were disconcerted to learn that Major Alexander Gordon Laing, eager to prove his theory that the Niger and the Nile were separate rivers, had already started for the interior. However, both men were welcomed as heroes. Denham in particular though becoming the object of public attention, which increased considerably after the publication of his Travels in Africa.   He became a frequent and honoured guest at the Home of Lord Bathurst, who thought so highly of him that he offered him a new and experimental appointment at Sierra Leone, that of superintendent of liberated African slaves on the West Coast.   He was given the rank of Lieutenant Colonel on 14th November, 1826, and then set out for the West Coast, reaching Sierra Leone in January, 1827. He spent some time on survey work, and towards the end of the year started on a visit of inspection to Fernando Po. Here he was to meet Richard Lander - bringing news from the interior of the death of his old colleague - Captain Hugh Clapperton. Early in May, 1828, Denham returned to Free Town, where he received the royal warrant appointing him lieutenant-governor of the colony of Sierra Leone. His reign though was to be a short one, for he immediately contracted fever, and died on the 8th of the month.

In June, 1825, Hugh Clapperton had been raised to the rank of commander, and then requested by Lord Bathurst to conduct a second expedition to the Niger, along with Captain Pearce, R.N., Mr Dickson, a surgeon, and Doctor Morrison, a navy surgeon and naturalist. Clapperton engaged Richard Lemon Lander, the Innkeepers son from Cornwall, as his confidential servant. For a man who had received a very poor education, then started his career by serving as a cabin boy, before being 'promoted' to the rank of Cook's mate, Clapperton had come a long way; but before covering in greater depth Clapperton's second expedition to Africa, let us return to the aforementioned African Traveller, Major Alexander Gordon Laing.

Laing was born in Edinburgh in 1793, being the eldest son of William Laing, A.M., and his wife, the daughter of William Gordon of Glasgow Academy. He was sent to Edinburgh University, then, in 1810, became an ensign in the Prince of Wales's Regiment. He later joined the York Light Infantry, serving in Antigua, where he was promoted to the rank of Lieutenant on 28th December, 1815. After other moves he was promoted to the Royal African Corps. Early in 1822 Sir Charles MacCarthy, the Governor of Sierra Leone, sent him on a mission into the Kambian and Mandingo countries, in order to ascertain the prospects of trade with the people of the area.

After staying at Kambia long enough to fulfil his instructions, he crossed the Scarcies to Melacourie, on the Melageah. He then made some diplomatic efforts to reconcile Amara, the Mandingo King, whom he described as a 'crafty Mohammedan,' with his arch rival, Chief Sannassee of Melacourie. He then returned to Sierra Leone, but on the 16th April, 1822 he set off again, on a long journey through the Timmannee and Kooranko countries to Falaba, the capital of Soolima, where he learned that there was a great deal of gold and ivory available. He was very well received here, and remained some months. He managed to ascertain the source of the Rokell, and was within three days travel of the supposed source of the Niger, but was not allowed to continue.

The situation on the West Coast at this time was extremely dangerous, for the grandly named West African settlements actually consisted of no more than Sierra Leone, which was little more than a shanty town, the tiny settlement at Gambia, and the Gold Coast. From this rather weak base the British made the fatal - but perhaps inevitable mistake - of getting involved in inter-tribal disputes, as a result of which they were soon bogged down in the Ashanti wars. Laing organised and commanded a large local force opposed to the Ashantee, whom he frequently engaged and defeated. The Ashantee though had an army of 10,000 fierce warriors, while the British could muster only 500 men from along the coast. Their Fanti allies proved to be unreliable, and the British were eventually overwhelmed. The Governor himself, Sir Charles MacCarthy, being killed in the action on the 21 January,1824, his skull being taken home by the Ashanti and used as a drinking cup. (These wars were to continue for a further two years, until a combined British-Fanti force eventually defeated the Ashantee.)

After the death of MacCarthy the chief command devolved onto Colonel Chisholm, who then sent Laing back home to report on the situation to Lord Bathurst, the Colonial Secretary.   While at home Laing began to prepare his journals for the press, which were subsequently published under the title, 'Travels in Timmannee, Kooranko, and Soolima, Countries of Western Africa, London, 1825. It was late in 1824 that Laing received his instructions from Lord Bathurst to undertake an expedition , by way of Tripoli and Timbuctoo, to ascertain the source and course of the elusive River Niger.

Full of enthusiasm, Laing left England on 5th February, 1825. He proceed to Tripoli by way of Malta, where he was treated with great respect by the Governor, the Marquis of Hastings. At Tripoli he became a close friend of the British Consul, Mr Warrington, and established an even closer friendship with his daughter, Emma Maria Warrington, who he married on 14 July, 1825 . The honeymoon was a short one, for two days later he set out for Timbuctoo, with Sheikh Babani, who undertook to get him to Timbuctoo in just ten weeks.

However, the ordinary route was considered unsafe, all of which obliged them to make a detour, which added one thousand miles to their journey. The travellers eventually reaching Ghadamis on 13th September. Laing was well received here, and remained in the town until 27th October. On the 3rd December he reached Ensals, a town on the eastern frontier of the province of Tuat, belonging to the Tuaric, where he repaid a friendly reception by caring for the sick. Thirteen months after leaving Tripoli Alexander Gordon Laing entered the ancient town of Timbuctoo, but not before being subjected to a savage attack, in which he was nearly murdered in his sleep; his terrible wounds amounting to twenty-four sword cuts, eighteen of which were exceptionally severe. A local Sheikh took pity on him, and gave him shelter, whilst he recovered - to a degree. After remaining in Timbuctoo for some time he left, but on the third night after leaving the ancient city he was attacked again, and this time decapitated. His journals and papers were never discovered. Sadly, his wife Emma died of consumption three years later. Articles which had belonged to Laing were still appearing in the Western Sudan well into the first decades of this century.

The second expedition to be led by Hugh Clapperton started for the interior from Badagry, in the Bight of Benin, on 7th December, 1825. The most humble member of this expedition being Richard Lemon Lander, engaged by Clapperton as his personal attendant. It was Lander though, not Clapperton, who was destined to succeed as a great explorer in his own right, and at last bring to a satisfactory conclusion the age-old mystery of the Niger.

Richard Lemon Lander was born on the 8th February, 1804, at Truro, Cornwall, where his father kept the Fighting Cocks Inn. His grandfather had been a famous Cornish wrestler. By chance he was born on the day that a Colonel Lemon won a local borough election, his parents, being keen supporters of this contestant, naming their son in his honour. After a rather basic education at 'Old Pascoes School,' Truro, he was put on board a sailing ship, going out to the West Indies as a page to a wealthy merchant. He returned to England in 1818. He then lived as a servant in the homes of several rich families in London, with whom he travelled on the continent. In 1823 he obtained a position as private servant to Major Colebrooke of the Royal Artillery, then a colonial commissioner. With Colebrooke he went to the Cape Colony, returning home with him in 1824. It was soon after this that the discoveries of Clapperton and Denham began to attract attention throughout Britain. Lander, who had already developed a taste for travel, was fascinated by what he heard, and, at the appropriate moment offered his services to Hugh Clapperton, refusing much better employment in South America.

At last the party set out, but a few days after leaving Badagry Doctor Morrison died. Other deaths soon followed, but Clapperton and Lander continued on their way, until they reached the city of Wow Wow, a place of some 18,000 inhabitants. Here they found the people to be exceptionally hospitable, particularly the Sultan, who was a mild unassuming man. In the town there also lived another powerful individual, Zuma, a widow , an ambitious woman who had her eyes set on ousting the Sultan from his exalted position. When the travellers arrived she immediately decided that a white husband would further enhance her status. Poor Lander was her first target, but he put up a very spirited resistance . She then turned her attention to Clapperton, who decided to make a run for it, leaving Lander behind with orders to bring on their baggage and meet him at Boussa. When Zuma found her intended husband gone she set off after him with a large entourage. The governor, thinking she had gone off to raise an army, then return with Clapperton and seize the throne, refused to let Lander go. Word then got through to Clapperton that his baggage, and Lander, were being detained - Clapperton returned. A few days later the widow Zuma also returned, in the same state and splendour that she had left Wow Wow in pursuit of the traveller. Things were explained to her, and, to her credit she was not the least bit offended, or vindictive. The Sultan gave her yet another lecture about her seditious and evil conduct; and then began to resume his former kindly attitude towards the two explorers, discussing with them the safest way for them to return to England. Eventually they and their baggage were allowed to depart peacefully, free at last from the passionate, over-ambitious, but above all, enormous, widow Zuma.

Clapperton and Lander, having escaped from the gentle dangers of Wow Wow, made their way to Boussa, the place of Mungo Park's death, before crossing over the river and entering into Nupe Country. Strangely, they made no attempt to descend the Niger, this because Clapperton had developed a strong aversion to this plan, and made no secret of it to Lander. His firm conviction now being that whoever attempted to go down the river would be attacked by the local people, and would never live to reach its termination. They crossed the river at Comie, finding themselves in a country that had just been devastated by a civil war. They passed through this area as quickly as possible, heading towards Guari, a stronghold in the hills, then on to Kano. On arrival here they found the place to be in a state of great agitation, for there were wars, and rumours of wars on every side. Clapperton made an attempt to reach Sokoto alone, leaving Lander and the baggage at Kano, but this plan was never carried out. A degree of opposition, and suspicion, about these continuous expeditions having set in. At the time the British considered it just a question of local jealousies, but it was far more than that.

The local Sultans were more far-seeing than the British appreciated, for they were in fact well aware of the situation in India, where the British had made themselves masters of the sub-continent, and trampled on all its local princes. They saw some ambitious design in the repeated missions sent by England - without any apparent motive. The court at Bornou, taking this view, accordingly wrote to Sultan Bello, advocating that he put the two explorers to death without further delay. Assurances were later given that Britain, and indeed all the European powers had no such evil designs on Africa, but subsequent developments demonstrate that the politicians at Bornou were very far-sighted !

Clapperton and Lander had not felt really well since they left the coast, particularly the former, whose health, at this point in time, began to deteriorate very rapidly. Lander was of the opinion that Clapperton's health had taken a real turn for the worse since he spent a night sleeping on the reedy banks of a stagnant ditch, and his morale was also low due to disappointments and bad treatment. Clapperton's Journal terminates abruptly on the 12 March, 1827, for his strength was now broken. On the same day he was attacked by dysentery, which he told Lander had been brought on by cold, caught by lying on wet ground, when heated and fatigued with walking. For twenty days Hugh Clapperton remained in a low and distressed state. Lander himself then contracted fever, and was unable to move. The two sick men were then cared for by Pascoe, a remaining member of the party, and one black slave. Towards the end of April Clapperton became alarmingly ill. Each day the faithful Lander read a portion of the New Testament, and the ninety-fifth psalm to him, which he seemed to appreciate. The end though was not far away, at length he called Lander to his side saying -

" Richard, I shall shortly be no more; I feel myself dying." Almost choking with grief Lander replied " God forbid, my dear master: you will live many years yet." " Don't be so much affected, my dear boy, I entreat you,"

Clapperton responding " it is the will of the Almighty; it cannot be helped. Take care of my journal and papers after my death; and when you arrive in London, go immediately to my agents, send for my uncle, who will accompany you to the Colonial Office, and let them see you deposit them safely into the hands of the Secretary."

Clapperton continued to give Lander further directions on how he should proceed after his death, but a few days later he breathed his last, this being in a small circular clay hut at Changary, near Sokota, on 13 April, 1827. Lander immediately sent to ask permission of the Sultan to bury the corpse, and he would point out the place where his remains might be deposited. Bello promptly ordered four slaves to dig a grave at the village of Jungavie, about five miles to the south-east of Sokota, and the body was then taken there. When all was ready, Lander opened the prayer-book, and, "amid showers of tears" read the funeral service over the remains of Hugh Clapperton. The Union Jack was then taken off, and the body lowered into the earth. Lander then wept bitterly, as he gazed for the last time upon all that remained of his generous and intrepid master - and indeed by now, very close friend.

Lander then returned, disconsolate and depressed, to his solitary hut, put his head on his hand, and reflected on his lonesome and dangerous situation. He was a hundred and fifteen days' journey from the coast , surrounded by many hostile people, with his only friend and protector mouldering in the grave, and suffering dreadfully from fever himself. In this sorry state he now had to plan his return route. At first it seemed that Bello had made up his mind to detain Lander, and he was in fact strongly suspected of being instrumental in the murder of the unfortunate Laing. However, on the representation of one of his officers, of the impolicy as well as the inherent injustice of such a measure, he let him go, and Lander eventually set off in the general direction of Kano. with the ultimate intention of making for the Bight of Benin.

On his way the King of Wawa made him a present of a beautiful mare, and afterwards the Sultan of Kiama gave him a pony, and told him that if his king wished to send any one to Bornou, he would see that he was conducted there by a safe route, without the necessity of going through the hostile Felatah country. In short, during the whole journey from Kano to Badagry, Lander experienced nothing but kindness from the local people; but here he became an object of hatred to a nest of villainous Portuguese slave-traders, who stirred up trouble for Lander, and nearly succeeded in having him killed. Their justifiable fear that the arrival of the English would eventually put an end to their obnoxious trade in slaves, being the obvious motivation for their actions.

Three of these merchants went to the King and told him and his principal men that Lander was obviously a spy, and, if allowed to leave, would soon return with an army and conquer their country. This, the incredulous people believed, and Lander was then treated with coldness and distrust by the king and his subjects, who seldom went to see him. The head men then got together in the fetish hut, discussed the issue, and decided that Lander had to be subjected to a form of trial, by drinking a poisonous "fetish" potion. On his way over to the appointed place Lander was surrounded by about six hundred very aggressive people, a great number of them armed with hatchets, bows and arrows, and spears. On entering the hut Lander was presented with a bowl, containing a liquid resembling water, which he was commanded to drink; and in a manner remarkably akin to the twisted logic of the European witch-hunters, the head man said, " If you come to do bad, it will kill you; but if not, it cannot hurt you." His options being extremely limited, Lander kept his wits about him, swallowed the contents without hesitation, then walked hastily out of the hut, through the hostile crowd, and back to his own lodgings. He then took some very strong medicine, and lots of hot water, which acted as anticipated, causing him to vomit violently. His stomach thus cleared, Lander felt no ill effects from the fetish. He was then informed that this bitter mix almost always proved fatal, Lander then stating -

" When the king and chief men found, after five days, that the fetish had not hurt me, they became extremely kind, and sent me presents of provisions etc., daily, and frequently said I was protected by God, and that it was out of the power of man to do me injury."

However, the Portuguese slave traders continued to make all efforts to stop Lander from communicating with his countrymen on the coast; but eventually word got through to Captain Morris, of the brig *Maria*, who, hearing that Lander was then at Badagry, kindly went himself from Whydah to rescue him, and convey him to Cape Coast. After having endured so much, and lived to tell the tale, the grateful Lander then wrote -

' Here I gave my faithful slaves, Aboudah, Jowdie, and Pascoe's wife, their freedom, who testified their sorrow at my departure, by heaping sand on their heads, and other marks of grief, peculiar to the African race. Colonel Lumley generously promised to give them pieces of ground and a small sum of money, and I have no doubt they will do well.'

From Cape Coast Lander embarked on the *Esk* sloop of war, and arrived in England on the 30 April, 1828. The man who had set out for Africa as a mere servant, was now rightly welcomed home as a conquering hero, which indeed he was. In the opinion of many Richard Lander was the most attractive of all the African explorers, his most charming quality clearly being the complete absence of pretension from his character. And, to his credit, there is not the slightest indication that he allowed his well-earned fame to alter his attitude. However, the mystery of the course of the Niger remained. The government therefore hit on the idea of sending Lander back to Africa, with instructions to follow the course of the river below Boussa. It was agreed that Lander could take his younger brother John with him, who was a printer by trade, but without any promise of reward by the government. And, unlike so many instances when a government makes a promise, which is promptly broken, the authorities kept to the letter of this parsimonious agreement!

The prime mover behind this expedition was John Barrow, second secretary at the Admiralty, who had become widely known for his sponsorship of Arctic exploration. After the death of Sir Joseph Banks in 1820, his place as unofficial patron of British exploration had been assumed by Barrow. He had visited South Africa, and in 1806 wrote a book about this venture, which, he felt, qualified him to speak as an expert on the entire continent of Africa. Barrow was still inclined to believe that the Niger flowed into a great lake - Tshad, and not the Atlantic Ocean. Richard Lander soon received very specific instructions on the aims of the expedition.

" Downing Street, 31st December, 1829

Sir,

I am directed by the Secretary Sir George Murray to acquaint you, that he has deemed it expedient to accept the offer which you have made, to proceed to Africa, accompanied by your brother, for the purpose of ascertaining the course of the Great River, which was crossed by the late Captain Clapperton, on his journey to Soccatoo; and a passage having been accordingly engaged for you and your brother on board the *Alert*, merchant vessel, which is to proceeding to Cape Coast Castle, on the western coast of Africa, I am to desire that you will embark directly on board that vessel......."

On arrival in Africa he was instructed to be very particular in his observations, and establish which rivers fell into the Quorra, and whether the whole or any part of the river turned to the eastward. If it continued to flow to the southward, he was to follow it to the sea, but if it went to the east he was to follow it, and he would probably find that it fell into Lake Tshad. If this was the case he was to explore around the lake as much as possible, but with due regard to his safety, then return by way of Fezzan or Tripoli. If, however, the river continued to flow to the east for some distance, but then turn off towards the south, he was to follow it until it reached the sea.

Amongst other things, he was advised to try and obtain any books or papers that belonged to Mungo Park, and to take every opportunity of sending down to the coast brief accounts of his progress. To ensure that such notes arrived he was further instructed that he was to furnish the bearer with a note, setting forth the reward he is to have for his trouble, and requesting any English person, to whom it was presented, to pay that reward, on the

63

understanding that it would subsequently be repaid by the British Government. The letter concluded with these words:-

" For the performance of this service, you are furnished with all the articles which you have required for your personal convenience, during your journey, together with a sum of two hundred dollars in coin, and in case, upon your arrival at Badagry, you should find it absolutely necessary to provide yourself with a further supply of dollars, you will be at liberty to draw upon this department for any sum not exceeding three hundred dollars. During the ensuing year, the sum of one hundred pounds will be paid to your wife, in quarterly payments, and upon your return a gratuity of one hundred pounds will be paid to yourself.

All the papers and observations which you shall bring back with you, are to be delivered by you at this office, and you will be entitled to receive any pecuniary consideration which may be obtained from the publication of the account of your journey.

I am, Sir, &c. &c.

(Signed) R.W. Hay "

On the 9 January. 1830, the Lander brothers left Portsmouth in the brig *Alert*, under the command of Captain Tyson, bound for Cape Coast Castle. They had a quick but boisterous and unpleasant passage out of forty-two days, arriving at their destination on the 22nd of the following month. Here they were pleasantly received by George Maclean, President of the Council, at Cape Coast, and the merchants living there. They also managed to engage old Pascoe and his wife, who had been employed on the last mission - together with Ibrahim, and two Bornu men, who could speak some English, and could also converse in the Haussa language. They then moved to Anamaboo, where they remained until the 4, March, when they took the opportunity of sailing in the *Alert* once more, then bound for Accra, where they expected to find a vessel that would take them on to Badagry, their starting point, in the Bight of Benin.

It was a British warship that eventually brought them to the coast off Badagry, where they were obliged to get ashore in a small canoe, this being the only way to get through the pounding surf. They were followed from the beach to the town of Badagry by a large group of local people, most of whom were roaring with laughter at the strange appearance of the Lander Brothers, for they had on their heads enormous straw hats, larger than umbrellas, while their bodies were draped in vast scarlet Muhammadan robes, belted in round the waist, full Turkish trousers and high boots!

The King of Badagry, who had been very friendly to Richard Lander two years previously now seemed rather hostile. He demanded large and expensive presents from the travellers, particularly greedy claims being made on their rum. It was in fact only when the stock of this desirable liquid was almost exhausted that he finally agreed to let them continue on their journey. On their way up country they passed many places of great interest, but before they had left the forest belt near the coast, they came to a deep hidden valley, which was exceptionally beautiful:-

" It is enclosed and overhung on all sides by trees of amazing height and dimensions, which hide it in deep shadow. Fancy might picture a spot, so silent and solemn as this, as the abode of genii and fairies; everything conducing to render it grand, melancholy, and venerable, and the glen only wants an old dilapidated castle, a rock with a cave in it, or something of the kind to render it the most interesting place in the universe. "

Early on 17, April they left Jadoo, and about mid-day arrived at a small pretty village called Pooya. They recorded that the country between these two places was particularly attractive, resembling a magnificent orchard. On their way they met hundreds of people, with vast numbers of bullocks, sheep and goats, together with fowls and pigeons, which were carried on their heads in neat wicker baskets.

They also noted that several of these travellers were loaded with packages of cloth, and indigo in large round balls. These people were all slaves, and were proceeding to the coast, to sell these goods for their masters. One old woman was unfortunate enough to slip, and let a large calabash of palm-oil fall from her head. Terrified of the punishment she would receive from her owner for this accident she, and her fellow slaves, began to cry and wring their hands in despair. By way of consolation the compassionate Richard Lander gave her a large clasp knife, which, he felt, would more than recompense her for the loss of the oil - and hopefully save her from some dreadful punishment. She wiped her tears away, and fell to the ground before him in gratitude.

Shortly after this incident John Lander fell sick, but on 20, April, when in the town of Assinara, he began to recover from the fever, but was still too weak to travel. The acting-governor of the town visited the brothers, and asked for their assistance in his efforts to expose a local sorcerer! It would seem this persons influence was being held responsible for making people pine away and die; women with children being especially singled out for his malevolence. These victims, it would seem, suddenly dropping dead without the slightest warning. The old man himself being very alarmed, asked the Landers to provide him with a charm to preserve him and his family.

The travellers pressed on, and by the 6 June they were at a place called Kakafungi, near the Oly River. John Lander was now so ill though that he could not mount his horse without assistance. At noon they left the town and headed north, through a stony and barren wilderness, at times the brothers falling behind the rest of the party, because they were unable to keep up with them. On Monday 7 June John seemed a little better, and at 8 a.m. they crossed the Oly River in a canoe they found tied to the bank. In the afternoon they passed a spot where their guides informed them a party of Felatahs, a short time ago, had murdered twenty of their slaves, because they had not enough food to support them.

It would seem this party had been despatched by Bello from Soccatoo to collect the accustomed tributes from the towns of Rakah and Alorie, but the inhabitants of the latter town shut the gates against them, and declared themselves independent of the Falatahs. On their way back to report to Bello they had to pass through Borgoo, where they encountered more opposition, the King of Kiama forbidding any of his people from selling them provisions. They were consequently obliged to find their way through a long and inhospitable wilderness without food. They dug numerous holes to find wild yams, and were no doubt reduced to a terrible state before they decided to kill their slaves. The Landers found the skeleton of one of these slaves, but think the story might have been greatly exaggerated, for they found that people in this area were very fond of presenting strangers with the most unfavourable idea of other local tribes.

After much suffering, and many more adventures, the explorers began to get near to the Niger. With commendable foresight the Landers then decided to head north in order to visit the Sultan of Yauri, in the city of that name; for they recognised that they would require his goodwill if they were to make a successful descent of the Niger. The usual long delays occurred, but at last the required co-operation was obtained.

The rather grudging co-operation of the Kings of Boossa and Wawa was also obtained by the Cornishmen in their epic attempt to descend the Niger in canoes, until they reached the sea. The Africans themselves must also have had an interest in the venture, for, strange as it may seem, the millions of people who had lived close to the great river for countless generations, were also not clear as to the full course of the stream, for political and geographical factors tended to confine each tribe or nation to their own particular stretch of the river.

Efforts to get started continued, with the Landers finding the wily potentates they were obliged to deal with sometimes co-operative, but also not above driving exceptionally hard bargains, taking full advantage of the fact that they were dealing with weary and isolated travellers. One first agreed to sell then canoes, but demanded payment in advance, and then did not deliver the canoes. He then passed the order on to someone else, who failed to keep to the agreement. At long last though all these problems were overcome, and, on 30, September, 1830, the explorers left Boussa, in two small leaky canoes; and within a short while reached the large and fertile island of Patashi - some forty miles below Boussa. John Lander later describing in very eloquent terms a typical scene as they floated rapidly downstream.

" Both banks presented the most delightful appearance. They were embellished with mighty trees and elegant shrubs, which were clad in thick and luxuriant foliage. Some of lively green, and others of darker hue; and little birds were singing merrily among their branches. Magnificent festoons of creeping plants, always green, hung from the tops of the tallest trees, and dropping to the water's edge, formed immense natural grottoes, pleasing and grateful to the eye, and seemed to be fit abodes for the Naiades of the River!"

At Patashi the local chief made them very welcome, lending them two better canoes so that they could proceed to a place called Leyaba, where they were to meet yet another important local potentate, this one styled in Hausa "Sariki-n-rua", or King of the River.

" Between nine and ten a.m. we heard a number of men singing and keeping time to the motion of the many paddles, but could see no one. However, in a very few minutes a canoe,.... propelled by above twenty very fine young men, whose voices we had been listening to just before, drew nearer. We were not only surprised at its extraordinary length and uncommon neatness, but likewise at the unusual display of pomp and show which we observed in her. In the centre a mat awning was erected, which was variously decorated, and on the front of it hung a large piece of scarlet cloth ornamented with bits of gold lace stitched on different parts of it. In the bow of the canoe were three or four little boys, of equal size, who were clad with neatness and propriety; and in the stern sat a number of comely-looking musicians, consisting of several drummers and a trumpeter, whilst the young men who had the management of the boat were not inferior to their companions either in decency of apparel or respectability of appearance. They all looked, in fact, extremely well. "

" As soon as this canoe arrived at the landing -place, the 'Water King' came out from beneath the awning, and, followed by musicians and a suite of attendants, walked to the hut, wherein all public matters were transacted.... When the usual compliments had passed on both sides, he informed us, with much solemnity, of his rank and title; he then alluded to the cause of his coming, which, he said, was to do us honour..... This being done, he presented us with a pot of excellent honey and two thousand kauris in money, besides a large quantity of kola nuts, which are cultivated in the country, and which are held in such great esteem, that the opulent and powerful alone have the means to procure them......"

The Lander brothers continued to float down the Niger for hundreds of miles, coping well with all the hazards of the river, which included numerous hidden rocks, lurking just below the surface of the water, shoals, rapids, and driving rain. Large, and potentially hostile animals, were also a constant cause for concern, in particular hippopotami. Here is their colourful description of an encounter with these beasts.

" we had paddled along the banks a distance of not less than thirty miles, every inch of which we had attentively examined, but not a bit of dry land could anywhere be discovered which was firm enough to bear our weight. Therefore we resigned ourselves to circumstances, and all of us having been refreshed with a little cold rice and honey, and water from the stream, we permitted the canoe to drift down with the current, for our men were too much fatigued with the labours of the day to work any longer. But here a fresh evil arose, which we were unprepared to meet. An incredible number of hippopotami arose very near us, and came splashing, snorting, and plunging all round the canoe and placed us in imminent danger.

Thinking to frighten them off we fired a shot or two at them, but the noise only called up from the water and out of the fens about as many more of their unwieldy companions, and we were more closely beset than before. Our people, who had never in all their lives been exposed in a canoe to such huge and formidable beasts trembled with fear and apprehension, and absolutely wept aloud; and their terror was not a little increased by the dreadful peals of thunder which rattled over their heads, and by the awful darkness which prevailed, broken at intervals by flashes of lightning, whose powerful glare was truly awful. Our people tell us that these formidable animals frequently upset canoes in the river, when everyone in them is sure to perish. These came so close to us that we could reach them with the butt end of a gun. When I fired at the first, which I must have hit, every one of them came to the surface of the water and pursued us so fast over to the north bank that it was with the greatest difficulty imaginable we could keep before them.. "

Below the confluence of the Niger with the Benue, which they passed on the 25, October, the Landers visited the town of Bokwa, where they were mistaken for a new type of pirate-conquerors like the Fulas. Some smooth diplomacy, and the services of a Muhammadan scholar saved the situation from degenerating into a fight, in which the Landers would have been in a 'no-win' situation. All involved eventually becoming the best of friends. At Damuggu, they also made such a good impression with the local chief that he agreed to give them better canoes for the continuance of their journey.

The Lander brothers continued downstream, passing the Warri branch of the river, until they came to the market town of Kirri. Here they encountered about fifty large canoes, full of men, all of them wearing European clothing, with the exception of trousers. They were also flying a variety of flags - including the Union Jack. At first the Landers felt overjoyed, but their fond anticipations vanished in a few seconds, when the first canoe met them, and their intentions became all to clear.

" A great stout fellow, of a most forbidding countenance, beckoned me to come to him, but seeing him and all his people so well armed, I was not much inclined to trust myself among them and paid no attention to him. The next moment I heard the sound of a drum, and in an instant several men mounted a platform and levelled their muskets at us. There was nothing to be done but obey; as for running away, it was out of the question, our square built loaded canoe was incapable of it, and to fight with fifty war canoes, for such we found them, containing each above forty people, most of whom were as well armed as ourselves, would have been throwing away my own and my canoemen's lives very foolishly."

Within a few moments all their luggage had been stolen. With amazing courage Lander then stood up and aimed his gun directly at their leader, but three of his men sprang on him and forced the gun from his hands. He was then robbed of his jacket and shoes, whilst other men attempted to carry away Pascoe's wife. Lander immediately seized hold of her, and with the assistance of other members of his party managed to drag her back into their canoe. He then encouraged his men to arm themselves with their paddles. Pascoe hit one of the raiders a savage blow, which forced the man to reel backwards and collapse. At last they managed to get free, and, luckily, none of the other canoes made the slightest attempt to assist their attackers. Richard Lander then resolved to follow these thugs to the market, where they appeared to be going, but did not meet with any success.

After this sad incident the explorers made a visit to the Ibo King. This 'Palaver' was attended by "King Boy", who was the son of an Ijo Chief, King Forday, whose domain covered an area of land at the mouth of the Niger. King Boy agreed to ransom the explorers for gun powder and trade goods, and to get them safely to an English vessel moored at the mouth of the Niger. For this last service though he demanded a further allocation of trade goods, up to a market value of fifteen slaves. Although this 'contract' was obviously entered into under duress, King Boy did at least intend to keep to his part of the bargain.

In November, 1830, the Ijo canoes took the Landers and their party down the central stream of the Niger to Akassa, where they found the English sailing vessel *Thomas* of Liverpool moored. At long last the mystery of the Niger was solved, by Richard Lander, the domestic servant from Cornwall, and his brother John, a humble printer. They had achieved immortality as explorers, but at this point in time they still had to get home. The behaviour of Captain Lake, master of the *Thomas*, now stood in the way of this objective. The explorers had not reached his ship at a very propitious moment, as four of the crew had just died of fever, and Lake and the rest of the crew were ill. The rather unpleasant old sea-dog then began to curse and swear, and with the most offensive oaths refused to honour Lander's bill, or to pay anything at all for him. Highly embarrassed by this unexpected turn

of events, Richard Lander then asked King Boy if he would mind taking
them on to the Bonny river, where other British ships were lying. Here he
was certain that he would find a Captain who would behave in a more
honourable manner; unfortunately though King Boy's confidence in the
integrity of British Captains had now been severely shaken. He refused to
take him, arguing that if one master had refused to redeem the promises
made by the Landers, they would not fare any better with others.

Lake eventually agreed to take Lander and his party away, but without
parting with any ransom money. King Boy returned to the shore in disgust. A
further complication then set in, when Lake refused to pay the African river
pilot his fee. It would appear that failure to pay fees was a recurring problem
faced by this pilot, this to the extent that he had felt obliged to mount a
battery of guns to cover the passage, just in order to enforce payment on such
occasions. Heavy seas, and an adverse wind, prevented them leaving the river
for some days, and rumours began to surface that King Boy was planning to
return with an armed band. Their situation was far from satisfactory, to say
the least, but on 27, November, Lake made a run for it, got past the battery,
narrowly avoided being wrecked on the breakers, then set sail for the island
of Fernando Po. Here the Landers eventually landed, where they were in
safety, for at Fernando Po in those days there was a British Admiralty
establishment for suppressing the slave trade, and a government
superintendent.

The Landers now had to face a long delay on the island before a passage
home could be arranged. John fell ill again, and whilst he was recovering the
superintendent, Mr John Beecroft, offered to take Richard Lander to the
Calabar river, in the colonial schooner *Portia*, where he was going to procure
stock for the use of the colony. John was left at Clarence, and they left for
Calabar on the evening of the 23, December. Beecroft was an interesting
character, whose remarkable career in West Africa began at Fernando Po in
1827, as the aforementioned superintendent. When the island was eventually
abandoned by Britain, he was to remain there to look after the interests of the
liberated slaves who had been settled there.   Richard Lander was to
accompany Beecroft twice to Calabar in the *Portia* before a passage home
could be arranged.

About 14, January, 1831 the brig *Thomas* touched at the island on her
way home from the Cameroons , her commander, Captain Lake thinking that
the Landers would be only too pleased to take a passage home with him. Not
surprisingly, the offer was refused, Richard recording his reaction in these
words " We have now been here seven weeks, and would certainly stay seven
more rather than put ourselves at his mercy again. We had experienced quite
enough of his care and kindness, and therefore declined his offer of taking
us." Had they accepted this offer the world would have heard no more of

Richard Lander, and he explains why: - " After waiting three days at the island, he (Lake) sailed at about six o'clock in the morning, and had not got more than a mile from the anchorage, when a large vessel with long raking masts suddenly appeared from behind a part of the island, and was seen in pursuit of him. We observed this vessel fire several guns at him, which at length made him take in sail and wait. We have no doubt that this vessel was a pirate, and our suspicions were confirmed the next day by seeing the two vessels lying becalmed close by each other. There was no signs of them the next day, and we saw nothing more of the *Thomas*. "

Captain Lake and his ship were never heard of again, thus confirming Lander's view that the ship had been taken by a pirate. It is also almost certain that Lake and his crew would have been made to 'walk-the-plank' - and the ship put into service as a slaver. Vessels that met this fate would then be filled with slaves and sent across the Atlantic. Should such vessels have met with a British man-o-war, of the West Africa Squadron, they would escape examination, as their appearance would be known, and no suspicion would have been provoked.

A few days after the loss of the *Thomas* arrangements were concluded to get the Landers back home on board the merchant ship *Caernarvon*, bound for Rio Janeiro, under the command of Captain Garth. At six in the evening of Saturday, 22, January, 1831 they said farewell to John Beecroft , Crighton, the British naval surgeon, Mr Beatty and other members of the British establishment on the island. The crew consisting of seven European seamen, two freed negroes, and one Krooman, besides the commander of the vessel and two mates. At noon the following day Owen Williams, seaman, died. On Wednesday 26th, Wells, the Captain's steward, and Jones, the second mate were taken ill with fever. The following day John Williams, seaman was taken ill with fever. The following Sunday Smith, seaman was taken ill, and Wells died. The situation continued to deteriorate, when, on Friday, 4, February, Captain Garth went down with fever, and Williams died. The weather was fine, with little wind, and they were making little progress over to the coast of America.

" Sunday, February 6th. - The chief mate taken ill with fever. So much are we reduced now, that the three black men, with my brother and myself, are all who are left to work the vessel, and only one of these, the Krooman, knows how to steer. Mr Stockwell is constantly employed attending to the sick."

On Monday 7, February Smith, seaman, died, and because of the sorry state of the crew, Richard Lander was constantly employed, both day and night in working the ship. He remained at the helm every night until 12 p.m. - going back to this task at 4 a.m. in the morning. To add to their troubles the vessel was completely overrun by rats, making life below decks very unpleasant. However, they continued to struggle across the Atlantic, and by

Monday, 14, March, they were off Cape Frio. That evening their only Krooman fell into the sea, and despite all their efforts they were unable to save him - but could hear his tragic cries for help over an hour later. Two days later they were becalmed, and started to drift towards the shore. They attempted to get the long-boat out to save themselves, but found they lacked the strength to lift her over the side. At this critical moment a breeze from the land sprang up, which enabled them to regain control of the ship. The breeze continued to favour them, and at 2 p.m. on Wednesday 16, March, 1831, they anchored in the harbour of Rio Janeiro.

The following day they paid their respects to Admiral Baker, the commander-in-chief of the South American Station, when they made known their situation, and asked for his assistance to get them back to England. Baker was kind and hospitable, and arranged a passage home for them in the *William Harris*, a government transport. A few days later , on Sunday, 20, March, they sailed for England, and on Thursday, 9th June, 1831 they arrived at Portsmouth after a very long and tedious voyage " and gladly landed with hearts full of gratitude for all our deliverances." All that remained now was to report their safe return, and their great discovery.

" Friday, June 10th. - Having left my brother at Portsmouth, I arrived in London this morning by the mail, and reported our discovery to Lord Goderich, his Majesty's Colonial Secretary."

Richard and John Lander were now acclaimed as national heroes, which factor did not appear to register with the noble Viscount Goderich, who was also president of the Geographical Society. On behalf of a grateful British government, he procured - by way of an appropriate reward for John Lander, a hero, but one of low social standing - a humble tide-waiters job in the customs house! John Lander lived for another eight years, dying on 16, November, 1839, from an illness originally contracted in Africa. He left a wife and three children. Richard Lander though was soon to return to Africa, on his third and final expedition.

On 14, November, 1831, the first meeting of the season of the Royal Geographical Society took place, Viscount Goderich being in the chair. The room was crowded to witness the presentation of his Majesty's first premium of fifty guineas, placed at the disposal of the Society, to Richard Lander, for his discovery of the termination of the Niger in the sea. Gooderich stated that he felt convinced that all would agree that this award could not have been more appropriately disposed of, than by conferring it on an individual whose courage and enterprise had achieved so much for the advancement of science. In a few words Richard Lander then expressed his deep gratitude for the reward bestowed on him. The second proposition at this meeting was also one of great historical significance, this being to incorporate the African Association with the Geographical Society, which was promptly carried.

CHAPTER FOUR THE NIGER STEAMSHIP EXPEDITION - 1832

Richard and John Lander had now proved that the Niger did not flow into a great lake, or across the African continent to join the Nile, but through its labyrinthine delta into the Atlantic. Their expedition had brought to a conclusion many years of exploratory work aimed at establishing the geographical outline of western Africa. As noted, it also brought to a conclusion the work of the African Association.

For the first thirty years of its existence the Association had been the only one of its kind in the world, but things were changing rapidly. In 1822 the French had founded the Societe de Geographie, then six years later the Germans established the Gesellschaft fur Erdkunde. More importantly though, in 1827 the Raleigh Travellers' Club was set up in London, with about forty members, many of whom were also members of the African Association. From this group came the suggestion to establish the British Geographical Society, which was founded the following year. The inaugural meeting being held on 16 July, 1830. John Barrow, a senior civil servant in the Admiralty agreed to undertake the spadework of the organisation, all of which brought to an appropriate end forty-three years active work by the African Association.

The far-reaching economic and social implications of the Landers' discovery was also noted by the merchants of Liverpool, who were eager to extend their area of trade in Africa. The notorious Liverpool slave trade had been abolished, and the emancipation of the slaves in the British colonies was about to take place. The Remorseless pressure of the British Abolitionists had also obliged the government to force anti-slavery treaties on one foreign power after another. A squadron of the Royal Navy now patrolled the West African coast, in an attempt to enforce these treaties, and all efforts were being made to offer free legitimate trade as an alternative to the slave trade. Steamships were now being developed as an alternative to sail, which made river navigation more viable. Macgregor Laird was an Abolitionist, a merchant and the son of a shipbuilder, thus bringing together in himself all the strands that were required to play the leading role in pending developments.

Macgregor Laird was born at Greenock, Scotland, on 19 October, 1809, his elder brother John Having been born there in June, 1805. They were the children of William Laird and his wife Agnes, the daughter of Captain Macgregor, the direct descendant of the legendary 'Rob Roy' Macgregor. The Laird family were well-to-do, being the owners of a large rope works.

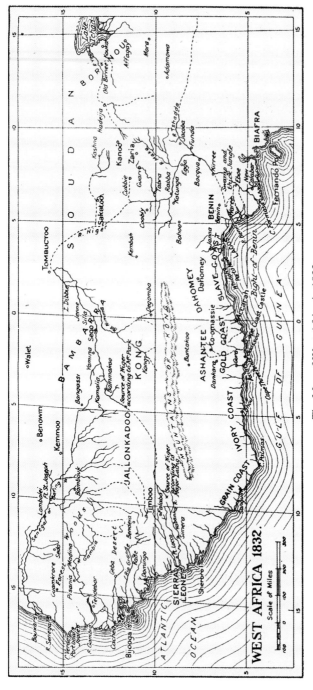

The Map of West Africa in 1832

74

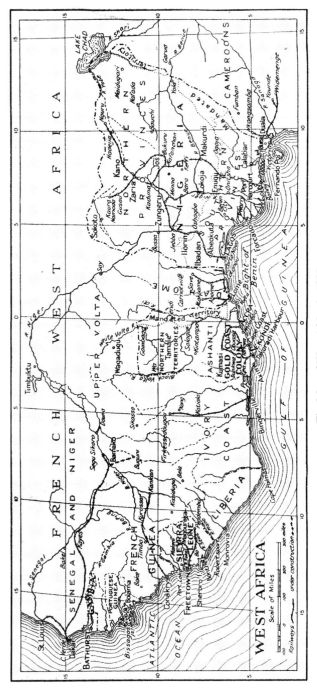

The Map of West Africa in 1932

75

In 1810 though it was decided that William and Agnes would move south to Liverpool, this in order to establish a branch of the family firm on Merseyside. On arrival in Liverpool they set up home in Bedford Street, and opened an office in Hill Street. He lost no time in establishing a rope works, and for good measure also became involved in the sugar trade. He also plunged into other ventures, becoming a director of two shipping companies, and the local agent for James Watt's steam engine. The use of steam for propelling ships was now well in hand, and William Laird, the astute young man of business, was quick to note these developments. Meanwhile, the brothers education had to be attended to, both youngsters being sent to the Royal Institution School, Liverpool.

Macgregor Laird did particularly well at this school, to the extent that his parents decided to send him to Edinburgh University to finish his education. He did well, but in 1829 he contracted typhus, the attack being a particularly severe one. His family came up from Merseyside to nurse him, and his intimate friend Doctor Thomas Briggs, whom Macgregor had known from infancy, and was just four years older than Macgregor, gave up work to attend his stricken friend. Thomas Briggs was the son of Doctor William Briggs, eminent physician of Duke Street, Liverpool. Macgregor Laird survived, in no small measure due to the attention of Briggs, but he was too weak to continue his studies, and therefore had to return to Liverpool with his parents.

In March, 1824 William Laird made extensive purchases of land around the Wallasey Pool, this being on the Wirral peninsular, on the opposite banks of the Mersey to Liverpool. The Laird family moved to Birkenhead, Wirral, and were then prime movers in the industrial and residential development of the town. In 1828 John Laird was taken into partnership by his father, and the firm, under the title of William Laird & Son, started to build small vessels. In October, 1829, they launched their first vessel, this being a lighter of 50 tons measurement, built to the order of the Irish Inland Company, for the navigation of the Irish lakes and canals. A similar vessel was to be launched three years later in 1832. From this humble start the long history of the world-famous Laird shipyard began. After completing his education Macgregor Laird joined his father and brother in this enterprise, but this was a post he was soon to relinquish, in order to organise an expedition .

Macgregor Laird - and many others - were of the opinion that the Landers had been treated shabbily by the government, and were anxious to rectify matters, and at the same time advance their own interests. Laird, together with Thomas Stirling, Joseph Hornby, Alexander Smith Jnr., William Dixon, Thomas Forsyth, and other Liverpool merchants set up the African Inland Commercial Company, in order to mount a steamship expedition to the Niger, it being agreed that command of this venture would be offered to Richard Lemon Lander. Lander consented, and the goods required for barter with the

Africans were selected by him. Ivory and Indigo seem to have been the chief things expected , which Lander assured the company could be obtained in the Niger Country at very little cost.

As a merchant Macgregor Laird immediately recognised the value of the Landers' discovery, seeing that the long-sought-for highway into Central Africa had been found, comparing it to the Rhine, the Danube, the Mississippi, or the Orinoko, in their respective countries. By introducing legitimate trade he also felt he was striking a blow at the slave trade. With these factors in mind the stated objectives of the expedition were to establish a permanent settlement at the junction of the Tchadda and Niger, for the purpose of collecting the products of the country.

The first plan put forward was to send out a large vessel to the Nun river, fitted out for the palm-oil trade, with a small steam - vessel to trade up the river.   Laird and Lander discussed this option, but this plan was soon abandoned. They eventually decided to fit out two steam-vessels of light draught, which would be able to make their way up river, and a sailing vessel, as a support ship, which would wait at the mouth of the river to receive their cargoes. Unfortunately no suitable steam-vessels were available, so they had no option other than to build them, which work Macgregor Laird organised. The keel of the larger vessel was laid on 28 March, 1832, and by incredible exertions she was launched just two months later, on the 29 May.   Her engine was a single one of forty-four horse power, which was manufactured by Fawcett and Preston of Liverpool, which firm also had a large financial stake in the venture.   She was 112 feet long, had a beam of 16 feet, and a depth of 8 feet, with a poop as high as the waist, to provide accommodation for the officers.

The smaller vessel was a highly experimental craft. With the exception of her decks she was entirely made of wrought iron. For reasons that are not altogether clear, she was built a considerable distance away from the Mersey, and consequently had to be conveyed through the streets of Liverpool on a large truck. As she made her way through the port, those involved with her construction were ridiculed. The pundits predicted that the long sea passage would work all her rivets loose, the heat of the tropical sun would bake her crew alive, and she would be destroyed by lightning! She was 70 feet long, beam 13 feet, 6.5 feet deep, with a small engine of just sixteen horse-power. The large boat was named *Quorra*, the smaller boat *Alburkah*, a Houssa word signifying blessing.

The crew of the *Quorra* consisted of twenty-six men, these being the Captain, 2 Mates, 1 Purser, 1 'Medical Gentleman' , 1 Boatswain, 1 Carpenter, 2 Engineers, 2 Firemen, 2 Stewards, 1 cook, 10 Seamen, and two apprentices. The crew of the *Alburkah* was formed of the Captain, 1 Mate, 1 Surgeon, 1 Engineer, 2 Firemen, 1 Steward, 1 Cook and 6 seamen. Total 14.

Allowing for all eventualities, including, it would seem, a small-scale war, Macgregor Laird also armed the *Quorra* with one twenty-four pound swivel gun forward, one eighteen-pound carronade, and eight four-pound carriage guns on the main deck, with a large amount of small arms, not only for the crew, but for the Kroomen they intended to recruit on the coast. The *Alburka* was more modestly armed, carrying just one nine-pound swivel gun forward, and six one-pound swivels on her sides. Both ships also had their sides armed with chevaux-de-frise, to resist boarders, and stop Africans from crowding the decks. No expense was spared in fitting the vessels out, goods and luxuries in abundance being made available for the officers and crews of both ships. Laird claiming that better found vessels had never left the port of Liverpool.

The sailing vessel purchased by the African Inland Commercial Company for the expedition was the *Columbine*, a brig of about 200 tons, only four years old, and well provided with stores. As a precaution, it was agreed that she was to accompany the steam-vessels on the voyage out, as, having been built expressly for river navigation, it was not actually expected that they would perform well on the Atlantic. Excitement mounted, as the day of departure drew closer, all of which was overshadowed by a serious outbreak of cholera in Liverpool, as a consequence of this development the expedition was ordered to proceed to Milford, and to remain there until it could be established that they were completely free from the disease. Their plan was then to proceed in company to the river Nun, calling at Cape Coast Castle for Kroomen and interpreters. In the event of them parting company their contingency plan was that they would rendezvous in the harbour of Port Praya in the island of St. Jago.

Macgregor Laird was now just twenty three years old, and, according to his eldest daughter, Eleanor Bristow Laird, more like his father than any of his other sons, the affection and sympathy between them being very strong. It had not been his original intention to accompany this expedition to the Niger, only to organise it. However, the prospect of going on an exciting expedition proved too great a temptation for a young man, and, despite his poor health he decided to go with Lander to the coast. One of the earliest letters which his daughter possessed, is the one in which he tells his father of the decision he has made to accompany the expedition to the Niger. This letter was undated, and had not been through the post. It was written some time early in 1832, probably soon after the expedition vessels were launched.

" My dear father,

I cannot be a hypocrite any longer, and much as I know my determination will grieve you and my mother, yet I do hope I am acting for the best..... I have made up my mind to accompany the African Expedition and nothing shall change it, it is the only chance I may ever have of distinguishing myself, and a nobler one I shall never have. I have not made up my mind rashly, but I have taken time to consider well of it, and if our speculation with Ericsson had turned out well, it was my intention to have tried it myself as soon as I could command the means. With regard to my personal risk, I feel assured that I shall run more by remaining at home, and the only thing that annoys me now, is that you will think me ungrateful for the kindness you have heaped upon me. I have now relieved my mind, and do hope upon consideration you will agree with me that it is the best for us all that I should go, it is a sure name, and a probable fortune, and I would sooner earn such a name than live in splendour and ease at home. You need not mention this to my mother or Mary for some time, as it will do no good, and only serve to make them miserable the longer. I would not have mentioned it to you now, if some business arrangements had not required it.

Believe me dear father
Your affectionate son
Macgregor Laird."

There can be no doubt that William Laird would have been grieved at his son's decision to join the expedition, for he would have been well aware that the risks were exceptionally high, and the chances of him returning alive, slender. Nevertheless, he did not attempt to stand in his way, and his sympathy and affection for him actually prompted him to draw up a new deed of partnership in the family business, which gave Macgregor a very substantial stake in the boiler making business at Birkenhead.

Before leaving Liverpool they were joined by Lieutenant William Allen, R.N. a naval officer for whom the Admiralty had requested a passage in one of the vessels, his task being to make a survey of the Niger. The company granted this request, despite the fact that they received no assistance or encouragement from any department of the government. The Admiralty remained pledged that no information should be given to the public by this officer without the express permission of the company. Lander then passed several weeks in Liverpool while the vessels were being prepared for sea, but left them a short time before they sailed, agreeing to join the expedition, of which he was to take command, at Milford.

The little fleet of three vessels, the *Quorra, Alburkah*, and *Columbine*, left Liverpool on Wednesday 19 June, 1832, the *Columbine* being towed out to sea by a steam vessel belonging to the City of Dublin Company. Before the pilot left the ship Captain Harris mustered all hands on deck; Macgregor being struck by the fine appearance of the crew, for all were picked men, from twenty-five to thirty-five years of age. But despite their obvious fitness only Macgregor Laird, and three others, were destined to survive.

After a very good passage of thirty-six hours the first vessel of the expedition fleet arrived at Milford, the rest some time later, where they were then detained until the 29th, awaiting the arrival of Richard Lander. On the 23rd July Macgregor wrote his farewell letter to his father, from which we note *his* intention to leave on the following day if Lander had not arrived! Had Richard Lander, in reality, now been relegated to the role of a hired guide, following Macgregor's decision to sail with the fleet ? His role as commander being a nominal one only, for public consumption. Had Macgregor Laird actually sailed without him there would have been a public outcry, which factor must have been pointed out to him. Perhaps a degree of jealousy did exist between them, but mutual respect seems to have been re-established, for Macgregor was later to write in his journal, "On the evening of the 29th we were agreeably surprised by the appearance of Mr Lander." His letter home reading as follows:

" Milford Haven
23rd July, 1832

My dear father,

I received your letter of the 21st inst. and much pleased to hear that William is getting over his attack; he requires to be narrowly watched and that I should think would be the only safeguard against a return as he is too young to have that command over his passions and appetites which he will naturally acquire in two or three years.

I had been rather uneasy about the *Columbine* but was much pleased by her arrival last evening about seven o'clock. All well.. By your letter I find Nuller is to be expected to-morrow, I have heard nothing from Lander but hope to meet him tomorrow per mail which arrives at 7 a.m. Tell John that I have engaged the second engineer of the *Vixen* P.O.P (Post Office Packet) at £6 per month, and have made Nullar the Chief Engineer. We had the *Quorra* and *Alburkah* under weigh today, and Nuller worked the engines for three or four hours remarkably well; he is a well-educated, respectable young man, and liked by all his messmates; with regards to Woods, I would not go in the same vessel with him, and as to Clarke I am astonished at John thinking of him after his behaviour to me; I feel perfectly confident in this arrangement, I hope it will meet with your approbation. If Nullar and Lander do not arrive tomorrow I will wait for neither (if the wind holds this way) as it is heartrending to be losing our time here with the wind as fair as it can blow. With regards to myself I must entreat neither you nor any of the family to listen to any reports which may appear in the newspapers respecting us, I feel confident in Harris and the crew; the former especially I hope will answer all our expectations, and I can assure the discipline into which he has already brought the crew, you would hardly believe in Liverpool. I do hope you will use your utmost endeavours even if the trade prove but moderate at first, to follow it up with vigour, it will ultimately prove beneficial to all parties.

This may be the last letter that I shall write to you, my dear father, I have been at times a disobedient and cruel son to you and my mother, I do entreat, I beg of you to pardon me freely and fully and if I ever return, I shall try my utmost to prove myself worthy of you.

Your affectionate son

Macgregor Laird."

There was still one short note to his father, sent ashore, one imagines, by the pilot, as it reads:

" Quorra. 150E. by South, off Scilly,
 Saturday 12 o'clock
      We left Milford at half-past eleven on Thursday evening and have had fine weather since. We are now in blue water and intend stopping the engine at twelve tonight. I am the only person on board who has been seasick, but I am now quite well or nearly so.

Love to all at home,

Your affectionate son,

Macgregor Laird."

The three vessels now headed south for Africa, experiencing fine weather as they crossed the bay. Twelve days after they had left Milford they were in sight of Madeira, which they sailed past without stopping. On the 17 August they anchored in Port Praya, where they found that the Cape Verd Islands were suffering from a terrible famine, arising from a lack of rain, none having fallen in any quantity for some three years. One thousand people had died in St. Jago, and upwards of fifteen hundred in Fogo, a smaller island. This was Macgregor Lairds introduction to a slave population, and he was disgusted to see men driven to their work, and women toiling up the steep hills which lead to the town, with heavy loads of salt upon their heads, many being in an obvious state of distress. On the evening of 19 August, the three vessels left the islands, glad to leave a place where they had seen so much misery without being able to alleviate it.

All the ships arrived at the Isles de Los on Sunday, 2 September, where they anchored between Factory Island and the mainland. The islands being well situated for trade, because of their proximity to the mouths of the rivers Rio Pongo and Rio Nunez. The day after they arrived H.M. Brig *Charybdis*, Lieut. Crawford commander, came in on her way to the Gambia; Crawford informing Macgregor that the slave trade was brisker than ever on the coast, and that he had been unfortunate in not being able to take any prizes. He also regretted having to go northward, where there was less chance of falling in

The "Alburkah" approaching the Nun River, 1832

with them.

On the 12 September, having taken on sufficient fuel, the Quorra ran up to Freetown, leaving the *Alburkah* at York. No sooner had they anchored off the port than the decks were crowded with Kroomen, anxiously seeking employment. The Kroo country extended from Simon River, along the coast to Cape Palmas, the inhabitants being noted for their loyalty, bravery, and skill as sailors. Macgregor also heard that these people were never taken as slaves, because of the unyielding spirit they always displayed. The Governor, Colonel Findlay, ordered that they should be supplied with provisions from the government stores, after which operation was completed they made plans to leave. On the 15th, having said goodbye to their hospitable hosts, they steered carefully across the shoals of St. Ann, and by Tuesday 19th they had made Cape Mesurado. On Monday 1 October they anchored off Cape Palmas, where they recruited a further ten Kroomen, these to compliment those that they had already engaged.

The expedition ships arrived at Cape Coast Castle on the 9th, where they received the greatest kindness and attention from the Governor, George M'Lean. They remained here until the 11th, when they left their anchorage under canvas, continuing on their course for the river Nun.(A mouth of the Niger) As usual on the coast, sickness soon struck, Captain Harries became very ill, as did George Curling the engineer of the *Quorra*. Dr. Briggs, old friend of Macgregor Laird, and now the 'Medical Gentleman' of the *Quorra*, treating both men. On the 17th, a black pilot, named Dedo, came on board offering to take the vessel into the river, but having heard a bad account of the Nun pilots, Macgregor Laird took the decision to take the gig and actually examine the bar, before proceeding. Eventually they got into the river, and proceeded up some miles until they came across the brig *Susan*, of Liverpool, loaded with palm-oil, and waiting assistance to leave the river. She had been lying there seven months, and had lost seven out of twelve of her crew. The ship looked in a deplorable condition, the surviving crew looking more like spectres than men. The commander informed Laird that he had purchased Lander's journal from King Boy, and had paid two hundred pounds for it, but Macgregor much doubted this story.

At four in the afternoon the *Columbine* came into sight, being informed on her arrival that she had missed the *Alburkah* the same night that they had left Cape Coast. That night Macgregor Laird was called by Doctor Briggs, and found Harries dying in his arms. He expired half an hour later. A few hours later the second engineer, George Curling, died with exactly the same symptoms. Harries had been well liked by his crew, and all the expedition people, and was greatly missed. The *Alburkah* then came over the bar, and on reaching her Lander informed Laird that he had buried a man the evening before, the symptom being similar to those suffered by Captain Harries.

The great expedition was now well under way, and on 21 October, 1832, they spent their first Sabbath on the Niger. Richard Lander came on board the *Quorra* to inform Macgregor Laird that he had in fact managed to recover his long-lost journal from the commander of the *Susan*, but he did not disclose what he had been obliged to pay for it. Macgregor very much wanted to see the daily journal of his adventurous voyage down the Niger from Boussa, but unfortunately he had not brought it with him, and although he tried he never managed to have sight of it. On the 23rd Macgregor was interested to note the arrival of the celebrated King Boy, the chief who had ransomed Richard and John Lander, and then conveyed them down river from Eboe.

By the 26th they had completed their arrangements for ascending the river, having reduced the draught of the *Quorra* to five feet three inches. King Boy then indicated his intention of remaining with them until they reached Eboe. They advanced up the river until they reached King Boy's Barracoon, or slave hut, which was about nine miles up-river from the bar. Here Macgregor was introduced to King Forday by King Boy, both described by Laird as ill-looking fellows, but uncommonly civil. On the 27th they were busy making their final preparations to proceed further up river. The black pilot who had been placed on board the *Alburkah* by King Boy then informed Richard Lander that the King had instructed him to take them up a branch of the river that was full of shoals, and, if possible, to run them aground. Armed with this vital information Lander took the *Alburkah* up the branch said by the pilot to be the best. It proved to have from two to three fathoms of water in it, and free from shoals. King Boy, and his father Forday were enraged by their determination to try this channel, indicating to Laird and Lander that they were up to no good. They left in a rage, promising to be back early the following morning. However, they did not show up on time, so the ships left without them. Soon the river increased in breadth, being on average about three hundred yards, with a depth of four to five fathoms. They now considered themselves to be fairly on the Niger, and thankful for having escaped the plot laid by King Boy for their destruction. They pressed on, Laird's description of the Nun Branch and it's creeks being much the same as other writers. He now spoke of the dreary mangrove swamps, and the 'miasmic' smells which always assailed them. After a while though he was pleased to report that the country began to improve considerably in every way. The splendid African oak and wild cotton trees appearing on the banks.

On the last day of October Macgregor was standing on the paddle box of the *Quorra*, watching the ever changing scene. He stepped down without care and ran a spike of the chevaux-de-frise through his foot. A seemingly trivial accident, but had infection set in there was little that could have been done to save him; fortunately it did not. They continued under steam until nine in the evening, but then had to stop the engines, it being impossible to continue in the dark. On the 1 November they started again at six in the morning. They made good progress, and had friendly visits from the chiefs of the villages that they passed. In the afternoon though a young member of the crew was taken seriously ill with an attack of ague. At eight in the evening, their fuel being expended, the *Quorra* dropped anchor. The crew had gone to rest, and Macgregor was making himself comfortable in his berth, when, at about 10.30, a canoe came alongside, and a note was brought to him from Richard Lander, by the pilot Louis. It was briefly as follows:-

"Sir, - The Eboes threaten to attack us tomorrow. I would thank you to have everything in readiness to resent an attack of whatever nature it may be,
Your obedient servant,
" R. Lander.
" P.S. They say we shall not pass this place, although there are not ten houses in the town."

Without waiting a moment, and taking care not to disturb the crew, Macgregor confided in Doctor Briggs, and together they got all the muskets and pistols loaded, and packed the cartridge boxes. In the meantime the Eboes had reviewed the situation, and decided not to delay their attack until the following morning. Within moments the right bank of the river, just seventy yards ahead of them, was ablaze with musket fire.

Lander, in the smaller *Alburkah*, hailed Macgregor in the *Quarra*, informing him that he was going to drop back; Macgregor responded by offering to take the *Quorra* between him and the line of fire, the offer being accepted without hesitation. Lander then sent his Eboe Pilot, Louis, over to the *Quorra*. Macgregor was suitably impressed with the coolness and self-possession of Louis. He could speak fairly good English, which pleased Macgregor, for he was then able to inform him that if he ran the *Quorra* aground he would blow his brains out. The message was received, and understood, but far from being alarmed by this threat Louis merely laughed, opened his jacket and showed Macgregor the butt-end of two pistols - indicating that two could play at that game.

Perhaps wisely leaving Louis to his piloting duties, Macgregor then gave directions for the heavy guns to be loaded with round canister, the men then started working the guns with devastating accuracy, and in about twenty minutes they had silenced the firing on shore. At daybreak the following day (2nd November,1832) the firing from the bush started again, and it was only then that Macgregor discovered that their opponents also had two heavy swivel guns! The *Quorra* opened fire on the town with all her heavy guns, but the shots did little harm, merely passing straight through the mud walls of

The confluence of the Niger and the Benue from Mount Patti

the huts, although they did manage to silence the firing.

The war continued. Lander hailed Macgregor, and they agreed to land and burn the town, by way of an example to all the rest. Accordingly, the gig under Macgregor's command led the attack, closely followed by Captain Miller in the cutter, and the launch, with eight volunteers. Doctor Briggs, with the officers of the ship, being left to keep up a heavy fire of musketry over their heads. They all stormed ashore with guns blazing, which forced the Eboes to retreat into the bush. Lander then arrived in the *Alburkah* and joined in the battle, which continued for some time. After things had cooled down Macgregor found time to muster his men, and was delighted to find that no one had been hurt. This was accounted for by the fact that the Eboes tended to fire from the hip, without bothering to take proper aim, but despite this lack of skill in using their deadly weapons, they had managed to hit the ships many times.

At nine they continued to make their way up the Niger, and when they were about three miles from their last anchorage they came to a small village. Here they were received with open arms by the chief, who was absolutely delighted on hearing that they had just destroyed his neighbours! It then transpired that the whole unfortunate affair had arisen due to a complete misunderstanding by the local people. The *Alburkah* had anchored off the town in the dark, and had fired a gun as a signal to the *Quorra* that she had done so. The locals imagined that it was firing on them, and so it all began - in much the same way that many battles and wars begin- over an imagined insult or threat.

At six in the evening, the battle over, they were all under weigh once more, now having several of the local chiefs on board, who had decided to take a ride up-stream, to their respective villages; the advantages of new technology clearly being recognised without undue delay. At six the following morning they were again under weigh, and at 9 a.m. they passed a magnificent branch of the river, about seven hundred yards wide, which they concluded might be the Rio Forcados branch, which falls into the Bight of Benin in Latitude 5. 28' N.

Preparations were then put in hand for a visit to King Obie. The launch and other boats were manned by Kroomen, dressed in Kilts and velvet caps, Lander himself being resplendent in a full general's uniform. Preceded by old Pascoe, Jowdie, and some other men who had accompanied Richard Lander on his former journey, they were all now returning in triumph to the scene of their former exploits. They made their way to King Obie's Court, and after a delay of some fifteen minutes he appeared, being a tall man with a pleasing appearance. He shook hands with Lander and Macgregor, then took his seat on the throne, with one on each side of him. The interview lasted for about fifteen minutes, Macgregor being very impressed with the gentlemanly

87

and agreeable manner of Obie. They received from him a bullock, five goats, and three hundred yams.

Early on the following morning of the 8 November, Macgregor was pleased to see a large fleet of canoes, numbering about one hundred to one hundred and fifty, leave the town, in order to collect palm-oil, and also gather yams, and bananas. It being the most gratifying proof of regular and honest industry that he had yet seen in Africa. At 1 p.m. they fired a royal salute in honour of King Obie, who went on board the *Alburkah* to visit Lander. General celebrations then took place, Macgregor being visited by the largest woman he had ever seen, who was about twenty five stone in weight, her personal charms being set off by a straw hat nearly five feet in diameter. Later they went ashore to visit her, finding her to be an intelligent, clever woman. They learned that she owned several canoes, which she employed trading on the river, both above and below Eboe. They established that the staple trade of Eboe consisted of slaves and palm-oil. The value of the slaves varying according to demand on the coast, but the average value of a fit young man of sixteen was about sixty shillings, and that of a woman something above this figure.

At 8 p.m. in the evening of the 9 November, 1832, they left Eboe, and by the light of a splendid moon made their way through some very difficult channels. They came to an anchor when about fifteen miles from the town, where they found themselves in the widest part of the river they had seen yet, its breadth being about three thousand yards.

They continued up river the following day, until they crossed the Benin branch, which they found to be eight hundred yards wide. The Bonny branch appeared to run in a south south-east direction. On the sandy point that formed its entrance there were a great number of temporary barracoons, and nine or ten canoes, and much evidence that a great trade in palm oil was conducted from this base. About eight in the morning they passed a smaller branch flowing in from the north-east. They pressed on, until two in the afternoon, then ran aground. The carriage guns and heavy chain cables were moved aft, to bring her down by the stern, the engines rammed into reverse, and they eventually managed to back off.

At 10 a.m. on the 11 November they came to an anchor, and Macgregor was informed that Mr Jordan, in the *Alburkah*, was going down with the fever. He was brought onto the *Quorra*, and then attended to by Doctor Briggs. Things rapidly grew worse, Briggs reporting to Macgregor, in the course of the evening, that four of his own crew were showing the same symptoms. At 11 a.m. the following day Macgregor Laird was also seized with fever, the symptoms in his case being a severe throbbing headache, a burning pain in the feet and hands, and a deadly sickness in the stomach. Briggs then fell sick, together with nine more of the crew. From this date until the 5 December, 1832 Laird's journal is a blank. More and more members of the expedition now fell sick and died. Laird was more fortunate than most though, for on the 5 December he was able to write in his journal that whilst remaining very weak, he was making a slow recovery. Richard Lander though remained healthy, Macgregor Laird writing that his behaviour during their sickness did him infinite credit. On the 8th Macgregor found himself well enough to take charge of the *Quorra* once more, but Briggs had become sick again.

On the 20th December, 1832 Richard Lander left the *Alburkah* at the junction of the Shary and Niger, and made his way to Macgregor Laird in the *Quorra*. He informed Macgregor that the navigation was tricky, but that there was plenty of water in the main channel. He also added that the inhabitants of all the towns he had visited had seemed delighted at the prospect of being able to trade directly with white people. The day after receiving this report Macgregor got under weigh and passed Bocqua, where the chief made them a gift of wood to fire the engines of the ship.

The small vessel then entered the great gorge of the Kong Mountains, where the peaks rise on either side of the Niger to the height of about three thousand feet. The channel here being extremely dangerous, because large blocks of granite lie in the stream, making eddies and shoals.   It was about four in the afternoon when the ship ground to a halt, having run onto one of these hidden shoals, but they got off again in about half an hour, and then came to anchor for the night, below one of the rocky islets that dot the river at the entrance to a narrow strait. In the morning they were under weigh again, and after a few minutes the river opened up, presenting a magnificent scene:

"An immense river, about three thousand yards wide, extending as far as the eye could reach, lay before us, flowing majestically between its banks, which rose gradually to a considerable height and were studded with clumps of trees and brushwood, giving them the appearance of a gentleman's park; while the smoke rising from the different towns on its banks, and the number of canoes floating on its bosom, gave it an aspect of security and peace far beyond any African scene I had yet witnessed. The confluence of the Shary was just in sight, and a range of low hills on the northern bank trended east-north-east; while on the western bank of the Niger were two remarkable isolated table-lands of a romantic and beautiful appearance, giving a finish to a picture to which no description can do adequate justice."

At 10 a.m. they suddenly grounded to a halt, the *Quorra* had stuck on a shelf of rock. The shock was actually so great that Macgregor expected the vessel to start leaking, and sink, but she fell off of her own accord, and showed no signs whatsoever of making water, so they continued on their way. An hour or so later though they ran on a sandbank when attempting to cross the river. They blew off the boilers to lighten the vessel, but this did not help. On the morning of the 23rd they made further attempts to lighten the ship, which eventually enabled them to get the *Quorra* off after some twenty-four hours hard-labour. They ran aground again soon after this incident, and to add to their troubles more members of the expedition died or fell sick. Laird and Briggs passed a thankful, but far from merry Christmas, stuck on yet another sandbank in the Niger. They were a few miles below what is now Lokoja.

Efforts to move the ship failed, and she remained fast for months. It was decided that they would remain with the stranded vessel, and started trading, by opening a market on the sandbank they were stranded on. Whilst still here, at the end of February, Macgregor's great friend, Thomas Briggs died. He left a widow, Anna Maria, daughter of Thomas Holme Maude, a descendant of Sir Robert Maude, of West Riddlesden, Yorkshire. The loss of Briggs was a great shock to Macgregor, and he became very depressed. To take his mind off things, ill as he was, he decided to set off to explore the Benue.

At a place called Fundah, on the northern bank of the river, Macgregor and his party were virtually kept prisoner by the local King who refused to let them continue on their way. To escape, Macgregor informed him that he intended to make a great fetish to his God, to know whether he should go or stay at Fundah. The King considered the matter, then informed Laird that he endorsed the proposal, and that he would attend, with all his priests, and summon his people to witness the event.

That evening an immense crowd assembled in the town, some people climbing onto walls, and the tops of houses, in order to get a good view of the proceedings. What Macgregor cunningly calculated they had not seen before, and would duly impress them, was a fireworks display! After much ceremony and ballyhoo Macgregor fired his pistol into the air, this being a pre-arranged signal for his companion Sarsfield, and their Kroomen, to let off some spectacular rockets. The effect was as expected, the people of Fundah, having no idea what was coming next, fled in all directions. The King, filled with terror, threw himself onto the ground. Macgregor, taking full advantage of the altered situation, promptly informed him that he would now be going back to his house - and taking all his men with him. After keeping the King in suspense for more than an hour, Macgregor sent word to him that he was ready to receive him, and his majesty was soon seated at Macgregor's feet!

To ram home the message, Macgregor then informed him that he planned one further trial, to see if he should stay or go, adding that his God would most certainly punish anyone who presumed to break his commandments. He appeared suitably impressed. Macgregor then took a small compass from his pocket, explaining to the King that if the needle pointed to him, as soon as it was placed on the ground, that he was to go from Fundah, if it pointed towards the King he had to stay. Macgregor, having taken great care to place himself in the correct position, put the compass on the ground, whereupon the needle obligingly turned towards him. Without further debate the King immediately agreed to release them.

The next day was spent in thankful preparation for their departure, with the exception of the heavy goods, and two barrels of gunpowder, everything being packed up for the carriers. Macgregor though was now a very sick man. At daybreak the next morning he had to be lifted on a horse. The small party then set off for a place called Potingah, their intention being to get there before the sun was high. Macgregor recorded his feelings about leaving Fundah in the following terms:

" I turned my back on a city where I had suffered both bodily and mentally more than I can describe, and from whence I took nothing but experience dearly purchased by an expenditure of time that would have allowed me, if I had ascended the Niger, to have reached Boussa."

Returning to Yimmahah, Macgregor then went downstream in the cutter, and rejoined the ships. Here, at the confluence, he had to wait six weeks, until the *Quorra* could be floated off by the rising river, and then the two ships joined up, going downstream on the 10th July 1833. The *Alburkah* was left at Idaah, with the expedition surgeon, R.A.K. Oldfield, and Richard Lander in charge, while Laird returned to the mouth of the river with the *Quorra*. The miserable remnants of the crew eventually reached Fernando Po on the 28th August, 1833. Macgregor, still seriously ill, had to be carried ashore. Without delay, he was then taken to the home of the Governor General, Colonel Edward Nicolls, a most remarkable man, who was destined to feature in the life of Macgregor Laird from this point on.

Colonel Edward Nicolls was born in 1779, and when Macgregor Laird met him in 1833 he had already been in action no less than 107 times! In 1803, in a small boat, with one gun and twelve men, he had beaten off a French brig of 16 guns and 120 men in sight of Havre de Grace, and managed to carry off two vessels which were under her convoy. On the 5th November, 1803, with a boat's crew of 12 men, he cut out the French cutter *Albion*, of six guns and 43 men, from under the guns of Monte Christo; in which action he took on the French Captain in single combat, but the latter put up a good fight, shooting Nicolls in the stomach. The shot passed round his body, and lodged in his right arm, leaving him severely wounded. Miraculously, he survived, and was duly awarded for this dashing exploit, by an ever generous High Command, who presented him with a sword of honour, value £30.00. He commanded the Royal Marines at the siege of Curacoa, in February, 1804, where he stormed and took Fort Piscardero, of 10 guns, and drove the Dutch troops from the heights. He then went on to serve in the Dardeanelles, Corfu and Egypt, his record in all these places being just as amazing.

On the 18, May, 1809, he landed with two lieutenants and 120 Royal

Clarence, Fernando Po, early 19th century

Marines on the island of Anholt where he defeated with the bayonet a force of 200 Danish troops, captured the island, and took upwards of 500 prisoners; for which service he received a letter of thanks, and was appointed Governor of the island. He served in North America during the war in that country, and raised and commanded a large force of Indians. He co-operated in the siege of Fort Bower in 1814, in command of a regiment of Creek Indians, and was three times wounded during the bombardment.

During his truly amazing career he had his left leg broken, his right leg severely wounded, was shot through the body and right arm, received a terrible sabre cut on his head, was boyoneted in the chest, and lost the sight of an eye in his last, or 107th action. (When Macgregor Laird was carried into his home in 1833 he was supposedly in his last post, prior to retiring on full pay, on 15, May,1835. His retirement though seems to have been short-lived, for he was soon back in the saddle, going on until he became a full General in 1854, and a Knight Commander of the Bath in 1855. All this though lay in the future - as did Macgregor Laird's marriage to his second daughter, Eleanor Hestor!)

Colonel Nicolls (Fighting Nicolls, as he was known to his men!) spent the next two months attempting to nurse Macgregor Laird back to health, and there can be little doubt that without this effort Macgregor would not have survived - although, on reflection, a degree of courage, and stamina, was clearly required in order to endure the Colonel's treatment, one example of which is worth citing. On a memorable night Macgregor was seized with cramp in the stomach and, struggling in agony, fell out of bed. Nicolls bounded into the room - made a split-second diagnosis, and concluded that some form of 'counter-irritation' would soon put matters right. Soaking a sheet of blotting paper in brandy 'Fighting Nicolls' placed it on Macgregor's stomach and set it on fire! This did cure the cramp, but Macgregor was so severely burned that he retained the marks of this 'remedy' for the rest of his life.

Despite such incidents Macgregor Laird and Edward Nicolls became very close friends. Macgregor at this time no doubt reflecting on the fact that he, the direct descendant of Scotland's legendary warrior, Rob Roy Macgregor, was now being nursed back to health by the greatest warrior in the annals of British military history. These two men were also united in their views on a crucial issue of the period. Both were dedicated and outspoken opponents of the slave trade - then so active on the coast; Fernando Po being the main British base for the elimination of the trade, all of which was then under the control of the Governor - Edward Nicolls.

Macgregor Laird remained at Fernando Po for two months, where he regained some of his strength, then, at the end of October, 1833, he set sail for Liverpool in the brig *Columbine*. With him went three survivors from the *Quorra*. The only other one, Harvey, being left in charge of her at Fernando

Po. The voyage home was a terrible one, made long by adverse winds, which were against the ship. One of the three survivors died at sea. When they were off the Welsh coast they met with a hurricane, and were nearly lost off Holyhead; but that danger was overcome, and, on 1st January, 1834, the ship arrived in the Mersey.

An eyewitness to Macgregor Laird's arrival stated that he came ashore wrapped in blankets, obviously still a very sick man, suffering from all that he had experienced. But he was alive, and welcomed home by a loving family. There was though to be no loving family reunion for one of the other two survivors who stepped ashore, for he died the day after landing.

While Macgregor Laird was making his way home in the *Columbine* Richard Lander and Oldfield remained in Africa, bravely planning the next phase of their pioneering, but ill-fated expedition. Early on the morning of the 4th August, 1833, the *Alburkah* was hove off the shoal, on which she had been grounded for so long, and at 9 a.m. got under weigh. Half an hour later they passed a place called Frenchwood, a point some three hundred and fifty feet high, that lies on the northern bank of the Tchadda.

They continued to explore the Tchadda to a distance of one hundred and four miles from its confluence, but on the 20th August they entered the Niger once more, having concluded this phase of the expedition. Oldfield noting in his journal that he had just been obliged to add the names of Smith, the engineer, Yarriba, George, and Lilly to the sick-list. They steamed past Mount Sterling, and the island off it, which was nearly covered with water. At this place three white men, a Krooman, and old Pascoe were interred. At 12.45 p.m. they anchored off a small town named Bangedy, where they found the local people were busy brewing beer from Dower-corn, which they boiled in large pots, each containing almost six gallons. Another local industry being the manufacture of red paint, from a wood of the same colour, which was brought from the Eboe country. From this place they had a wonderful view of the majestic Kong Mountains, Oldfield describing the scenery as being extremely picturesque and beautiful.

At 6.35 a.m. on the following day they got under weigh for a place called Cuttum-Curaffee. As they made their way along the Niger a small canoe came alongside, containing an old woman, the mother of an African, John Thomas, who had served as steward on board the *Quorra*. She tried to sell Oldfield and Lander some fish, as she had been with the steamers when they were aground, and had usually kept them supplied with fish. They threw her a few coppers, which upset her, and Lander, feeling hurt by her reaction, determined to take her back to Egga, the country she came from, an area which they would be obliged to pass on their return. This poor woman had been the victim of her own blind faith in the power of a 'Maghony' (charm) - which she thought rendered her invulnerable to all sharp tools and cutting instruments.

94

The local King soon heard about her claims, and determined to put the power of her extraordinary charm to a suitable test. He desired a man to take an axe, and see whether this wonderful *Maghony* would protect her from its effects; reasoning, with admirable logic, that if it did so, such a charm would give his soldiers a great advantage in all future battles. The woman was brought to the King, taken to a specially prepared room, and in full view of many spectators, her leg was laid on a block. A powerfully built man then raised an axe above his head, and brought it down with great force, making contact with the ill-fated leg just below the knee. The result of which was as might have been expected. To the poor woman's great horror, and in a manner which clearly shocked all present, her leg flew to the other side of the room. She survived this horrendous attack, but, not surprisingly, lost faith in her charm, and was then obliged to crawl about on her knees. Oldfield decided that when he reached Fernando Po he would see if he could make arrangements for someone to make a wooden leg for her.

On the 1st September, they anchored off a large town named Eggaginee, where about thirty canoes, containing a great number of interested people met them. The following day a solid mass of local Africans assembled on the banks, gazing at the strange vessel; and then some climbed into canoes, and began paddling around them. Several of them said they had heard of the white man's boat, but they did not think it would be so large. In the afternoon Oldfield and Lieutenant Allen went ashore, and were soon surrounded by a great crowd . They then passed through a kind of glen, where there were piles of bones, and a number of jars, stacked one above the other. They learned that this was the place used for the execution of malefactors, and that very recently two people had been obliged to drink poison, or as they expressed it taken fetish water. This mode of punishment - as already noted - then being very common in West Africa.

They continued to make their way back down the Niger, and on Tuesday, 29th October, 1833, they passed another branch of the Benin river, which was about five hundred yards wide, the Niger itself becoming visibly narrower. They steamed past the branches of two rivers leading into a creek, and St. John's river, communicating with Brass. At 7.30 p.m. they anchored off Barracoon House - all hands giving three hearty cheers - for they were now within sight of salt water. Still having a little rum left on board, they drank to their many absent friends, with as much sincerity as they could muster under such circumstances. The following day King Boy came on board, and his men were given hatchets, who then obliged by helping the crew cut wood for the boilers.

On Thursday, October 31st, after getting their wood on board, they got under weigh, but a major problem lay ahead, for they still had to cross a very dangerous bar. They survived however, and at 8 p.m. they anchored within

95

six miles of the shore, and off the Bonny river. Here though they suffered a disaster. The Kroomen, when taking in the foresail, allowed it to become entangled with the paddlewheel, by which it was torn to shreds. They then had another serious mishap, this being the loss of their only anchor. They ordered the steam to be got up immediately, but only had an hour's fuel left on board. Whilst they were doing this they drifted into three fathoms of water, among the breakers. The little iron vessel laboured strenuously against the powerful swell. Lieutenant Allen, who now had temporary command of the vessel, to take her to Fernando Po, determined on standing out to sea, to get a good offing. Six signal-guns of distress were fired, but they were not heard by any English vessel, or the pilots at Bonny.

They were short of drinking water and food. Soon their fuel ran out, and Allen was obliged to get some jury-masts rigged, and some awnings ready to be converted into sails, which then enabled them to go at the rate of two or three knots per hour. On the afternoon of Saturday, November 2nd, 1833, they were about fifty miles from Fernando Po when a vessel came into sight, which, to their delight, proved to be the *Quorra* herself. A boat was lowered, and Colonel Nicolls, Governor of Fernando Po came on Board. The *Alburkah* was immediately taken in tow. Nicolls then informed Lander and Oldfield that the *Columbine* had remained at Fernando Po for about three months, but had left for England about a month ago, with Macgregor Laird, and three survivors of the *Quorra*. Harvey, one of the *Quorra's* men, had been left in charge; and a young man named Sarsfield, from the *Alburkah*, had remained to take care of her engines. At 8.30 p.m. - on this fateful day - they received an anchor, which they joyfully dropped in Clarence Bay, Fernando Po. Another stage in this great expedition was at a close.

No sooner had they reached Fernando Po than Oldfield fell seriously ill. Lieutenant Allen, having completed his survey of the Niger for the Government then indicated that he wanted to return to England as soon as the opportunity arose. Oldfield managed to recover, and it was then agreed that he would go again up the Niger, while Lander, who, after visiting Cape Coast and Accrah for Cowries, was to follow him, and rejoin him on the river in about six weeks. All efforts were then made to prepare the *Alburkah* for her next trip up the Niger. They received stores on board, left by Captain Beecroft, and a Chief Officer, and men, to navigate the vessel.

At 10.30 a.m. on November 10th, 1833, the *Alburkah* was, for the third time, under weigh for the Niger. The yards of His Majesty's brig *Curlew*, Captain Trotter, were manned, and they were saluted with three great cheers from her as they passed by, which they returned as they left the bay. On Sunday, 17th November, they entered the Bonny, to the surprise of the local King and his people, who inquired if they had come down the "big river," meaning the Niger. Here, to their distress, they came across three Spanish slavers in the river, one of which had taken slaves on board the preceding night; but hearing that H.M.S. *Brisk* and *Curlew* were off the river, they sent them on shore again.

On the morning of the 24th November, they fell in with the *Quorra*, under the command of Captain Fuge, but with Richard Lander on board, which had been sent out unexpectedly by Colonel Nicolls, with men, provisions and some despatches, which the Crown cutter had brought from England. They stayed together for three days and then parted company. This being marked by a salute of seven guns, and three hearty cheers from the crews. Shortly after their departure Oldfield got under weigh for the Niger, and at 2 p.m. entered Louis' Creek, but promptly managed to run the vessel aground. On Wednesday, 4th December, they were well up-river, being near the towns of Subercriggee and Hyammah - a fateful place for Richard Lemon Lander, who was soon destined to be attacked there.

They continued to explore the Niger Country until the middle of March, 1834, when one of Chief Abbakoka's sons gave Oldfield some provisions, and also informed him that a man named Hadgeegoo had a paper for him from Richard Lander. This was so sudden and unexpected that Oldfield stated " that it would be utterly beyond my power to describe my sensations at the intelligence." Half an hour later he had the pleasure of receiving a letter from Richard Lander, which read as follow:-

"River Nun, Jan. 22nd, 1834.

Dear Sir,

Having an opportunity of writing to you by King Boy, who will give it to King Obie to forward to you, I will avail myself of it. I was coming up to you with a cargo of cowries and dry goods worth four hundred and fifty pounds, when I was attacked from all quarters by the natives of Hyammah, off the fourth island from Sunday Island. (which is Eighty-four miles from the Nun) The shot were very numerous both from the island and shore. Mrs Brown and child were taken prisoners, whom I was bringing up to her husband, as well as Robert the boy. I have advanced King Boy money to go and purchase them; and the vessel will call here immediately, as I am going to Fernando Po to get the people's wounds attended to.

We had three men shot dead; - Thompson, second mate of the cutter, one Krooman, and one Cape Coast man. I am wounded, but I hope not dangerously, the ball having entered close to the anus and struck the thigh bone: it is not extracted yet. Thomas Oxford is wounded in the groin: two Kroomen wounded dangerously, and one slightly. I am sorry to say, I lost all my papers, and everything belonging to me, the boat and one canoe; having escaped in one of the canoes barely with a coat to our backs, they chased us in their war canoes, and all our cartridges being wet, so that we could not keep them off. They attacked us at 3 p.m. on the 20th January, and left us at eight at night. We pulled all night, and reached the cutter on the 21st. We are now under weigh for Fernando Po.

I remain,

Your most affectionate Friend,

(Signed ,) R.L. Lander

To Surgeon Oldfield,

Alburkah Steamer, River Niger. "

On receipt of this letter Oldfield noted in his journal that he rejoiced to learn that the wound Richard Lander had received was not dangerous. This, alas, was far from the truth - the wound was a very serious one - from which Lander was not to recover.

Surgeon Oldfield, and the crew of the *Alburkah* continued to explore and trade on the river, until June - when they were, once again at the place were Thomas Briggs, Senior Surgeon of the expedition had been buried. Oldfield then availed himself of the opportunity of placing a board, which he had prepared in readiness, at the grave of his late colleague. It was inscribed,

To the memory of

Thos. Briggs, Esq.

Senior Surgeon of the Niger Expedition.

Who departed this life,

Feb. 8th, 1833.

R.A.K.O. May 11th, 1834

The 12th June, 1834, found the *Alburkah* anchored off the town of Iddah. Here Oldfield took on board the forge, and all the other items that he had left behind when passing in April. Oldfield then fell ill, suffering from dysentery, which he attributed to having got wet one night during a tornado, at Addacoodah! The ship ran aground - once again - but on the 23rd they succeeded in their efforts to get the vessel off. They anchored, and then spent some time repairing the fireplace.

To get back down the river they were now faced with the problem of passing the town of Hyammah, the place where Lander had been attacked. To complicate matters Oldfield could not recollect the exact location of the place, but late in June he felt convinced that they were fast approaching it, this opinion being not entirely subjective, for he noted that there seemed to be an increasing number of well armed, and hostile looking Africans lining the banks of the river. With commendable foresight Oldfield saw to it that all the guns, nine in number, were double shotted, and the numerous muskets fixed

98

round the quarter-deck were all ready for instant use. Each man was then armed with a cutlass, and a brace of pistols, and stationed by the heavy guns.

The town of Hyammah then consisted of about four streets, built on the left bank of the river, a few hundred yards away from the branch which Oldfield understood led to the Bonny. Oldfield was advised that the town, and the two adjacent towns, could probably not have raised more than four hundred and fifty men, and not more than two hundred musket, but these were more than enough to prevent the *Alburkah* passing, should they have had time to organise a hostile attack.

With the steam pressure raised to the maximum, and all guns manned, the *Alburkah* raced towards Hyammah. Within moments she had passed close under the town, and so sudden was her appearance, and so short the time that elapsed until the vessel was out of sight, that the hostile residents of the town had no time to recover themselves from the surprise - let alone organise an armed attack. At 9.30 p.m. they anchored in Louis' Creek, at the mouth of the Niger, where they could hear the noise of the surf breaking on the beach. The night was dark, so Oldfield considered it prudent not to attempt to proceed any further till day-light.

At ten in the morning of the next day they got under weigh, and at 12.15 anchored off Barracoon House, in the River Nun, after having been only thirty-two hours fifteen minutes under weigh from Iddah. Overcome with joy, at seeing this well-remembered spot, Surgeon Oldfield and his crew then gave three cheers for their safe return down the Niger. On Sunday, June 29th, the pilot Footman came on board, bringing with him a letter from Colonel Nicolls, addressed to Oldfield, which advised him on the sad death of Richard Lander, who had died from the wounds he had received at Hyammah.

" Dear Sir,

You will no doubt be much annoyed at hearing that Mr Lander died of the wounds he received in an attack that was made upon him in a most treacherous manner by the natives of Hyammah. I am in hopes that this may reach you at Eboe, as it will put you on your guard. As you pass keep well in the centre of the river, and, if possible, steam quickly past them. I send this to King Boy, with a request that he forward it to you. Come with all your people as soon as you can to Fernando Po, and my best wishes herewith to ensure your safe return, &c. Tell Brown his wife was taken, but I understand that King Boy has ransomed her. I shall see him in a day or two, and will write you again. Hoping to see you soon, and in good health,

Believe me to be truly yours,

(Signed) Edward Nicolls,

Lieut-Col. Commander and Superintendant.

Quorra, in the Nun, April 24th, 1835.

To Surgeon Oldfield, or the Officer in charge of the African Inland Company's Affairs in the River Niger. "

Oldfield noted, with some bitterness, that the 'rascally' pilot Footman had detained this letter until he had arrived back, making no attempt to forward it as requested. So far as Lander was concerned, Oldfield felt that he had been just too trusting, and had his generous heart allowed him to be more suspicious, he would have been better prepared for murderous attacks. The loss of Lander was indeed a tragedy, for as Oldfield noted, he had been a valuable member of society, and an enterprising, and persevering traveller. In the very best sense of the word he had also been a gentleman, liked and respected by all who knew him, and a man who had in turn, liked and respected the African people.

Early on the morning of the 1st July they crossed the bar of the Nun, and then, on reaching the open sea were tossed about in the heavy swell. When off Old Calabar river, at noon on the 8th, a brig was observed, which Oldfield at first assumed to be a palm-oil vessel. He only had two hours supply of wood left so headed for her, in an attempt to obtain more fuel. However, as they got near to her she hoisted the Spanish flag. She was a large ship, with nearly eighty men on board, and mounted six guns and a large carronade. The vessel was in fact a slaver, and would be planning to take away between five and six hundred enslaved Africans. These ships planned to be on the coast during July and August, when the new yams came into season, on which the slaves could be fed whilst on the dreaded 'middle-passage.' Needless to say, Oldfield obtained no co-operation from the master of this vessel, who, no doubt suspected them of being a tender to a British anti-slavery patrol man-of-war. All of which spotlighted the great humanitarian responsibility carried by Colonel Nicolls, at this time, in his efforts to mount opposition to this evil trade.

They arrived at Fernando Po in the evening of the 9th July 1834. Colonel Nicolls invited Oldfield to his house, where he was to remain during his stay at Fernando Po. The Kroomen were paid off, and the *Alburkah* was moored alongside the *Quorra*. On the 11th August Oldfield embarked on the *Mars*, Captain Irving, and they immediately got under weigh for England. On the 8th November, Oldfield landed at Falmouth, after a very pleasant voyage. On the 18th, he reached London, but in a very poor state of health, as he put it - " having suffered much in my constitution from exposure to climate and all kinds of privation, and the only European left alive of the crew of the *Alburkah* who left Fernando Po in November.

Macgregor Laird refused to publish an account of this historic expedition until Oldfield returned, and their " Narrative of an Expedition into the Interior of Africa, by the River Niger, in the Steam-Vessels *Quorra* and

Alburkah in 1832, 1833, and 1834 " could be produced together, and eventually published by Richard Bentley in 1837. The first quarter being written by Laird, the remainder by Oldfield.

The expedition was a commercial failure, and the loss of life terrible, but between them, Lander, Laird and Oldfield had made history. Surgeon Oldfield had made the first recorded treaty between the African Inland Commercial Company and the chiefs of Iddah. More importantly though, they had proved, together, that the Niger was navigable for steamers; that normal trade was possible, and there was now hope that this legitimate trade would eventually displace the one in slaves. Above all other considerations, Macgregor Laird considered these facts well worth the enormous cost in lives, suffering and money. Oldfield and Laird concluded their narrative with a powerful and moving chapter demonstrating their opposition to the slave trade, and their views on the benefits of proper trading relations with Africa. It also contained a strong condemnation of previous British involvement with Africa.

" From the commencement of the sixteenth century to that of the nineteenth in protecting and fostering the slave trade, - by legislative enactments, in granting premiums to the importer and bounties to the slave-holder, we (Great Britain) endeavoured by all means in our power to demoralise and disorganise Africa. During that time we have been the means of destroying life to a frightful extent, - of desolating whole districts, of annihilating all the domestic relations, changing the love of parents for their children to that of animals for their offspring. We have refused to take anything from them but slaves, and have turned round and reproached them with indolence for not cultivating their own soil. We have debased and degraded them to the level of animals, and taunted them with mental incapacity. We have heaped on them misery and suffering, contumely and scorn. We have denied them instruction, and accused them of ignorance. We have abused them for idleness while fattening upon their labour, and have turned round with the Pharisee and said, - God I thank thee, I am not such as these. "

The melancholy mortality list and the poor trading returns of this expedition for a time daunted the Liverpool merchants, but Laird maintained his faith in the basic soundness of his project, though he henceforth held that ships in the Niger trade should be manned by Africans, the officers alone being Europeans. Interest in the Niger soon revived; a Glasgow merchant, Robert Jamieson, in 1839 built and sent out the steamer *Ethiope*, which, under Captain Beecroft, ascended the river until stopped by the Boussa Rapids. Commercially, however, this expedition fared no better than Laird's. Next was to come the imposing and ill-fated government expedition of 1841, designed, according to Queen Victoria, to make arrangements with the Chief Rulers to suppress slavery, and establish lawful commerce.

A LIST OF THE MORTALITY ON BOARD THE QUORRA
& ALBURKAH

Alburkah

Joseph Hill, captain.

Josiah Jones, mate.

William Unwin, carpenter.

William M'Kensie, boatswain.

Joseph Drakeford, engineer.

James Smith, fireman.

John Gelling, fireman.

John Smith, fireman.

James Smith, Cook.

Abraham, boy.

Joseph Huntingdon, second mate.

Francisco, seaman.

Hugh Dunlevie, engineer.

William Miller, carpenter.

Samuel Harvey, seaman

Quorra

G.L. Harries, R.N. Captain.

James Goldie, first mate.

William Edelstone, second mate.

Thomas Belfrage, gunner.

Hugh Cosnaham, seaman.

William Gardner, seaman.

William Morgan, seaman.

James Breen, seaman.

William Davies, seaman.

James Swinton, carpenter.

John Addy, cook.

Master A.G. Clarke, apprentice.

Duncan Campbell, fireman.

John Johnson, Fireman.

William Ram, cabin steward.

John Gillingham, 2nd cabin steward.

Walter Miller, first engineer.

George Curling, second engineer.

John Grey, boy.

James Fardey, cook.

Thomas Parry, boy.

Richard L. Lander.

Thomas Briggs Esq. M.D.

Richard Jordan, clerk.

Between eight and ten Kroomen died, chiefly from poison.

SURVIVORS
Alburkah

R.A.K. Oldfield, surgeon.

Thomas Orford, Seaman.

Charles Jeffrey, coloured man.

Thomas Sarsfield, steward.

Quorra

Lieutenant W. Allen, passenger.

Macgregor Laird

Alexander Hector, purser.

Thomas Harvey, seaman.

William Kirby, seaman.

CHAPTER FIVE   ABOLITIONISTS, EMANCIPATORS & SLAVERS

The Lander - Laird - Oldfield expedition lasted from 1832 to 1834, these being crucial years in the struggle to end slavery. During this period the highly influential Abolitionist Movement in Britain succeeded in their long struggle to see slavery abolished throughout the British Empire. By the Celebrated Act of The Imperial Legislature, passed in 1833, compulsory labour (slavery) was summarily abolished throughout the British Empire. The effects of this Act were mitigated by the fact that it was not immediately enforceable until some years after this date. West Indian Planters were also given the option - if they so chose - to implement a system known as 'apprenticeship' as a sort of interim system, between the formal abolition of slavery by the above Act, and the slaves complete freedom.   To their credit the planters of Antigua - men who had profited by the system for generations - decided that enough was enough, laid aside all claims to 'apprenticeship', and gave their negroes freedom. This example was not followed in other colonies.   The owners then received compensation - for their loss of 'property' - to soften the blow, which in many cases exceeded the value of their estates; the British Tax Payer footing the bill.

    The implementation of the above Act created an immediate shortage of labour throughout the British Empire, which soon brought into existence the 'Coolie Trade' whereby free Indian Labourers were recruited in the sub-continent and shipped to America and the West Indies; notably by James Nourse & Company, and Messrs Sandbache Tinne and Company of Liverpool. These firms claiming, with some justification, that the Indian workers and their families were shipped out under very carefully controlled and humanitarian conditions, with a guarantee of a 'return passage' and therefore this trade bore no resemblance whatsoever to the slave trade. Some Abolitionists were to give this matter their consideration, remaining unconvinced by these arguments; but at the actual time of Emancipation, the anti-slavery men, then led by Thomas Fowell Buxton, turned their attention to the state of West Africa.

    The Royal Navy was now highly active in opposing the slave trade, the British anti-slavery patrol occupying about 20% of our naval strength.   Just two years after the Laird - Lander expedition, 6,000 men could be regarded as being engaged in anti-slavery work, manning between fifty and sixty ships. Over 3,000 of these men, with twenty-six ships, were on the North American and West Indies station, 2,000 men on the South American station, with about fourteen vessels, and 1,000 men on the Cape and West Africa station.   In spite of all this Buxton and the Abolitionists were shocked to hear that the slave trade was actually increasing - not declining, as might be expected!

Buxton and his supporters drew the obvious conclusion that more ships, and in particular powerful steamships should be made available to the anti-slavery squadron, but he also realised that the British policy of imposing anti-slavery treaties on other nations would have to be stepped up, and efforts made to see that legitimate trade replaced the slave trade. He also proposed that agricultural settlements should be established at various places on the West Coast, so that the African Chiefs, who had profited for so long from the slave trade, would willingly sign treaties abolishing the traffic in their own enslaved people, and then start trading in palm oil and other agricultural products. The Abolitionists were not being unrealistic, for they were well aware that slaves were in great demand, and were therefore the most profitable commodity that the African Chiefs could deal in. Buxton drew attention to the fact that on one notable occasion the Chiefs had been incited to set fire and destroy 30,000 palm oil trees, in an act of revenge against the British, as this legitimate venture was upsetting the more profitable trade in slaves! Buxton was also astute enough to make it clear that he was not advocating a policy of imperialism, merely wishing to organise a system of Christian Agricultural mission stations in West Africa. It was this philosophy which was to lead to the mounting of the government backed expedition to the Niger in 1841; to begin the first settlement of the kind that he proposed. It was doomed to failure, for all the Europeans were attacked by malaria, and forty-eight of them died. However, the struggle against slavery, by the Abolitionists and Emancipators, was to continue, at which point in this story about West Africa it would be appropriate to summarise the long history of a movement with such a direct bearing on the development of this area.

The story of the years of struggle, dating from 1676 to the close of the 19th century, but in particular during the years 1787 to 1841, under the leadership of Wilberforce, Buxton, Clarkson, Sharp, Sturge, Lushington, Rathbone and their thousands of supporters, may , as the great Irish historian, William Lecky once observed, ' be regarded as among the three or four perfectly virtuous acts recorded in the history of nations.' Lord Roseberry, when commenting on British efforts to put an end to slavery stated that - ' This country when it stands before history, will stand, when all else has passed away, not by her fleets and her armies and her commerce, but by the heroic self-denying exertions which she has made to put down the iniquitous (slave) traffic.'

This great Christian crusade was eventually instrumental in bringing to an end the vulgarity and barbarity of a social system based on the continuing enslavement of black Africans. (Although it has to be said, that according to the United Nations definition of the term , slavery is still rife today, at the close of the 20th century, under one guise or another.) Nevertheless, the anti-slavery movement had positive effects on British society. Rex Coupland, in his biography of Wilberforce noting that -

"it founded in the British people a tradition of humanity and of responsibility towards the weak and backward black peoples whose fate lay in their hands. And that tradition has never died..... It was nothing less, indeed, than a moral revolution; and those who see the world's life as a whole, as an intricate, shifting complex not only of states and nations but of continents and races, discordant, yet interdependent, heterogeneous, yet all belonging to one human family, will give a high place in history to the Englishman who did so much to bring about that revolution."

These sentiments remain valid - despite the crude Imperialistic scramble for Africa which loomed on the political horizon, which was to astonish everyone, including the German Chancellor Bismark, who, at the close of the 19th century, complained that he was being led into a 'colonial whirl' - and the French Prime Minister, Jules Ferry, who called it a 'steeplechase into the unknown'. In 1880, near the close of the 19th century most of the African continent was still ruled by Africans - and only partly explored, at least by those of European origin. Just two decades later five European nations had established over thirty colonies, or 'protectorates', through which they dominated the lives of over 100 million black Africans. Open slavery had been suppressed, only to be replaced by a system of imperialistic exploitation, which was, so far as Britain is concerned, exemplified by the rise of men such as Cecil John Rhodes. However, in the days of Wilberforce and Buxton, this sorry development lay in the future.

Those who sought to abolish the slave trade were known as Abolitionists; those who sought to abolish slave owning as Emancipators. As the movement developed both sections became known as Abolitionists. This movement came to dominate British colonial policy, eventually producing administrators such as General Charles Gordon, of Khartoum, Sir George Grey, and then Baron Frederick Lugard, who was to become Governor General of Nigeria in the early years of this century; and Sir Alan Burns, who was to act as Governor of Nigeria in 1942. His celebrated *History of Nigeria*, first published in 1929, being an authoritative and sympathetic work, which on several occasions has been quoted in the Nigerian courts.

However, the cultural atmosphere of the late 18th, and the early 19th centuries was decidedly unfavourable to the Abolitionists. The period was marked by the spiritual atrophy of the Churches, which gave rise to feelings of indifference to slavery, injustice, and human suffering in general. They were also up against the politically powerful vested interests of the British slave owners, who did all they could to discredit individual Abolitionists, and undermine their cause in general. Nevertheless, the stout-hearted

Abolitionists soldiered on, motivated by a literal and humanitarian interpretation of Christianity. Christianity was eventually to win this victory, but only after a struggle which lasted for more than five decades. In the 2,000 year history of the Christian faith, which guided all the actions of the Abolitionists, it is clear that it never achieved anything greater.

The penetration of Africa by all the aforementioned explorers opened up this continent - for good or ill - to all the impacts of western religion, education and commerce. So far as the religious factor is concerned, the Church Missionary Society, in particular, was to carry on its work in Western Africa from the days of the early pioneers, guided by the same humanitarian Christian ethic that motivated Wilberforce and his colleagues. This was to lead to missionary involvement in the 1841 expedition. A summary of the Abolitionist movement, from the days of Godwyn and Richard Baxter, in the 17th century, will put all these historical developments into proper perspective.

Between 1670 and 1680 Godwyn, who was a clergyman of the established church, and Richard Baxter, a famous Non-conformist, spoke out strongly against slavery. The former describing eloquently, the brutality of slavery, as he had witnessed it in Barbados, the latter protesting against the slave-trade, denouncing those who were involved in it as robbers and pirates. These writers were soon followed by Southern, Hutcheson, Foster, Wallis and others. Bishop Warburton, in 1676, then preached a notable sermon, denouncing those who "talk, as of herds of cattle, of property in rational creatures!"

John Wesley, the founder of Methodism, born at Epworth, Lincolnshire, in 1703, after studying at Christchurch, Oxford, took orders in 1725. He made his way to Georgia, then the West Indies, where he witnessed the workings of slavery at first hand. He then declared American slavery to be the vilest that ever saw the sun, and constituted the sum of all villanies. He had nothing but contempt for slave dealers, considering them to be man stealers; and the worst of thieves, in comparison to whom high-way robbers and house-breakers were comparatively innocent! On his return from America he set up the Methodist Church which then took a strong stand on the issue.

The Society of Friends, established in the middle of the 17th century, under the leadership of George Fox , with the Methodists, were also quick to take a stand against slavery. In 1724 they passed a resolution condemning both the slave trade and the holding of slaves, this despite the fact that at this time some Quakers were participating in the trade. In 1758, when it was clear that this, and other gentle admonitions had not sufficed, in thirty-one years, to purge the Society from involvement in slavery, the following resolution was adopted:

"We fervently warn all in profession with us, that they carefully avoid being in any way concerned in reaping the unrighteous profits arising from the iniquitous practice of dealing in negro or other slaves, whereby, in the original purchase, one man selleth another, as he doth the beasts that perish, without any better pretension to property in him, than that of superior force, in direct violation of the Gospel rule, which teacheth all to do as they would be done by, and to do good to all. We, therefore, can do no less than, with the greatest earnestness, impress it upon Friends, everywhere, that they endeavour to keep their hands clear of the unrighteous gain of oppression."

In Britain though there had always been a minority who considered slavery was a crime against humanity. During the reign of William 111, Sir John Holt, the then Chief Justice, took the view that any slave who entered England should automatically become a free man. His judgement had little effect, as slave-owners continued to advertise for and recover runaway slaves. The position of these owners was in fact strengthened in 1729, when the Solicitor General and the Attorney General turned their attention to this issue. After due consideration they declared that a slave did *not* become free by coming to Britain, and remained the property of his master. There were a minority of people in Britain who were not willing to accept this interpretation of the law, and they soldiered on, against all odds. Opposition to slavery also existed in the Church of England, but they were a minority - voices crying in the wilderness. Bishop Warburton denounced in strong language, those who were involved with slavery, proclaiming from the pulpit that those who talked of 'herds of cattle, of property in rational creatures.' could not consider themselves Christians.

It was later in the 18th century that Granville Sharp, evangelist, humanitarian and leading anti-slaver began to argue the case against slavery in the English Courts. His crusade began in 1767, for the release of an individual slave, which was soon followed by efforts to overthrow slavery itself throughout the British Empire, but particularly in England. His most celebrated case concerned the slave James Somerset, who had been brought to England in November, 1769, by his master, Charles Stewart, from Virginia, and after some time had elapsed, made a bid for freedom by leaving him. Stewart had him seized, and carried on board the *Ann and Mary*, Captain Knowles, so that he could be taken to the British colony of Jamaica, and there sold as a slave.

On 7 February, 1772, the case was tried in the King's Bench, before Lord Chief Justice Mansfield. The crucial question at issue was - ' Is every man in England entitled to the liberty of his person, unless forfeited by the laws of England?' This was affirmed by the advocates of Somerset; and Mr Sergeant Day, who opened his case, broadly declared 'that no man at this day *is*, or *can* be, a slave in England.' The case dragged on, Mansfield showed signs of wavering, but by this time the eyes of the British public were focused on

Granville Sharp

Thomas Clarkson

William Wilberforce, aged 29

him, all awaiting, with great interest, the decision of the Court. He delayed judgement, and twice threw out the suggestion ' that the master might put an end to present litigation, by manumitting the slave.' Judgement was demanded, which was given on 22 June, 1772. Mansfield decided as follows:

"Immemorial usage preserves the memory of *positive law*, long after all traces of the occasion, reason, authority, and time of its introduction are lost, and in the case so odious as the condition of *slaves*, must be taken *strictly*: (Tracing the subject to natural principles, the claim of slavery can never be supported.) The power claimed by this return never was in use here. We cannot say the cause set forth in this return is allowed or approved of by the laws of this Kingdom, and therefore the man must be discharged."

The decision was a momentous and historic one, for it meant that once a slave set foot on British soil he became free. Thus was the guilty fiction of legal slavery in England exploded, but only after it had been acted upon as though it were a truth for decades. This was considered the starting-point of the movement for the abolition of the Slave Trade, and Slave System, which for years had been fundamental to the plantation economies of the great European powers, Latin America, and, the British North American colonies. So far as the latter were concerned, the time was a significant one, for they had just broken away from British rule, searching for liberty, justice and equality, proclaiming that ' all men under God are equal...' - although many years were to pass, until the time of the American Civil War, in the 1860's, when the Union Forces, under the Leadership of President Abraham Lincoln, eventually managed to crush the slave-based Confederacy, and finally bring to an end slavery in America.

Things were clearly on the move, for just four years after the Somerset case, in 1776, a motion was moved in the House of Commons that 'the slave-trade is contrary to the laws of God and the rights of man.' It failed, clearly being ahead of its time, but the fact that such a motion was placed at all was historically significant. Undaunted, Granville Clark, with ardent social reformers such as William Wilberforce, M.P., and Thomas Clarkson, carried on the struggle against slavery. In 1787 they banded together and established the Society for the Abolition of the Slave Trade. Wilberforce became the leader of this Society, and he presented several Bills to Parliament between 1788 and 1796, designed to prohibit the further importation of slaves into the British colonies in the West Indies. The Bills never became law, but at least something was accomplished, it being agreed that bounties should be given to all masters and surgeons of British slave ships, whose human cargoes escaped disease and excessive mortality. Wilberforce soon gained the support of William Pitt, the then Prime Minister, in his crusade against slavery, as well as that of other powerful and influential Members of Parliament, but still many years were to pass before he was to secure a vote for abolition.

Other external factors now began to alter the entrenched attitudes of the British Establishment. In France, for decades, the court had revelled in every form of costly luxury and debauchery. Crowds of courtiers, worthless and dissolute men, hung about the palace, and lived in the most extravagant style - mainly at the public expense. The people, ground down with taxes to pay for all this vice and luxury - rose up. The Bastille was stormed on 14 July, 1789, and the King and Queen were then executed - for denying them 'Liberty, Equality and Fraternity.' The French revolution caused such radical concepts to be discussed throughout the world - but particularly in Britain. From 1779 Wyvill's Yorkshire movement took the leading role in organising petitions for Parliamentary reform. The working people were demanding the vote, and a democratic society. In 1780 the Society for promoting Constitutional Information was formed, and it welcomed Paine's *Rights of Man* no less than it did the American and French revolutions. The Industrial Revolution was now marching arm in arm with a great international social revolution; all marked by the rapidly increasing number of newspapers and journals that were appearing - particularly in Britain. In this heady liberal atmosphere, the concept that negroes were part of the human race, and just as entitled to freedom as all other men, and that slavery was evil, was becoming accepted.

But new ideas, isolated from other social and economic developments, would not have been enough to bring about the radical changes required to end the slave trade. The aforementioned Industrial Revolution was making Britain the first Industrial nation of Europe. By 1780 Mathew Boulton had entered into partnership with James Watt, symbolically linking the scientist-inventor with a captain of industry; and it was the Laird family who were foremost in putting this new technology to maritime use, and in a manner that had enormous social implications for West Africa. By 1780, though enclosures were in full swing, England had ceased to be corn-exporting, and was becoming, on balance, a corn-importing country - so great was the consumption by the new working class, whose formation dates from these years. Britain was fast becoming the 'workshop of the world'. What she required now was a constant supply of raw materials for her ever expanding, urban based, industries, and more and more overseas markets in which to sell her manufactured goods.

By the close of the 18th century the value of the slave trade to Britain's economy was declining rapidly, although many remained blind to this fact, this due, in part, to the disproportionate influence of the ' Plantation Lobby'. The economic arguments against abolition - and even emancipation - were already failing to ring true even in the closing decades of the 18th century. Scores of new industries were rising up to provide a route to prosperity for the bourgeois, and the aristocracy. The more politically aware now began to realize, that in a rapidly changing world, Abolition no longer posed a threat to the economic stability of Britain. It has been said that abolition of the slave trade succeeded only when economic considerations coincided with the moral crusade of the British Abolitionists, but this, once fashionable view, does not give due credit to these crusaders. It has to be noted that advanced nations without such an active anti-slavery lobby participated in slavery, and the slave trade, for many years after Britain took a strong stance against the system. Slavery continuing in the French colonies until 1848, in the United States until the 1860's, in Cuba till 1886, Brazil till 1888, and in the Portuguese colonies of Angola and Principe until 1908. Clearly, abolitionist activity combined with these economic developments, uniting into an historical development, which eventually brought down traditional forms of slavery.

However, at the time of the American Revolution - and before - the Abolitionist movement in North America was also well established, and was to gain in power and influence, until the Union victory in the American Civil war eventually brought about the downfall of slavery in the United States. All of this had tremendous implications for West Africa. Three years before the Revolution began the Abolitionist Samuel Hopkins produced a plan for training freed Negroes of the North American colonies as colonizers and missionaries for Africa. This policy was to give rise to the establishment of Liberia. Eight years later, in 1781, Cornwallis surrendered to the United States at Yorktown, and in the same year Thomas Jefferson revived a plan for the *gradual* abolition of slavery in the United States. But although Jefferson wanted to free the slaves, he did not want the freed slaves to remain in North America! His plan embraced the concept of 'methodical deportation' and subsidised colonization in Africa of freed slaves, all of which complimented the proposals advanced by Hopkins. The fact that very few freed slaves actually wanted to return to Africa, being conveniently ignored; nevertheless, his intentions were honourable.

At the time of the American Revolution the American colonies had a large population of freed slaves. Some of the Negroes had been liberated by their owners, but many more had run away from their owners, and gained sanctuary in non-slave territories. Long before the close of the 18th century many Americans had become active Abolitionists, considering slavery immoral. During the 1790's the Congress of the United States began enacting laws designed to put an end to the slave trade between the United States and foreign powers. During the early years of the 19th century Congress passed more laws which were aimed at bringing to a close all slave importation. Sadly though, these laws were continually violated. In 1818 slave-trading was eventually defined as piracy, by Congress, and the following year another

Act was passed which provided that Negroes captured from slavers should be "safely kept, supported and removed beyond the limits of the United States." Meanwhile the population of freed slaves was growing. All of this eventually led to the establishment of Liberia - supposedly a refuge for freed American slaves, which it has to be said was not a great success.

Meanwhile, another, more radical, black 'Abolitionist' by the name of Denmark Vesey. was gaining support in America. He was a freed slave, who lived and worked in Charleston, and he was undoubtedly a most remarkable man. A skilled tradesman, he also spoke English, Spanish, German and French. He had a profound understanding of the scriptures. Vesey used the Bible to prove that God was opposed to slavery, then set himself the monumental task of organising a slave uprising!

In 1821 he began to recruit conspirators for the revolt, and after much effort he mustered a following of about eight thousand slaves. In April, 1822 he set the date for the revolution, this being the second Sunday in July, the basic plan being to mount five separate attacks upon the town of Charleston. Plans had to be changed, and then a slave turned informer. This led to the arrest of Vesey and thirty-seven of his leaders, all of them being hanged. The planned revolt had failed, but news of it soon spread throughout 'The Deep-South' like wildfire, frightening all the plantation owners. Repressive legislation was then rushed through, which, amongst other things, prohibited the educating of negroes, and the 'congregating' of slaves. Like Spartacus, the great freedom fighter of the Roman Empire, Denmark Vesey had failed in his bid to secure freedom for those held in slavery; but the torch of freedom was now well and truly lit, and it could not be extinguished. On the other side of the Atlantic the torch of freedom was then being firmly grasped by the great Abolitionist, William Wilberforce.

William Wilberforce was born on 24 August, 1759. He attended Hull Grammar School, but when his father died he was sent to his uncle William, who had a house at Wimbledon. He then attended a school at Putney. His mother brought him back to Hull on hearing that an aunt was 'perverting' him to the cause of Methodism! To cure him of this subversive influence he was placed under the care of the Rev. K. Baskett, master of Pocklington Grammar School. He forgot his Methodism, and in spite, or because of this, became very popular. In October, 1776, he was sent to St. John's College, Cambridge, where he struck up an acquaintance with William Pitt.

On leaving Cambridge he decided to go into politics, an expensive business in those days. In September, 1780, he was elected for Hull, but only after spending about £8,500 pounds on his election expenses! In London he joined several exclusive clubs, including the 'Goosetree' where he strengthened his friendship with Pitt. In Parliament Wilberforce invariably supported Pitt, their friendship developed, Pitt eventually taking rooms in the house at Wimbledon, which after his uncle's death, belonged to Wilberforce. Wilberforce stood by his friend during the struggle in the early part of 1784, and on the dissolution of Parliament went to Yorkshire to stand in the same interest. In the next Parliament he supported Pitt with undiminished zeal. Wilberforce returned to support Pitt's proposals for reform by February, 1785. This friendship was to be of crucial importance, in the development of the British Abolitionist movement.

Later in 1785 Wilberforce went abroad again, and met his mother at Genoa. On this and other journeys he was accompanied by Isaac Milner. They studied religion together, the result being Wilberforce's 'conversion,' and a resolution that in future he would lead a strictly religious life. He advised Pitt of his new and improved state of mind, who received this information with 'delicate kindness' - and although not 'converted' he was not alienated by his close friends declared change of attitude.

In the session of 1786 Wilberforce carried through the House of Commons a bill for amending the criminal law. It was rejected in the House of Lords, though many compliments were paid to Wilberforce for his benevolent intentions. The attention of philanthropists was then being drawn to the question of slavery, particularly after Granville Sharp had won the Somersett Case in 1772. The following year, in 1787, a settlement was established on the West Coast of Africa by the English Society for the Abolition of the Slave Trade. This was not a great success at the time, but indicates that public support for Abolition was growing. In the same year, an Anti-Slavery committee, mainly composed of Quakers, of which Sharp was president was established. Wilberforce, now moving independently towards an Abolitionist position, felt moved to accept the parliamentary leadership of the cause. The committee remained independent, but Wilberforce worked closely with it. From this point on he worked tirelessly in the House to bring in legislation banning the Slave Trade. Pitt, soon converted to the cause, becoming a strong ally. In 1791 Wilberforce joined in the Sierra Leone Company, suggested by Granville Sharp.

During the parliament elected in 1796 the abolition question made slow progress, and in April the following year, Charles Ellis, working in the interest of the planters, tabled a motion which recommended that the colonies themselves should be instructed to introduce measures leading to the *gradual* abolition of the trade. Pitt strongly opposed this line, declaring that every one was now agreed that the trade should be abolished, but he lost, the motion being carried by 93 to 63. Pitt died in January, 1806, but the new government of Fox and Grenville was generally in favour of abolition. Eventually, a resolution in favour of abolition was carried by 115 to 14 on the 10 June, 1806. The Bill for abolishing the slave trade was finally introduced in the House of Lords in January, 1807, and was carried.

It was sent back to the Commons in February, when it was debated again, the Solicitor General making a memorable speech, in which he stated that Wilberforce 'would that day lay his head upon his pillow and remember that the slave trade was no more'! The House then rose to cheer the great crusader, but Wilberforce was so overcome with emotion that he was like a man in a dream - he hardly noticed! The motion was carried by 283 to 16. The Bill receiving the royal assent on 25 March, 1807. This had immediate implications for Liverpool, a town with an interesting and varied history,but then the European port most heavily engaged in the slave trade with West Africa.

In 1700 the town of Liverpool had a population of about 5,000, the port owning about seventy vessels, which gave employment to 800 seamen. When George 1 ascended the throne in 1714 Liverpool had a population of 10,000 persons, with a mayor, aldermen, and town council; with two representatives in the House of Commons; and a hundred small ships were registered at the port, which gave employment to about 1000 men. One single dock being sufficient for the accommodation of its commerce. By 1750 the population had risen to 18,000.

The rise of new industries had brought about this growth in population. Sugar refineries were well established, shipbuilding yards were active on the shore - to the north and south of the docks. There were many rope works, and several iron foundries. Liverpool was also becoming world famous for the production of watches. The Liverpool potteries provided employment for many skilled workers, turning out fine blue and white delft, the main works for this product gaining an international reputation for excellence. In the year 1737 The Duke of Bridgewater, whose estates lay at Worsley, five miles from Manchester, got a private Act of Parliament to improve a stream, leading from his pits at Worsley, to the Irwell, along which his coal could be carried to the neighbouring town. In 1758, the great engineer Brindley, acting for the Duke, undertook the construction of the Bridgewater canal to link Manchester with Liverpool. The River Weaver, from the salt-pits of Cheshire to the Mersey, was made navigable in 1720, and the Sankey Canal, from the coal-fields to the same river were made navigable in 1758. The Cheshire salt, then brought to Liverpool for export, was of exceptionally high quality, and soon put an end to the manufacture of salt from sea-water. Foreign nations now looked to Liverpool for the supply of this basic commodity. A circle drawn round Liverpool included coal-fields covering 2,466 square miles, one pit being within eight miles of the port. From these deposits Liverpool developed as a major exporter of coal - much of it being shipped to Ireland, Liverpool in fact dominating all trade across the Irish Sea.

Other major 'industries' which provided much employment to the people of Liverpool were privateering and smuggling! For a period of about one hundred years the port being heavily involved in privateering, notably, against the commerce of the French and Americans - 120 privateers being fitted out by Liverpool merchants at this time. It was reckoned in 1778, by a committee of the House of Lords, that, during the war then going on, 773 British vessels had been captured, whilst we had taken 904 American vessels. The value of this property, amounting to two million sterling - on both side, went, as prize money to the captors, not being restored to the commercial and industrial capital of either side. The second war with America, from 1812 to 1815, inflicted even more damage on British shipping; whilst the effect of the war with Napoleon was to prevent any considerable increase in the number of Liverpool vessels.

In 1757, 106 Liverpool vessels were employed in the smuggling trade, and they are said to have brought to the port an annual profit of £250,000. As the goods exported for this 'trade' were largely paid for in Spanish gold, pistoles and doubloons became common currency in Liverpool. The smuggling was based on the Spanish dominions in Central and South America. The Spanish government was trying to control its colonial commerce, this in order to keep out foreign competition. In practice this led to Spanish smugglers frequenting the ports of Jamaica, buying goods which the Spanish authorities refused to let them buy at home. On the other hand the Liverpool smugglers did their best to evade the Spanish customs, in order to trade directly with Mexico and Cuba. This trade though did not outlive the middle of the 18th century, as the issue led to a war between Spain and England. In 1747 an Act of Parliament forbade foreign vessels to frequent British West Indian ports, which drove away Spanish smugglers from Jamaica, and also brought to a close the Liverpool based smuggling industry. Other industries soon rose to fill the gap.

This leads to the great importance that the cotton trade was to play in the development of Lancashire and Liverpool; the 'dark satanic' mills of the county being driven by the steam engine, developed by Watt, using coal from the neighbouring pits. The spinning wheels being superseded by the steam-driven machines of Arkwright, Hargreaves and Crompton in 1770. At this date the annual importation of raw cotton into Liverpool was only 6,000 bales, but this figure was 100 times greater in 1860.

The cotton trade began with the East, not from the West, probably in the time of Queen Elizabeth, when Turkish Merchants brought cotton- wool to be worked up into garments, after being spun by hand on the ancient spinning-wheels. With mechanisation of the trade came the demand for a more consistent supply of raw material. This demand was met by the United States, whose plantations in the 'Deep-South' were manned by slave labour, and continued to be so until the time of the American Civil war in the 1860's. The situation now being an ironic one, for as Liverpool moved away from formal involvement with the slave trade, the port itself, and indeed Manchester and Lancashire, were, during the first part of the 19th Century, to become ever more dependent on a fibre produced by slave labour; all of which brings us to that once most lucrative branch of Liverpool enterprise - the slave-trade with West Africa.

In the early days of the English slave trade London and Bristol had a near monopoly on the business, and from 1698 to about 1730 Bristol began to gain on London. During these four decades Bristol merchants were investing more and more of their capital into, what was euphemistically known as, 'The Africa Trade'. They felt obliged to do this because Liverpool Merchants, with close access to goods manufactured in Manchester, were undermining her direct trade with the West Indies. When exactly the Liverpool slave trade began, and how it expanded, must remain a matter of guess-work, for the merchants had much to gain by making false Customs entries, this being to avoid a 10% duty on their trade, which was payable to the Royal Africa Company until 1712.

Liverpool merchants of this period were particularly skilled at evading a variety of laws. They broke Navigation Laws by exporting Irish manufactures direct, and consistently evaded duty on their return cargoes of West Indian or American produce, by landing it in the Isle of Man, from whence it could be smuggled in at leisure. They were in fact evading most duties payable in Liverpool itself by a system of bribery. These Merchants were also well known for being tight-fisted with their captains, crews and agents; many of them having served their time at sea, and consequently were very hard men. These points being made by a Liverpool writer in 1795:-

"The reason why the port of Liverpool could undersell the merchants of London and Bristol, was the restriction on their outfits and methods of factorage. The London and Bristol Merchants not only allowed ample monthly pay to their captains, but cabin privileges, primage, and daily port charges; they also allowed their factors five per cent. on the returns, and their vessels were always full manned by seamen at a monthly rate. The Liverpool merchants proceeded on a more economical but less liberal plan, the generality of their captains were at annual salaries, or if at monthly pay, four pounds was thought great wages at that time, no cabin privileges were permitted, primage was unknown amongst them, and as to port allowances, not a single shilling was given, while five shillings a day was the usual pay from Bristol, and seven and sixpence from London. The captains from these ports could therefore occasionally eat ashore, and drink their bottle of Madeira; whereas the poor Liverpool skipper was obliged to repair on board to his piece of salt beef and biscuits, and bowl of new rum punch, sweetened with brown sugar.

The factors instead of a rate per centum, had an annual salary, and were

116

allowed the rent for their store, negro hire, and other incidental charges; therefore, if the consignments were great or small, the advantage to the factor suffered no variation. The portage was still economical, their method was to take poor boys apprentice for long terms, who were annually increased, became good seamen, were then made second mates, then first mates, then captains, and afterwards factors on the islands. This was the usual gradation at that time, whereby few men at monthly pay were required to navigate a Liverpool vessel. This note is not meant invidious to the conduct of the proceedings of the traders at that time, nor to that of the present day, which is said to be similar in most instances, the African outfits excepted, nor are the remarks ideal, they are from the author's positive local observations, and are indispensable to an elucidation of this part of the history, that the cause may plainly appear, which enabled Liverpool to sell her Guinea cargoes nearly twelve per cent less than the rest of the Kingdom, and at the same time return an equal profit."

By these means Liverpool adventurers managed to take the trade away from London and Bristol merchants, and for a period of about 80 years managed to win for the port the unenviable distinction of being the main slave-trading town of Europe. To put this into perspective, in 1701, one hundred vessels were employed in this trade from London, which figure dropped to forty-five vessels by 1705. Liverpool appears to have entered the trade in 1709, when one small vessel of thirty tons went to Africa, traded goods for fifteen slaves, who were then taken across the Atlantic and sold. No serious increase in the trade occurred until 1730, when new regulations came into force, and Liverpool merchants promptly sent to Africa fifteen small vessels, of the average burthen of 75 tons each. The actual number of slaves taken across the Atlantic by these ships cannot now be established with any accuracy; but the profits must have been good enough to encourage further investment, for in 1837 we find that 33 ships had cleared from Liverpool, bound for the West Coast. Just over a decade later this figure had increased to seventy five named ships, with space to carry 23,200 slaves. The typical slaver of this period being a snow or brig of 250 - 300 tons. The owners and masters often being respectable church or chapel-goers, who saw nothing in the trade which was incompatible with their Christian faith.

Other readily available statistics show that in 1752 there belonged to Liverpool 88 vessels employed in the 'African Trade' - but there were also 124 trading directly with the West Indies, American and foreign; 28 plying between different ports in Europe; 21 in the Cheshire - London cheese trade; 101 coasters and Irish traders; and 80 sloops and flats on the river; making a total of 442 ships actually *registered* at Liverpool in 1752. This would indicate that just under 20% of Liverpool owned ships were active in the trade, 80% otherwise engaged - or at least not *directly* employed in slavery. Although the

117

ships employed in the 'Africa Trade' would, undoubtedly, have represented a higher proportion of the *tonnage* registered at Liverpool at this time.

Gore's Liverpool Directory states that 74 Liverpool vessels sailed for Africa in 1764, with 141 sailing for America in the same year. Interestingly though, it also notes that Liverpool had inwards a total of 766 ships, and outwards 833, these figures being the total movement of *all* ships using the port in this year, not merely those *registered* at the port. On this basis it can be seen that in 1764 8.88% of sailing from Liverpool were to Africa, and 91.12% to other destinations. To add further perspective to these figures it should be noted that on Sunday, 19 February,1791, 350 vessels sailed out of the port on *one* favourable tide. Whilst these figures help to keep this disgraceful issue in proportion, as they relate to all Liverpool trade, others show just how bad things were nationally, at this point in time, on the whole question of slavery.

The 'Gentleman Magazine' of 1764 estimated that there were about 20,000 black slaves then living in London alone, and these slaves were openly sold on the exchange. These unfortunate men, women and children, were branded with a distinguishing mark, and then secured with collars and padlocks, Adverts. appearing in the press for "silver padlocks for Blacks or Dogs; collars &c." Other notices offering substantial rewards for runaway slaves. This being just three years before Granville Sharp brought the James Somerset case to court.

Writing in 1907, Professor Ramsay Muir estimated that 878 round voyages were made by Liverpool trading vessels to the West Coast, during the eleven years from 1783-1793. These ships carried 303,737 slaves from Africa to the West Indies; and sold them for £15,186,850. After allowing for agents commission etc., purchase of slaves and other costs, the net annual profit going to Liverpool slave-traders - during the period under consideration being £300,000 per annum. This though did not complete the picture, for after selling the slaves the holds of the vessels would be filled with sugar, rum, tobacco and other West Indies produce, which yielded further substantial profits. From these statistics we can see that, although the trade was seasonal, on average, 79.81 ships sailed, *outward* bound for Africa, each year, from Liverpool - or say one every 4.57 days - with one returning during the same period. The average profit - per round voyage - on slaves alone - therefore being £3,758. The profit per slave carried being £10.86p. This shows that, on average, each ship would have carried 345.94 slaves on each crossing, and under horrifying conditions.

However, if we relate these statistics to those produced by Henry Smithers, writing in 1825, we will see that in 1788 some 991 vessels cleared from Liverpool, bound for Ireland alone. This would suggest that the Liverpool slave trade, even when at its zenith, represented a smaller

118

proportion of the sum total of Liverpool commerce than might have been expected; but the figures spotlight the crimes of those merchants engaged in the trade, and their collective guilt must never be underestimated. The worst feature of the trade being the notorious 'Middle-Passage'.

The trade was a 'triangular' one, the vessel first taking manufactured goods to the coast, and trading these items for slaves. The ship would then embark on the 'Middle-Passage' taking her human cargo to the West Indies. Here the holds would be cleared of the 'slave-decks' and the vessels loaded with plantation produce for the final leg of the voyage - back across the Atlantic to the home port of Liverpool. The export cargo, in the early years of the 18th century was usually composed of muskets, swords, gunpowder, flints, knives, clothes, shoes, rum and brandy. By the later years cotton goods were included, and the cargoes sometimes included fancy hats, mirrors and diamond necklaces. All these items being highly prized by the traders and the African Chiefs. Provisions for the voyage would usually be obtained from Ireland on the outward voyage, and then the course would be set for the West Coast. Many of the slaves would be obtained from the Niger country, being held in stockades, awaiting the arrival of the ships. When the ship was fully slaved, the Middle-Passage - the second part of the triangular voyage - began. Crossing the Atlantic could take as long as 51 days, and the slaves were crammed together below decks all night, and in rough weather. How many survived depending on the behaviour of the master and crew, the length of the voyage and the weather. At Jamaica, Antigua or other places in the West Indies, the slaves were landed and sold, and then the ship loaded with sugar, rum, and other plantation produce for the homeward run back to the Mersey.

As to the actual conditions for slaves on the 'Middle-Passage' - an eyewitness, Falconbridge, once a surgeon on a slaver, who then gave evidence against the trade, paints a grim picture. He tells us that as soon as the male negroes were brought on the ship they were immediately fastened together by handcuffs on the wrist, and irons riveted on their legs. They were then stowed below on platforms, often being packed so close together that they could only lie on their sides. Here fights would break out, as the desperate captives attempted to get to water or toilet buckets placed at the end of the narrow low platforms. Falconbridge goes on to describe the disgraceful catering arrangements;-

"In favourable weather they are fed upon deck, but in bad weather their food is given to them below. Numberless quarrels take place among then during their meals; more especially when they are put upon short allowance, which frequently happens. In that case, the weak are obliged to be content with a very scanty portion. Their allowance of water is about half a pint each, at every meal.

Upon the negroes refusing to take sustenance, I have seen coals of fire, glowing hot, put on a shovel, and placed so near their lips as to scorch and burn them, and this has been accompanied with threats of forcing them to swallow the coals, if they any longer persisted in refusing to eat. These means have generally the desired effect. I have also been credibly informed that a certain captain in the Slave-Trade poured melted lead on such of the negroes as obstinately refused to eat their food."

The Africans were far more affected by sea-sickness than the European crews, and suffered so badly from it that they frequently died. The exclusion of fresh air below decks also made life intolerable for the slaves. Most ships had air ports, but whenever the vessel met with bad weather they had to be closed, making the slave decks unbearably hot. The confined air soon became stale, and with excreta and urine, running about, sickness soon developed. Deaths soon occurred, and often the dead would remain chained to the living. Granville Sharp brought forward a case which aroused public attention to the horrors of this passage. In his memoirs we have the following account taken from his private memoranda:-

"March 19, 1783. Gustavus Vasa called on me with an account of 132 negroes being thrown alive into the sea, from on board an English slave-ship". "the circumstances of this case could not fail to excite a deep interest. The master of a slave-ship trading from Africa to Jamaica, and having 440 slaves on board, had thought fit, on a pretext that he might be distressed on his voyage for want of water, to lessen the consumption of it in the vessel by throwing overboard 132 of the most sickly among the slaves. On his return to England, the owners of the ship claimed from the insurers the full value of those drowned slaves, on the ground that there was an absolute necessity for throwing them into the sea, in order to save the remaining crew, and the ship itself. The underwriters contested the existence of the alleged necessity; or, if it had existed, attributed it to the ignorance and improper conduct of the master of the vessel. "

The contest of these financial interests, in open court, brought to the public attention the brutality of this detestable plot, but it also exposed the horrors of the trade itself. From statistics kept by several vessels, it appears that out of 7,904 slaves purchased on the coast, 2,053 perished on the Middle-Passage. In one document the figure is put at 20%, and in the case of the ship *John* the rate of mortality was actually 50%. So horrible were the conditions that the slave-ships had to be constructed with a view to preventing the negroes from ending their miseries by plunging into the sea. The public then began to hear other horror stories about the trade, particular mention often being made about the barbaric behaviour of some masters. One Captain, enraged by a child who refused to eat, had him flogged, and then he ordered the cook to place the youngsters feet in boiling water. This brought off the skin and nails. Four days later the child died. Another Liverpool Captain related to some friends at Buxton how a female slave on his ship became upset because her child was sick. " Apprehensive for her health, I snatched the child from her arms, knocked its head against the side of the ship, and threw it into the sea." Facts about such monsters, glorifying in their unparalleled brutality, once made public, brought further support to the Abolitionist cause, then led nationally by Wilberforce, and later by Sir Thomas Fowell Buxton.

In Liverpool itself there was also a small group of men who dared to speak out against the trade, among them being William Rathbone, the second of that name, Doctor James Currie, and above all the great scholar, William Roscoe. Born in 1753, he published a poem, 'The Wrongs of Africa', in 1787, and in 1788 a pamphlet entitled 'A General View of the African Slave Traffic,' in which he denounced the evil, though in very temperate language. He then devoted much time and effort to writing his celebrated 'Life of Lorenzo de' Medici'. In October, 1806, Roscoe was elected M.P. for Liverpool. He sat for only a few months, but had the pleasure of being able to speak in favour of Wilberforce's Act which abolished the slave-trade. After this he returned to Liverpool, and was welcomed by a mob with staves and brickbats. He did not return to Westminster, but he was always proud of the fact that he had been able to cast his vote in favour of abolishing a trade which had brought wealth into Liverpool, but at the expense of all civilised values.

The Slave Trade ended on May 1, 1807. The last ship to sail from Liverpool on a slave-trading voyage being the *Mary*, under the command of Captain Hugh Crow, who had been born in the town of Ramsey, in the Isle of Man, in 1765. Crow always claimed that the trade was not as bad as many suggested, and that he had always treated his 'passengers' with care and respect. The *facts* about the trade painted a different picture, most people taking the views of this apologist for slave trading with a large pinch of salt. The 400 negroes taken across the Atlantic by Hugh Crow, on this voyage, being the last (officially recorded!) shipment of slaves sold by British merchants to work the estates of the West Indies.

Even before Abolition came, other industries had developed in Liverpool, which meant that the prosperity of the port, as a whole, suffered but little, when Abolition finally arrived in 1807. From the years 1750 to 1765 a very extensive fishing industry was established in the area. A whaling industry was also established in Liverpool, which began to develop rapidly in the closing decades of the 18th century, it being recorded that three ships were sent out to the Greenland and Davis's Straights in 1764. By 1788 this had increased to twenty-one vessels, with a total tonnage of 6,485.

In 1792 the number of Liverpool ships engaged in the 'African Trade' was 136, the tonnage 24,544, giving an average figure of 180 tons burthen per vessel. This represented just 8.33% of the tonnage which *entered* the

Captain Hugh Crow

port in this year. Whilst the traffic had increased in absolute terms by 1804, relatively it was then playing just a minor part in the British export market. As the Journal of Negro History has pointed out, by 1804 only 2.5% of English capital engaged in foreign trade was then invested in the slave trade. Hence, the old argument that the traffic was essential to Britain's continuing prosperity - pushed so vigorously by the Liverpool Merchants engaged in the trade - had, even then, lost all validity.

Some of our best poets and writers had also given their support to the Abolitionist cause, among them being William Cowper, who attacked the slave trade in 'The Task,' and later wrote three poems, the best of these being 'The Negro's Complaint.' Pope, Thomson and Defoe also made their contribution, as did the great William Wordsworth, with his sonnet to Toussaint L'Ouverture. A great many women made, or at first attempted to make, their contribution to the cause; but the Abolitionists occupied too early a page in history to allow women a prominent share in the task. Wilberforce apparently regarded public agitation by women as 'undesirable' - whilst Buxton sought their *silent* co-operation only - through prayer! The Committee of the British Anti-Slavery Society not even admitting women members until 1905.

Out in the Atlantic though things improved more rapidly. From 1807 onwards, Britain alone of the great maritime powers of the 19th century, refused to allow her ships to carry slaves. The Anti-Slavery Patrol was established, and the Royal Navy then began the monumental task of stopping the traffic in slaves. This work they maintained, throughout the greater part of the century, until the Atlantic slave trade was finally extinguished. In 1842 the West Africa Squadron contained five steamers, but it was not until three years later that the Admiralty really began to accept this new technology. The screw steamer *Rattler* being sent to join the paddle steamer *Alecto*, then already working with the patrol. However, to the end of its days, the Anti-Slavery patrol of the Royal Navy relied mainly on sailing ships, some of them being captured slavers - built for speed. This helped, for many of the ships the Admiralty provided for this work were designed for hard service in northern waters, whilst many of the slave ships were Baltimore built clippers, designed to cope with the light airs of the South Atlantic. As noted, the Royal Navy had a sort of advance base on the Spanish island of Fernando Po, which was under the command of Colonel Edward Nicolls, at the time of the 1832-34 Laird - Lander expedition.

In 1814 Wilberforce was delighted to hear that the French Government had prohibited the slave trade from north of Cape Formosa. Soon afterwards Napoleon returned from Elba, then proclaimed a total abolition, which was afterwards accepted by the government of restoration. At the close of 1821 Wilberforce's health began to deteriorate, and though advised by his doctor to avoid demanding work, he still insisted in taking part in anti-slavery agitation. In March, 1823, he issued an 'appeal' which was followed by the formation of the Anti-Slavery Society, which still continues the good work down to this day, now being the oldest established human rights organisation in the world   On 16 March, 1824 he spoke again on the question of slavery, but on the 19th was taken seriously ill.

On 15 May, 1830 he made his last public appearance at a meeting of the Anti Slavery Society, when Clarkson was present and moved that Wilberforce should take the chair. He became ill again in May, 1833, gradually became weaker, and died on 29 July, 1833. In compliance with a requisition signed by all Members of Parliament, whose names could be obtained at the time, he was buried at Westminster Abbey on 5 August. Leadership of the Anti-Slavery Movement was then passed on to Sir Thomas Fowell Buxton.

Buxton was born on 1 April, 1786, being the eldest son of Thomas Fowell Buxton of Earl's Colne, Essex., by a daughter of Osgood Hanbury, of Holfield Grange, in the same county. Significantly, his mother was a member of the Society of Friends, and a woman of great intelligence and energy.   He married in 1807, and then worked in the office of Truman, Hanbury, & Company, the brewers, of London. He became active in social issues, then, in 1818, he was returned to Parliament as the M.P. for Weymouth, then developed an interest in the Abolitionist cause. In May, 1824, Wilberforce formally requested Buxton to become his successor, as Buxton had been a very active member of the African Institution. Buxton worked hard for the cause, and in 1831 brought forward his resolution for the abolition of slavery. He showed that in 1807 the number of slaves in the West Indies was 800,000, while in 1830 it was only 700,000. This indicated that the slave population had suffered the loss of 100,000 in these few short years. The necessity for emancipation was conceded, and at the opening of the session of 1833 Lord Althorp announced that the Government would introduce a measure. Eventually, on 28 August, the Bill for the Total Abolition of Slavery Throughout the British Dominions received the Royal assent.

In 1839 Buxton published his famous work 'The African Slave Trade and its Remedy,' in which he recommended, as already mentioned, the concentration on the coast of Africa of a more efficient naval force; treaties made with the African Chiefs, under which they would agree to stop trading in slaves; and the actual purchase of Fernando Po, from the Spanish, so that the island could be better used to establish legitimate trade, and operate more effectively as a base for the Royal Navy.

He then became the prime mover in establishing the Society for the Extinction of the Slave Trade and the Civilisation of Africa. Related to this development, the Government resolved to send three ships to explore the Niger, these being the Gun Boats, *Soudan, Albert* and *Wilberforce*, built by

Macgregor Laird's elder brother John, at the family shipyard in Birkenhead. The vessels being launched in 1840. As will be noted, Macgregor Laird strongly disapproved of this expedition, correctly predicting that it would be a disaster, but Buxton pressed ahead with his plans.

During the 1840's, and 1850's the Liverpool Movement for the Abolition of Slavery continued to develop, Macgregor Laird taking up the issue, when he was called to give evidence before the Parliamentary Select Committee on the West Coast of Africa, in June, 1842. Before the Committee Laird stated that he felt that there were two ways in which the trade could be put down, the first being by declaring slave trading piracy. Related to this he wanted the Royal Navy to be allowed to use more force, he also pointed out that the slaver would not generally fight, for if they were taken, there was no real punishment for them, they did not face imprisonment, and these men therefore ran no personal risks. " I do not think anything will do, unless you give the British Government, who are the only honest parties in this, the power of dealing with the crews of those slave vessels, under whatever flag they sail."

Macgregor Laird pressed for the establishment of legitimate trade, and a 'reverse proposal' by which he thought that attempts should be made to see if 'tropical produce' could be put on the market more cheaply by free labour, in the British colonies, and thus undermine the market for slave produced sugar etc., coming from Cuba and Brazil. He also wanted to see an emigration of free labour from the West Coast to the Colonies, but only in steam ships, and under Government control. He saw these people working for a few years in the colonies, and then returning to Africa, bringing ideas back with them, which would help develop agricultural production in their homeland. The idea did not gain acceptance - at least with Africans - but as noted, free Indian Labour was taken to the colonies, at a later date, and by Liverpool ships, belonging to the Sandbache Tinne fleet.

In 1853 a public breakfast was held in Liverpool to commemorate the centenary of the birth of William Roscoe. Speech after speech was delivered, praising his literary talents and his many gifts to the city, but the tribute that would have pleased him most was the following:-

"For nearly thirty years he carried on his battle (Abolition) against selfishness, wealth and power, almost without allies..... Had it not been for William Roscoe, the people of Liverpool would scarcely have had anyone to warn them that man-stealing was a crime; but he gave them no rest; and though he had first to struggle against contempt and then against the rage of baffled avarice, he never allowed the claims of business nor the delights of literature to deprive him of the time needed to defend the rights of those amongst whom he lived.... For nearly thirty years the position of Roscoe in Liverpool was nearly as painful (though not as dangerous) as that of an

Abolitionist would be at the present time at Charleston or New Orleans."

The tribute to Roscoe alludes to the situation in the United States in the 1850's when the battle to win freedom for the slaves, then working the plantations of the 'Deep South' still had to be won. As history has recorded, this issue led to the election of Abraham Lincoln, on an Abolitionist ticket, but his election was soon followed by the secession of South Carolina, Mississippi, Florida, Louisiana, Alabama, Georgia and Texas from the Union, who formed themselves into the Confederacy, in order to perpetuate the slave system. The long and bloody Civil War then began, which was eventually won by Lincoln and the Union, thus bringing down slavery in the States.

During this period the Confederacy had many friends on Merseyside, which is not surprising, as the port, and the Lancashire Cotton Industry, were dependant on slave produced cotton. However, we should never forget that the Abolitionist movement, was also then very active in Liverpool, and enjoyed mass support. This movement being led by John Cropper, Hugh Stowell Brown, and C. Wilson, then President of the Liverpool Emancipation Society Their humanitarian efforts being in the tradition established by Roscoe, which remain as a lasting tribute to all the decent people of Liverpool, who stood for the abolition of slavery in the 19th century.

CHAPTER SIX   MACGREGOR LAIRD AND
THE AGE OF STEAM

Whilst Macgregor Laird had been away in Africa his father and brother had been busy at Birkenhead, making shipbuilding history. In 1833 they had produced an iron paddle wheel vessel, named the *Lady Lansdowne*, for the City of Dublin Steam Packet Company. She had an exceptionally strong frame, and was plated to the standards of a sea-going vessel, although she was only intended for navigation on the River Shannon. The vessel was 'shipped' out to Ireland in sections, not launched in the normal manner; the reason being that as a completed vessel she would have been too large to pass through the canal at Limerick.

Further experience in iron steamship construction had also been gained by William and John Laird, for they had also been busy, at this time, building the *John Randolph*, a paddle steamer for use on the Savannah River in America. Like the *Lady Lansdowne* she was built in sections, not launched. She was powered by a condensing engine, made by Fawcett, Preston & Company, of Liverpool, which was exported with the Laird built hull. After being assembled in America she became the first iron ship seen on American waters. She was a very successful vessel. She left Savannah on 11 August, 1834, on her first voyage, under the command of Captain Creswell. She had two flat barges in tow laden with 8,000 bushels of salt - in all a cargo of about 200 tons, arriving in Augusta just seventy two hours later. She had maintained a speed of five miles per hour upstream. Returning with a cargo of 1,500 bales of cotton, with the current behind her, she made eight miles an hour. The skills acquired by William and John Laird, in this work would, in a few short years, be put to good use in building specialised vessels for Macgregor Laird, and others, designed to advance the exploration of the Niger. At which point it would be appropriate to take a glance at the age of steam.

The history of steam navigation, which the Laird family were now advancing, goes back a long way. Papin, who was driven from France by the revocation of the Edict of Nantes, describes, in 1690, a steam cylinder, and, as one of its uses he mentions the propulsion of ships by paddle wheels. Towards the close of the 17th century Papin made contact with Thomas Savory, a noted inventor, and Thomas Newcomen, a blacksmith of Devon. Together thy produced a marine engine which was used to propel a steamboat on the River Fulda, Germany.

Thirty years later (1736) Jonathon Hulls, of Berwick-on-Tweed, received a patent for the first steamboat, of which there is any authentic record. Hulls was modest enough to concede that it would not be practical to place his new invention in anything other than a tow-boat, as it took up too much room, and he also advised potential clients not to use the vessel in stormy conditions. There appears to be no real evidence that Hulls actually managed to get anyone to build a steam-boat, along the lines he proposed. Sadly, his patent brought him nothing but ridicule, and he died in London a very poor man.

Between 1770 and 1780 Jacques Constantin Perier, a very capable engineer, is said to have tried a steam boat on the Seine, while in 1776 and in 1783 the Marquis De Jouffroy d'Abbans made experiments with steam vessels on the Rivers Doubs and Saone. Unfortunately no accounts of his experiments were published until thirty years later, although there is little reason to doubt that he obtained some measure of success.

In the same year, but on the opposite side of the Atlantic, a Mr Fitch experimented with a steam boiler on board a small nine ton vessel on the Delaware river, getting his invention to propel the vessel with paddles. Four years later he had a much larger boat built, which he fitted with a twelve inch cylinder. With this vessel he is reported to have made the trip from Philadelphia to Burlington at an average rate of seven miles per hour. In 1790 he considered making an even bigger boat, but his plans failed. Like Hulls, his contemporaries considered him to be crazy. He died in 1798.

About this period, 1787, Patrick Miller, Laird of Dalswinton, Scotland, devoted much of his time to experimenting in naval architecture. James Taylor was a tutor to his son, and he had been making experiments with steam, and helping Miller with his experiments. They debated the issue, and one thing led to another, until they met with William Symington, an engineer of great ability, who was given the task of building a steam engine. In the autumn of the same year the engine was completed and placed in a small pleasure-boat. "Nothing," says Miller in his narrative, "could be more gratifying or complete than the success of this first trial." The following year a larger boat was put on the Forth and Clyde canal; and in December, 1789, " and in the presence of vast number of spectators the machinery was put in motion." At the commencement of the last century Symington was employed by Lord Dundas to build for him a steam tug for use on the Forth and Clyde canal.

Through the support of Lord Dundas, Symington was able, in 1803, to fit up a new steamboat for the Firth & Clyde Canal Company, which was named the *Charlotte Dundas*. She was used to tow a couple of barges on the canal, and performed exceptionally well - in fact too well, the " agitation of the water by the paddles was found to wash down the banks in an alarming manner." For this reason the vessel was taken out of service, and left to rot on the banks for many years, being regarded as a monument to misdirected ingenuity!

Amongst those who had seen the *Charlotte Dundas* in motion was Robert

Fulton and Henry Bell of America. They entered into negotiations with the English firm of Boulton & Watt, and obtained from them the main working parts of a trial engine, which was delivered to them in the United States in 1806. The following year it was placed in the famous *Clermont* and proved a great success as the world's first passenger steam-boat, running on the Hudson River between New York and Albany. The *Clermont* being the pioneer of a large steam boat service ultimately established on the inland waters of the United States.

In 1808, a steam boat called the *Comet* was tried on the River Clyde, in Scotland, by the aforementioned American, Henry Bell. She was by no means a successful speculation for Bell, but she carried many passengers up and down the river. A monument being erected to Bell, on the banks of the Clyde, honouring him as the father of public steam-navigation in this country.

On the North American continent things now began to develop rapidly, In 1809, the *Accommodation*, the first steam-boat on the St, Lawrence, was launched, another soon followed . Two years later, the *New Orleans* was built at Pittsburgh, for service on western waters. In 1813 two new steamers, the *Car of Commerce* and the *Swiftsure* started a service on the St. Lawrence, and in 1816 eight steamers were at work on the Hudson, with another five steaming up and down the Delaware. In 1817 the first steam-boat ran from New York to Newport, and in the same year the first steam vessel was put into service in Boston Harbour.

It was also in 1817 that an interesting steam vessel made her appearance on the Mersey, this being the small ferry-boat *Etna*. The Tranmere Ferry Company placed advertisement in the local press in April, which informed the public that the Etna had commenced running, and could take on board, for the crossing, carts, Carriages, Horses and Cattle of every description - "without the trouble hitherto experienced in the Common Sail Boats." It is actually doubtful whether many animals or carriages could have been carried, for the *Etna* was a very small boat, and not famous for its stability.

In the meantime however, the Laird family, and their various partners, had not been letting the grass grow under their feet. In 1814 they set up an important company, which later claimed to be the oldest steamship company in the world. The several firms of Alexander A. Laird & Sons, Thomas Cameron & Co., and MacConnell & Laird, later becoming unified into a large concern known as the Laird Line. The first vessel owned by the founder of the company being the *Brittania*, a small paddle-wheel steampacket, built like all the vessels of her time of wood. The second steampacket built for the company being the *Waterloo*, built in 1816. These vessels plied between Glasgow, Greenock, Gourock, Rothesay, Tarbert and Inverary.

Alexander A. Laird, after whom the Line was named, was then a well-known shipbroker in Greenock, and when the famous St. Georges Steam

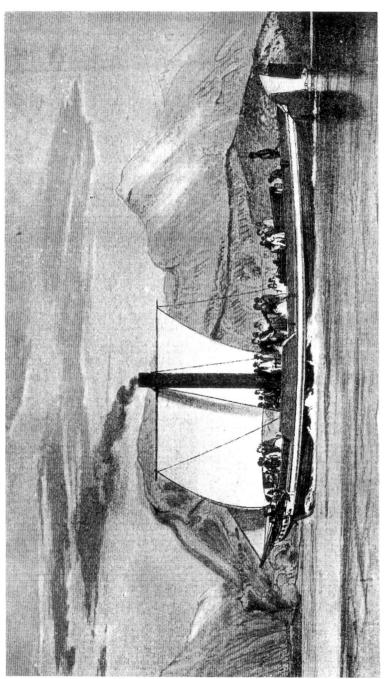

The "Comet"

Packet Company commenced operations in 1821, the first steamship service was established between Liverpool and Greenock, Laird being appointed agent for the company at the latter port. The actual founder of the Company being Joseph Robinson Pim. In 1825 Laird established a fortnightly service between Glasgow and Inverness; the steampacket employed being the *Stirling*. It was though through a vessel owned by the St. George Company that Macgregor Laird, with his partners, was destined to make world maritime history - but in 1834 this still lay a few years in the future.

The expedition to Africa had completely undermined Macgregor Laird's health, and before he could even consider building a new career for himself he had to recover his strength. His parents, William and Agnes Laird, did all they could to help their son, but his condition continued to be a cause of great concern. Within weeks of his return his father took him to Cheltenham, where, at that time, there was a notable doctor, who, it was felt, might be able to help him. "Mineral Waters" then being considered the remedy for a great variety of ailments; and Cheltenham, being a noted spa, it was hoped that going through the well-established ritual of "taking the waters" would also help him. Whilst at Cheltenham Macgregor wrote the following note to Mrs Nicolls:

"Madam"

I have the honour to enclose a note of introduction from Colonel Nicolls, which I regret I am prevented from indisposition from presenting in person. When I left Colonel Nicolls in October he was in excellent health and spirits, but I am sorry to say there appeared little hope of his being able to leave for England till March.

Allow me, Madam, to express to you my gratitude for the unceasing and unvarying kindness shown to me, and the miserable remnants of my crew by Colonel Nicholls, I may literally say that I was a stranger and he took me in; to him I am indebted for my life, and may God grant, Madam, if your son has ever the misfortune to be placed in the same situation, he may meet with as kind a friend. I expect to be in London in ten days, when I will do myself the pleasure of waiting upon you.

I have the honour to be, Madam,
Your most obedient and grateful
Macgregor Laird

The following day another letter arrived in the small house in Francis Street, Woolwich, where Mrs Nicholls was living with her family; this one being from William Laird. He stated how the kindness and attention that Colonel Nicholls had extended to his son had, without doubt, saved his life. He concluded this note with the assurance that their son, Macgregor, and indeed all the Laird family, would always retain a sense of obligation to her and her husband.

Early in February, 1834, Macgregor Laird made his way down to London, and on the 10th of the month the first account of his great expedition to the Niger was given to the Royal Geographical Society; by the Secretary, from information given to him by Macgregor, who was present, but too unwell to give the report himself. At the conclusion of the report there was much cheering for the hero of the Niger, and he was unanimously elected a fellow of the society, this being carried by acclamation.

Whilst in London for this memorable event Macgregor lost no time in paying his respects to Mrs Nicolls. Her house in Francis Street being near the Marine Barracks, most of the neighbouring houses being occupied by Officers' families, each one having a pleasant view over the Thames. The family at that time consisting of three grown-up daughters, Alicia, Ellen and Anna, and two younger daughters, Jane, aged 15, and Bess, aged 13, and Richard, a school boy. The eldest son, Edward, being away from home at the time, serving as a midshipman. Sick as he was, Macgregor was not slow to notice that Ellen was extremely beautiful. A blue-eyed blonde, then just twenty-one years old, she was straightforward, intelligent and shy. Macgregor fell in love with her at first sight, but two more years were to pass before he felt confident enough to ask for her hand in marriage.

Later that year Colonel Nicolls left Fernando Po, and returned to his home at Woolwich, but much broken in health by his long stay in Africa. In his outspoken zeal for the repression of the slave trade, Edward Nicolls had made enemies of those who still had a vested interest in perpetuating the slave trade. Unfortunately for Nicolls, some of them had also made their way back to London at this point in time, and were clearly waiting for a suitable opportunity to settle old scores with the Colonel. They wasted no time in trumping up charges against him which, though false, were not easy to answer. Nicolls was a courageous, honest soldier, not a business man or accountant. Because he was extremely honest himself he had clearly taken insufficient precautions to prove himself so when dealing with many of the dubious characters who then frequented the west coast of Africa. What these charges were is not clear, apart from the fact that they were connected with money.

Without much ceremony the all-time hero of the British Army was arrested and taken to the Fleet Prison, and this when he was so ill that it was feared that he might die on the way. It was at this sad time that Macgregor Laird acted like a son to him, and to a large measure repaid his debt of gratitude to him, thus forging further bonds between the two families. As soon as the Colonel was arrested Macgregor found lodgings for the Nicolls family near the prison, these being in Melina Place, a small row of houses just opposite Balham. Until Edward Nicolls was finally released the family were to spend a very trying time in that small London house. During this traumatic period Macgregor was to call regularly, giving help and comfort to the family. He wrote letters, and did all he could to secure the release of his friend.

Exactly how long the Nicolls family remained at Melina Place is not clear, but what is known is that they had returned to Woolwich by February, 1835. Colonel Nicolls was cleared - and a free man once more - the machinations of his devious enemies having been defeated; mainly, one imagines through the help of Macgregor Laird. Without a doubt, his comrades in the Royal Marines must also have made every effort to help him, and been outraged by the affair. What the army actually thought of the charges is made abundantly clear, by the fact that when he returned to the marines they lost no time in promoting him to Major General, and he ended his illustrious career as General Sir Edward Nicolls, K.C.B.

More problems though were on the way for Macgregor Laird. He had agreed to take Lieutenant William Allen on the Niger expedition on the strict understanding that he did not publish an account of this privately funded venture. The terms were accepted, but it now transpired that Lieutenant Allen wanted to break this agreement. Laird, understandably, took exception to this, and took steps to prevent Allen proceeding. He went to see Lord Aukland about the affair, who promptly asked Captain Beaufort to lay the correspondence before him.

Soon after this Macgregor Laird was contacted by the Admiralty, Mr Woods, the Secretary, requesting him to attend a meeting at which the matter could be resolved. Further correspondence was handed to Woods, making the issue absolutely clear. This was taken to Lord Aukland by Woods, who after a short while returned. He asked Allen to wait outside in an anti-room, then turned to Laird and said " Mr Laird, I see clearly that you have the right to prevent Mr Allen publishing at all, but I hope you will agree to compromise the matter?" Macgregor responded by stating that after what had transpired that was impossible, but to show that he had no ill-will towards Mr Allen he informed those present that he had no objection to Allen publishing twelve months after he, and Oldfield, had published their work on the expedition. When informed of this decision Allen began to grumble, but he got no support from Woods, who pointed out to him that Laird did have the right to stop him publishing at all.

As soon as the issue with Lieutenant Allen was resolved Macgregor Laird began to turn his attention to business matters, in particular the establishment of a transatlantic steamship line. The trans-Atlantic passenger trade at this time being mainly in the hands of the American Packet Ship Lines, whose sailing ships made regular crossings of the Atlantic from Liverpool to New York, Boston, and other American ports. They were regular in the sense that they would attempt to sail from Liverpool on a set day each month, but being totally dependant on variable winds and weather conditions, no regular arrival date could be guaranteed. The most famous of these was the Black Ball Line,

The *Clermont*, 1807

The *James Watt*, 1821

134

who first established a service between Liverpool and New York in 1816, with four small ships. The masters and officers of these vessels had a commendable reputation as mariners, but a notorious record for "hazing" - that is bullying and beating their crews.

In 1835 Captain Charles Marshall became the managing owner of the Line. Marshall being a man who had arrived at the top the hard way. He had served his time on a Nantucket whaler, but it was nine years before he obtained his first command. After leaving the whaling trade he commanded three packet ships, the last one of which was the *South America*. Marshall died in 1865, but this line of sailing packets was to continue in business until the 1880's. Only then was competition from steam able to drive him out of the trade.

Other Lines of sailing packets operating out of Liverpool in the 1830's, engaged in the trans-Atlantic trade, being the Red Star Line, the Swallow Tail and the Dramatic. The Red Star was owned by Messrs Byrnes, Grimble & Company. Messrs Fish, Grinell & Co., also established themselves in the trade in the 1830's - their first ships being the *Silas Richards, York, George*, and *Napoleon*. It was in fact in the late 1830's that Captain E.K. Collins established his famous Dramatic Line of Liverpool packet ships, then afterwards gave his name to the Collins Line of steamers. Such was the state of the trans-Atlantic passenger trade in the 1830's, when other men, including Macgregor Laird, began to consider the possibility of establishing a steamship line to cross the Atlantic.

Among others considering this issue was Isambard Kingdom Brunel, then serving as engineer to the Great Western Railway Company. The story goes that in October, 1835, the directors met at the Radley Hotel, London. Here one of them commented on the great distance the line would traverse from London to Bristol, whereupon Brunel responded "Why not make it longer, and have a steamboat go from Bristol to New York and call it the *Great Western?*" The idea, although expressed half in jest was a sound one, and, as history has recorded, was soon to be acted on. News of this proposal soon reached the ears of a thirty-one year old graduate of Yale College, Junius Smith. Although he had studied and practiced law, his family were established at New York in the importing and exporting business, and Junius himself had for some time been interested in the possibility of establishing a steam ship line to cross the Atlantic. When a case took Smith to England he acted as the representative of his brother's firm, continued to live in England, married and reared a daughter. Smith had already put forward one plan for a line of steam packets to run from London to New York, this being in June, 1835, but on hearing of the Great Western proposals in October, revised his plans. In November he floated a company known as the British and American Steam Navigation Company, with a capital of £500,000.

The *Great Western*, 1821

The *British Queen*, 1821

136

Smith had originally planned to float a company with a capital of £100,000, but clearly prompted by the Great Western development, had raised this sum to half a million. In order to obtain this additional capital - to built bigger and better ships - Smith had been obliged to increase the number of Directors, and consequently reduce his own measure of control. The enlarged board met on 27 November, among them being Henry Bainbridge, Colonel Aspinwall - American Consul at London, and, interestingly, Joseph Robinson Pim, a director of the St. George Company, and the Dublin Steamship Company, organisations in which William Laird had a direct interest! Macgregor Laird was also present, as one of the directors, and as the Company Secretary, would soon be playing a leading role in the day-to-day management of the firm. The activities of Messrs Smith, Laird and Brunel would soon be attracting the attention of a then forty-eight year old shipowner in Canada - his name being Samuel Cunard!

The links between the newly established British and American Steam Navigation Company, and the already established St. George Steam Packet Company are significant, for it was to be the *Sirius*, a ship of 703 tons register, and 320 horse power, owned by the latter company, but later to be placed on charter to the British and American Company, that was to make maritime history - with her celebrated crossing of the Atlantic. Before this notable event though ideological battles had to be fought, by Macgregor Laird, and his competitor, Isambard Kingdom Brunel - with the Rev. Dionysius Lardner, L.L.D. F.R.S.

Among a great many other things, Lardner was the author of a book on the steam engine, editor of an encyclopedia and a prominent member of the British Association for the Advancement of Science. Clearly a man to be reckoned with, he arrived in Liverpool in the winter of 1835, and from a lecture platform, on 14 December, poured several gallons of verbal cold water on those planning steam ship links between England and New York.

Doctor Lardner was convinced that an earlier plan to run steamers from Valentia to America *was* possible, for by this route the longest sea stage would be from thence to St. Johns, Newfoundland, a distance of just 1,900 miles. He solemnly predicted that vessels of 800 tons with engines of 200 Horse Power, would be the best for this crossing, "but, the utmost limit of a steam voyage might be taken at 2,550 miles; but even this could not be reckoned upon." As to the project that Smith and Laird were engaged in, of making the long crossing from Liverpool to New York, Lardner had no hesitation in saying it was "perfectly chimerical, and they might as well talk about making a voyage from New York or Liverpool to the moon."

Unfortunately for Smith, Laird, and the other directors of the British and American Company, many investors respected Doctor Lardner's opinions. Moreover, his preference for the Valentia route was supported by a

Parliamentary Commission in 1829. But the name of the Laird family was now well known in ship building circles, in particular as it related to steam ships. William and John Laird had by now built six steam paddle vessels, these being the *Lady Lansdowne*, the *John Randolph*, the *Garryowen*, and the *Euphrates, Tigris* and *Chatham*, the last three having been built for the Hon. East India Company. Macgregor Laird also had the distinction of having designed the steamboats *Alburkah* and *Quorra* for the now famous Niger expedition. If Lardner was a man to be reckoned with, so was Macgregor Laird, who lost no time in responding to the opinionated Doctor. In a letter published in the Liverpool Albion on 28 December, 1835, and signed "Chimera" - Macgregor Laird took Lardner to task for his dogmatic views. He said:-

"By what process of reasoning Dr. Lardner has fixed the ultimate size of steam vessels for the Atlantic at 800 tons and 200 horse power does not appear, which is more to be regretted, as it must be a peculiar one, from the size of the vessels very little exceeding that of several in the coasting trade, and the power being much less; but I am not bound to take this for granted particularly as all my experience has proved that we have never had to complain of the size of the vessel if the power has been proportionately increased...... The *Leeds*, it appears, makes the voyage from Bordeaux, a distance of 1,600 miles, with one supply of coals. The *Leeds*, is, I believe, 420 tons and 140 horse power.

Now, the distance from Portsmouth to New York is 3,000 nautical miles or 3,500 statute miles, a little less from Liverpool. Suppose the *Leeds* be trebled in capacity.... it is not necessary to treble her power, as double horse-power propels more than double bulk; but allow her 300 horse-power..... I take consumption of coals at 30 tons per day, and a mean speed of 10 miles per hour, and at expenditure of 525 tons of common coal, or 420 of Langennich, I have landed my passengers at New York, Portsmouth or Liverpool in something less than fifteen days...........

I hope I have made my point, Mr Editor, I have proved that it is easier to go from Portsmouth or Liverpool to New York than to the moon; that it is more convenient to go direct than through the first "gem of the sea" - and last, though not the least consideration, that if we wish to go at all by steamer, we had not better wait for the Valentia Railway. "

It was clearly a great advantage to the British and American Company to have Macgregor Laird as one of the directors, but this was to annoy Junius Smith, whose ego was badly bruised, when he discovered that the public were assuming that Macgregor Laird was the man who had originally conceived the idea of establishing the Company, and was now the prime-mover! However, despite everything, the great race to conquer the Atlantic by steam was now on. The Great Western Steam-Ship Company being formed in June,

1836. Three months later the British and American Company contracted for the first of their ships. She was to be the *Royal Victoria* - a vessel of 1,800 tons, designed to cross the Atlantic in 15 days, on 480 tons of coal.

Soon after this though, the *Great Victoria* was renamed the *British Queen*, in honour of young Queen Victoria. Unfortunately for the British and American Company the firm who had contracted to build her engines then went bankrupt. As work was proceeding rapidly with the *Great Western* a substitute had to be found without delay, if they were to win the historic race to get a steam ship across the Atlantic.

Smith, Laird, and other directors of the British and American Company were not prepared to allow this problem to beat them. Without delay, they chartered a steamship from the St. George Company, which was easy enough to arrange, as the Laird family had an interest in the company, and Messrs Pim, Beale and Twigg were directors of both firms. Formalities were soon attended to, and the British and American Company soon found themselves in control of the recently launched *Sirius*, which at 703 tons register, and 320 horse-power, was, without doubt, the best ship in the St. George Company fleet. As history has recorded, the *Sirius* subsequently beat the *Great Western* in the race across the Atlantic, all of which was gratifying for Macgregor Laird, Junius Smith and their fellow Directors, but somewhat less so for Doctor Dionysius Lardner.

All in all the late 1830's were a busy time for Macgregor Laird. Whilst the main focus of his attention had been centred on the fortunes of the British and American Company, he was also active with his elder brother John, at their Birkenhead yard. Macgregor designing the *Rainbow*, which they were building to the order of the General Steam Navigation Company. Launched in October, 1837, this 581 ton vessel was then the largest iron ship to be built. She was to operate for many years on the London - Antwerp run, and was the fastest vessel of her day. Just before this vessel was launched though Macgregor Laird found time to marry Ellen Nicolls. The marriage taking place in London on 1 August, 1837

It was also at this time, in the summer of 1837, that the Laird-Oldfield "Narrative of an expedition into the Interior of Africa by the River Niger, in the Steam-Vessels *Quorra* and *Alburkah* in 1832, 1833 and 1834 " was finally published in two volumes. Macgregor's narrative only occupied a portion of the first volume, the remainder being taken up with the journal of Oldfield, the surgeon of the expedition. Macgregor always had a high regard for Oldfield, who he saw as a true comrade. Macgregor was advised that his narrative would have had more success if published separately, and of course it could have been produced at less expense - and earlier. Characteristically though, he ignored this advice, because he thought this plan would have been injurious to his fellow explorer, Oldfield.

The *Sirius*

Before the close of 1837 it seemed likely that Macgregor and Ellen Laird would be leaving England, to take up residence in Australia. Colonel Torrens M.P., a first cousin of Mrs Nicolls, was at that time editor of the famous Globe Newspaper, a supporter of the Government, and very much involved in colonial affairs. It therefore may have been at his suggestion that an offer was made to Macgregor Laird to go out to Australia as its first Governor. Exactly what the terms of this seemingly very attractive offer were remains something of a mystery, but as they stood they were not acceptable to Macgregor, who proposed certain conditions.

The offer though had thrown the Laird household into a state of turmoil, for Ellen Laird made it abundantly clear that she did not wish to go - whatever the terms might be. She was later to tell her daughter that she cried for a week at the prospect. Her fears were soon allayed, for the Colonial Office would not accept Macgregor's terms - whatever they may have been, but he thanked Colonel Torrens in the following note:-

" 78 Cornhill
Saturday 16 December, 1837

My Dear Sir,
Your note of yesterday gave great satisfaction to my wife and was no disappointment to me. Her Majesty has within her realm five hundred men as good as me, who will jump at the office without any conditions, but I cannot afford to be a warming pan for any man. The only person I consulted was an acquaintance of yours, and one who has a great practical knowledge of foreign governments; he thought the conditions rather moderate than otherwise, which it seems you do not, so I can only repeat that I feel grateful to you for making the offer to
Yours very truly
(Signed) Macgregor Laird "

Despite, in effect, declining a remarkable offer, Macgregor Laird had a very great interest in colonial development. He counted amongst his friends Edward Gibbon Wakefield, the British statesman and colonist. After a period spent in the diplomatic service Wakefield took part in the colonisation of South Australia, went to Canada as secretary to the Earl of Durham in 1838, and played a leading role in the colonisation of New Zealand. In 1837 an association was being formed in London, which Macgregor Laird must have been aware of, if not active in, which gave effect to the ideas of colonial development put forward by Wakefield. Two years later this association was to become the New Zealand Company, its purpose being to obtain land from the Maoris for British settlement, a project which was to lead to the appointment of Captain William Hobson, as Lieutenant Governor of New

Zealand. Laird was very much taken with the ideas of Wakefield, whose theories of " the proper way in which to occupy the earth that God had given to the children of men" had so much to do in shaping the social development of both Australia and New Zealand.

Macgregor Laird, like so many Victorians, had an almost naive faith in the benefits of colonial development, and honest international trade, a view rarely shared by those whose ancestral lands were being earmarked for this attention. At Waitangi in 1840 Captain William Hobson, Lieutenant-Governor of New Zealand met the Maori Chiefs, who accepted British sovereignty, but only in return for the guarantee of their rights and land. Thirty years later the Maoris, under such leaders as Rewi and Te Kooti, were to be engaged in armed struggle, in an effort to defend themselves, and the earth that they felt God had given to their children, against the colonists, who had little regard for guarantees given to them by Hobson.

In 1837 though, all this lay in the future, which makes the contradiction in Laird's philosophical position more understandable. Laird bitterly opposed slavery in Africa, but the arrival of Wakefield, Hobson, and their fellow colonists in Australia and New Zealand was to lead to the impoverishment, and virtual enslavement, of the Australian Aborigines and the Maoris of New Zealand. Macgregor Laird was now to turn his attention back to Africa once more.

In January, 1838 he was honoured by a visit from Buxton, who expressed his horror at the iniquities of the foreign slave trade, then so active on the West Coast of Africa. He told Macgregor of his intention to try and get a Parliamentary Inquiry into the system pursued on the coast of Africa. What Buxton wanted to know from Macgregor Laird was, if the slave trade was put down, would the Africans have the natural resources which would enable them to procure the goods they now paid for in the sale of slaves? How productive was the soil, could production be raised to enable them to trade in agricultural produce, rather than their fellow men ? Laird was to give Buxton his answer to these considerations in two letters, the first of which was written in London on 27 February, 1838.

Macgregor informed Buxton that the legitimate trade then existing on the West Coast of Africa was mainly conducted through the British or Dutch Factories, or the African Chiefs, based at the mouths of the principal rivers. From the British settlement of St. Mary's in the Gambia there were exports of hides, gold dust, gums, mahogany, rice and ground nuts. A similar trade was being conducted on the River Rio Nunez, by a notable house of London traders. However, here Macgregor pointed out to Buxton that the delta formed by the Rio Nunez, Rio Grande and Rio Pongo was very extensive and fertile, but at this time the area was frequented by slave vessels, making legitimate trade very difficult.

Fifty miles from Sierra Leone lay the delta of the Jeoonz Boom, Kileam and Galunas rivers, which ground had about 1,00 to 1,500 miles of the richest alluvial soil, capable of growing all manner of tropical produce, including rice. But, sadly, Macgregor had to inform Buxton that " At present it produces nothing but the first description of slaves, of which great quantities are exported from the rivers, under the very nose of the Mixed Commission Court."

The Cape Palmas area, Buxton was informed, was inhabited by the most extraordinary race of men in Africa, the Kroomen. Although their land was extremely poor and rocky, and could produce no exportable produce, Kroomen would not buy or sell slaves, nor allow themselves to become slaves. Their attachment to their poor land was great, and they were patient, enduring, faithful and brave, to the point of rashness.

From St. Paul to Cameroons, and from thence to Cape Lopez, lay "the richest country that imagination can conceive." Here there existed forty to fifty rivers of all sizes, discharging their waters into the Atlantic Ocean, forming a vast alluvial plain of about 180,000 miles in extent. It was from here, Laird stated, that most of the exportable goods were produced. All the palm oil was obtained from this area, half the ivory, camwood and other dyewoods. Here though, it had to be kept in mind, that all these rivers were infested with slavers, who were constantly interfering with legitimate trade, and rendering the collection of palm oil and other produce difficult and dangerous. Yet, despite these problems, and unprotected by a single British settlement, exports continued to rise, this being from 4,700 tons of palm oil in 1827 to 13,945 tons in 1834. Of interest to Buxton though was the horrifying fact that during this period the area in question had also 'exported' 200,000 slaves.

Macgregor informed Buxton that he had a low opinion of the Coastal Chiefs in this area, and their subjects. They monopolised all trade, but the goods were produced by other Africans, further up river. The country above the delta areas was highly cultivated, growing rice, millet, Indian corn, tobacco, cotton and indigo. Macgregor stating that he considered the people of these areas to be very superior to other Africans; each town having its pits for dyeing robes, blacksmiths and other tradesmen were common, and the people had a general eagerness to trade.

Macgregor concluded his long letter by stating that he hoped men could be found who would enter into trade - with the Africans - without the hope of profit, and with the prospect of loss, who would in fact subscribe their money and consider it was a gift to the advancement of Africa. Such behaviour would, after a few short years, not only lay the foundations for a better society, Macgregor felt, but lead to good commercial development, improve the moral and physical character of the Africans, and leave a way open to converting them to Christianity. His plans for Africa were based on trade being a cure for all evils, provided this was placed in the hands of particularly high-minded, and well funded traders. Alas, such men are few and far between, and others far less noble, were to follow Macgregor Laird, and other explorers, out to Africa. Laird wrote a second letter to Buxton on 13, March, 1838, Buxton replying to him six days later:-

"To M. Laird Esq.
Norhripps Hall,
Near Aylsham, Norfolk   March 19,
1838
Dear Sir,
        I am much obliged to you for both your letters. I am hard at work on the subject and shall be ready on my arrival in London next week to show you what I have been doing and to ask, upon a variety of points, your very valuable assistance. I think it hardly worthwhile for Mr Jamieson to come to town at present; the time is not arrived as yet for making that commercial effort which he suggests. It is not till the public mind shall be saturated with the horrors of the slave trade, that we shall get support enough to undertake it, but I doubt not that eventually we shall resort to the adoption of his plan. I never felt more interest in anything than in the slave trade enquiry, which now occupies me, especially in the new light in which your voyage has placed the subject.
                              Yours very truly
                                    (Signed) T.F. Buxton "

        On May 18, 1838 Ellen and Macgregor Laird's first child was born, a girl. She was christened Eleanor Bristow, after her grandmother, Mrs Nicolls. Macgregor Laird now had much to occupy his mind, a young daughter, Buxton and Africa, and last but not least, the affairs of the British and American Company.
        The *Sirius* had managed to beat Brunel's *Great Western* in the race across the Atlantic, but she was never designed for this service. The directors of the British and American Company were now eagerly awaiting the launch of *British Queen*, to replace the chartered St. George Company ship. The *British Queen* was, at long last, floated out of the Limehouse Dock on the high tide of 23 June, 1838. This was, without a doubt a great occasion in British maritime history. The feast laid on to mark the occasion was attended by some three hundred guests, among whom was the Prime Minister of the Day, Melbourne, the Governor of Canada, Sir F.B. Head, and the ubiquitous news man, James Gordon Bennett, from New York. The installation of her engines still remained to be done, but this by Robert Napier in Scotland, not Messrs Curling & Young, her builders in London. Whilst the *British Queen* was waiting to have her engines fitted, and the *Great Western* was laid up in

Thomas Fowell Buxton

dock, on 7 November 1838, the Admiralty placed a small advertisement in the Times:

"Steam vessels required for conveying Her Majesty's Mails and Despatches between ENGLAND and HALIFAX and NEW YORK. "

This small notice was to be instrumental in changing the history of trans-Atlantic steam ship development, for it was read by an enterprising resident of Nova Scotia, who wasted no time in responding, his name being Samuel Cunard; all of which had serious implications for the future of the British and American Company.

The British Queen eventually sailed from London on 10 July, 1839, with Captain Roberts in command, she attracted much attention, for she was the largest ship afloat. Among the 200 passengers on board were Junius Smith, and Macgregor Laird. It was a proud moment for both men when she eventually entered New York harbour, to another tumultuous reception. James Gordon Bennett visited the *Queen* shortly after her arrival and had a glass of sherry with Captain Roberts, Laird, and Smith.

The *British Queen* remained at New York - alongside her rival the Great Western - until 1 August. On this day the two famous ships left the dock at the end of Clinton Street, less than thirty minutes apart. About 100,000 spectators watching as they left, many lining the water-front as far as the Battery. Hundreds of thousands of dollars were bet on the outcome of this second great steam ship race; all of which added to the excitement of the day. In the event the *Great Western* took just 13 days to get back to her home port of Bristol, whilst it took the *British Queen* another twelve hours to get back to her base at Portsmouth.

Neither of these pioneering ships were to stand up well to the rigours of trans-Atlantic work; both having to undergo extensive repair and alteration work during the winter of 1839 - 40. Business was now very bad for the British and American Company, the directors pinning all their hopes on a new ship under construction for the company, this being the *President*. They were fighting a losing battle though, for by now Samuel Cunard had won the Admiralty Mail Contract, and with it a substantial subsidy, which was to give him the edge over all competitors.

Throughout the year of 1839 work on the *President* continued. She was eventually launched in September, Ellen Laird being given the honour of christening the ship. It was not a happy event, a thief stole her watch and chain, and moments after the bottle had been broken over her bows, the ship moved forward, then stuck. It was only after considerable effort that she was later got into the water. Ellen felt that this was not lucky, and always refused to name another ship.

The *President* performed reasonably well, but never quite lived up to the expectations of Laird or Smith. She had a good passenger list on her maiden voyage to New York in August, 1840, but it took her 17 days to get to America, and 17 to get back. She lumbered across the Atlantic, and returned once again, being a long way from breaking any records. The 11 March, 1841, found the ship in New York once again. On that day Captain Roberts, veteran commander of the *Sirius* and the *British Queen*, stood on her paddle-box as she left New York. On board were a large number of passengers, some of them very well-known people. This was the last the world was to see of Captain Roberts, his ship, crew, or passengers, for the *President* was to be seen no more. Strangely, long before there was any cause for concern, Captain Robert's brother, and the Agent of the company in New York both dreamed, on the same night, that they saw the ship, a confused crowd on the deck, Captain Roberts on the bridge giving orders, and then she suddenly disappeared.

Anxiety about the *President* increased, as she became overdue. Rumours were rife, it being presumed that she had been blown south, others putting forward the theory that she had put into the West Indies for extra coal, Macgregor's belief being that she had run into an iceberg and sank instantly. Eventually an investigation was held in New York. From this it was concluded that she had been lost in a great storm on 12 March, when between Nantucket Shoals and George's Bank. Another report tabled at this hearing indicated that a Portuguese brig had sailed within three miles of a steamer, significantly sailing under sail alone, her huge paddles not rotating, and no smoke coming from her funnels - this being on 23 April. At this time there were very few steamers, like the *President*, with two funnels, so this may well have been the ill-fated ship.

The real fate of the President may never be known. What is known though is that the loss of this ship was a terrible blow to the already shaky British and North American Steamship Company, for the firm did not survive this sad loss by many months. Laird and Smith had indeed done the work of pioneers, but the Government had given the mail contract to Samuel Cunard, and this, with the loss of the *President*, put an end to this bold venture. Meanwhile, John Laird had been busy at Birkenhead building ships for another ill-fated venture, the Government backed expedition to the Niger.

CHAPTER SEVEN   THE NIGER EXPEDITION OF 1841

The Government backed expedition to the Niger of 1841 was under the personal patronage of the Prince Consort. The principal object of the expedition being to put an end to the Slave Trade, by entering into treaties with the African Chiefs, " within whose dominions the internal Slave Trade is carried on, and the external trade supplied with its victims." The state of the trade at this point in time was indeed alarming, prompting Buxton to note in his celebrated book, 'The African Slave Trade and its Remedy" that:

" I am driven to the sorrowful conviction, that the year from September 1837 to September 1838, is distinguished beyond all preceding years, for the extent of the (slave) trade, for the intensity of its miseries, and for the usual havoc it makes on human life."

Having brought public attention to the extent of the slave trade, Buxton then put forward his 'Remedy', which would be by:-

Impeding the Slave Trade.

Establishing legitimate commerce.

Promoting and teaching modern methods of agriculture.

Imparting religious and moral instruction.

For all of this he suggested the augmentation of the British naval force employed in the suppression of the Slave Trade, and concentration of that force on the coast of Africa, thus forming a chain of vessels stretching from Angola to The Gambia; and, as noted, a 'chain' of treaties with the African Chiefs.   It was with a view to furthering these objectives that the "Society for the Extinction of the Slave Trade and the Civilisation of Africa" was established. It was composed of noblemen and gentlemen - " of all shades of political opinion" under the Presidency of His Royal Highness Prince Albert. After due consideration the Society agreed to send a deputation to Lord John Russell, Her Majesty's principal Secretary of State for the Colonies, with a strong recommendation that an expedition should be sent out to the Niger, with Commissioners empowered to form the proposed trade and anti-slavery treaties with the most influential Chiefs on the coast, and on the banks of the main rivers. All of this the Government agreed to, and then arrangements were put in hand to have the required ships built.

After consulting with Capt. Trotter, Sir Edward Parry of the Admiralty, stated that he was of the opinion that the expedition would require three vessels, two larger, and one smaller one. The two larger to be 136 feet long, with a draught of water not to exceed 4ft 9inches, powered by two 35 horse-power engines, the smaller to be 110 feet long, with a draught of water not to exceed 3ft., with just one engine of 35 horse-power. The estimated expense of building and equipment the three vessels being £35,000. It was also noted that it would be necessary to supply the expedition with suitable articles as presents for the Chiefs, which cost was not included in the above estimate. The annual charge for paying and victualling the officers and men being put at £10,546.

In his long report on this issue, Sir Edward continued by making it clear that in his opinion it would be 'highly expedient' to contract with one iron shipbuilder for the vessels and engines, provided the selection of the engines, as well as their plan of construction, was strictly subject to the approval of the Admiralty. He continued:-

"And as there are only two or three individuals who understand the peculiar art of iron shipbuilding, and Messrs Laird of Liverpool, are the most eminent and experienced in this line, I recommend that they be desired to furnish plans and estimates for this undertaking. Messrs Laird have already built several iron vessels for enterprises of this nature; among the rest, for the Euphrates expedition; and one of these gentlemen being an African traveller of considerable reputation, they would not only bring to the subject much more information and experience than any other person can possess, but would also take a deep personal interest and pride in making the vessels in all respects fit for this important undertaking. I may add, that Messrs Laird are now under contract with the Admiralty for furnishing an iron steam vessel for a Dover packet, with her engines and everything complete for sea, in the manner above recommended."

Sir Edward concluded his report, dated 14 November, 1839, by drawing attention to the fact that as these vessels would be built specifically for river navigation, they could not carry out with them, across the sea, all that would be required for such a large expedition. His view being that a transport ship would also be required to convey all that was required out to Africa, and then some goods could be put on board the steamers at the mouth of the Niger, and the remainder landed at Fernando Po, or some other convenient place, for future use.

This development was followed by Lord John Russell's letter of 26 December, 1839, to the Lords Commissioners of the Treasury, in which he gave a comprehensive view of the appalling increase of the Slave Trade, and amongst other points stated:-

"My Lords.- The state of the Foreign slave trade has for some time past engaged much of the attention of Her Majesty's confidential advisers. In whatever light this traffic is viewed, it must be regarded as an evil of incalculable magnitude; the injuries it inflicts on the lawful commerce of this country, the constant expense incurred in the employment of ships of war for the suppression of it, and the annual sacrifice of so many valuable lives in this service, however deeply to be lamented, are not the most disastrous results of this system. The honour of the British crown is compromised by the habitual invasion of the treaties subsisting between her Majesty and Foreign Powers for the abolition of the slave trade, and the calamities which, in defiance of religion, humanity, and justice, are inflicting on a large proportion of the African continent........"

"I find it impossible to avoid the conclusion that the average number of slaves introduced into Foreign States or colonies in America and the West Indies, from the western coast of Africa, annually exceeds 100,000....."

"the number of slaves actually landed in the importing countries affords but a very imperfect indication of the real extent of the calamities which this traffic inflicts on its victims. No record exists of the multitude who perish in the overland journey to the African coast, or in the passage across the Atlantic, or of the still greater number who fall sacrifice to the warfare, pillage, and cruelties by which the slave trade is fed. Unhappily, however, no fact can be more certain, that such an importation as I have mentioned presupposes and involves a waste of human life, and a sum of human misery, proceeding from year to year, without respite or intermission, to such an extent as to render the subject the more painful of any which, in the survey of the condition of mankind, it is possible to contemplate."

Lord Russell continued his report by stating that it was essential that new preventative measures were brought to arrest the foreign slave trade at its source, and with this in mind he proposed establishing new commercial relations with the African Chiefs, within whose dominions the internal slave trade of Africa was carried on, and the external trade supplied with its victims. The basis of these agreements being the abandonment and absolute prohibition of the slave trade, and the establishment of normal trade links with Britain. The Chiefs who gave the most cause for concern being those whose countries were adjacent to the Niger and its great tributary streams. He therefore endorsed the proposals to send out an expedition that would ascend the river by steam boats, and which would be responsible for establishing 'factories' at various points. From these bases he felt legitimate commerce could be conducted, and that the Chiefs would then realize that there were methods of employing their people that were more profitable than converting them into slaves, and selling them for exportation to the slave traders.

Plans were then endorsed for the construction of the ships by John Laird, and arrangements put in hand to give chief command of the expedition to Captain H.D. Trotter, R.N. with Captain William Allen, R.N. - late of the Laird Lander expedition- being his 2nd in command. After what had already transpired between this officer, and Macgregor Laird, one can imagine that the latter was not pleased with this appointment. In fact Macgregor Laird was, with many others, bitterly opposed to the expedition being mounted at all; this despite the fact that his brother had contracted to build the required ships for the venture. This opposition was centred on the practicality of the expedition, and the potentially high risk of death from fever and malaria, which Europeans had little or no resistance to; this conclusion being drawn from his own practical, and bitter, experiences on the river.

So far as William Allen is concerned, it is interesting to note here that he was born at Weymouth in 1793, and entered the navy as a volunteer in 1805, and, as a midshipman, was present at the passage of the Dardenelles in 1807. He became a lieutenant in 1815, and, after taking part in the Laird - Lander expedition he was promoted to commander in 1836. With Trotter, and T.R.H. Thomson, the Surgeon of the pending expedition, he was later to publish a narrative of the expedition.

Work soon began on the construction of the ships at the Laird yard in Birkenhead, and other arrangements were put in hand. Then, on 1 June, 1840, there was held in the Exeter Hall, London, one of the most momentous gatherings ever to be held in that famous building. It was a meeting to mark the first anniversary of the Society for the Extinction of the Slave Trade, and for the Civilisation of Africa. The public were informed that his Royal Highness Prince Albert of Saxe-Coburg, who only four months before had married the young Victoria, had accepted the office of President of the Society, and would take the chair at the great meeting. The demand for tickets was unparalleled, with tickets changing hands at exorbitant prices two days before the event. On the day itself Exeter Street and the Strand were blocked for hours by the vast number of carriages bringing supporters of the Society to the great event. At 10 a.m. every part of the hall was densely packed with, what the Times reporter described as, a 'highly respectable' audience. He continued: " The number of ladies predominated, and their personal beauty and elegance of costume enhanced the *tout ensemble* of a truly interesting *coup d' oeil*." The organist then gave a powerful performance of the voluntary on the organ, to set the stage, and at 11 a.m. precisely his Royal Highness Prince Albert, with Fowell Buxton, Dr. Lushington, and other leading members of the committee, appeared on the platform. The whole company stood up, and clapped and cheered, with the men throwing their hats into the air, whilst the 'elegant ladies' discreetly waved their handkerchiefs.

Among the people who thronged the great hall was the Ambassador of France; The Duke of Norfolk, the Earl of Ripon; Lord Worsley, seven bishops, Sir Robert Peel M.P.; William Ewart Gladstone M.P.; Doctor Bowring, and a young medical student, then unknown, David Livingstone, who, in the same year, under the auspices of the London Missionary Society, was to go out to Bechuanaland, South Africa; where he would become associated with the great Scottish missionary, Robert Moffat, whose daughter he was destined to marry. Among other things he was also to have dealings

151

Captain William Allen, R.N.

with John and Macgregor Laird in the future.

His Royal Highness was then ushered to the chair by the committee, and on reaching it the great organ thundered out the national anthem, which was followed by loud and long cheering. A silence then fell upon the huge audience, as the Prince Consort rose to make his first public speech in English, and with a very slight foreign accent he opened the business of the day. As reported by the Times, his Royal Highness said :-

"I have been induced to preside at the meeting of this Society from a conviction of its paramount importance to the great interests of humanity and justice (cheers.) I deeply regret that the benevolent and persevering exertions of England to abolish that atrocious traffic in human beings, at once the desolation of Africa, and the blackest stain upon civilized Europe, have not as yet led to any satisfactory conclusion. But I sincerely trust that this great country will not relax in its efforts until it has finally and for ever put an end to a state of things so repugnant to the spirit of Christianity, and to the best feelings of our nature. (Tremendous applause) Let us, therefore, trust that Providence will prosper our exertions in so holy a cause, and that under the auspices of our Queen (cheering for some minutes) and her Government, we may at no distant period be rewarded by the accomplishment of the great and humane object for the promotion of which we have this day met (Loud and long-continued cheers.)

Thomas Fowell Buxton then came forward, and noted with some satisfaction how well attended the meeting was. He spoke for some time, then moved the first resolution:-

"That notwithstanding all the measures hitherto adopted for the suppression of the foreign trade in slaves, the traffic has increased and continues to increase under circumstances of aggravated horror, and prevails to an extent which imperatively calls for the strenuous and combined exertions of the whole Christian community to effect its extinction."

The meeting could see that the resolution acknowledged that efforts to bring an end to the trade, or even reduce it, had not met with success, which raised the question, what was the state of Africa? The point was made that local religions embraced human sacrifice, and that the continent was a 'universal slaughterhouse' with thousands being taken each night in slave-trading raids, and then forced to march across the burning sands of the great dessert, or herded onto slave-ships on the west coast. The debate continued, with the meeting acknowledging the fact that they wanted to convert the African people to the Christian religion, and introduce legitimate trade.

The meeting continued, and then Daniel O'Connell M.P. the Irish patriot and politician, known as to his admirers as The Liberator, entered the room from a door at the back of the platform. At this point in his career he was organising his fellow Irishmen into the Catholic Association, and calling for the repeal of the Union, which made him a very controversial politician, loved by his admirers, and hated by the pro-Union establishment, and notably Sir Robert Peel. His entrance was greeted by 'slight applause' - which increased when his presence became more widely known, but also some cries of objection from those who opposed his political views.

The Venerable Archdeacon Wilberforce, son of the great Emancipator, then spoke, and received a good reception, which was followed by another contribution by Buxton. He made the point that, in his view, God had used secondary instruments as the means of introducing Christianity, the commerce that Britain was engaged in merely being God's way of spreading the true religion, each trading ship carrying with it the boom of everlasting life.

Sir Robert Peel then rose to speak, to a great round of applause. After going through the formalities of expressing his 'pure delight' that his Royal Highness had sanctified this great cause, he drew the attention of the audience to the fact that Britain had just voted £20,000,000 to put an end to the slave trade, but there was still need of combined and increased exertions. He also wanted to bring to the minds of those present, the fact that this grant had done nothing more than rescue Britain's own character from imputation. Then, to emphasise the horrors of the trade, Peel read from a document that was not prepared by any anti-slavery association, but was "The shipping List of the Cape of Good Hope" - a commercial paper not professing any sentiments, but merely recording commercial transactions. It was dated 17 March, 1840, and one of its columns was devoted to the capture or wreck of slave ships. To an attentive audience he read the last article, in order to bring home the real horrors of the trade:-

"On the 24th January, 1840 during a hurricane from the south-east, two slavers, a ship and a brig, were wrecked at Mozambique harbour, but the crews of both and 200 slaves on board the brig were saved. The ship had arrived the preceding day, and had not taken in any slaves. It was reported that the brig, commanded by a Spaniard, had originally 900 slaves on board, but during the hurricane the hatches had been battened down, and on opening them 300 were found to have died from suffocation. Again the hurricane came on; the hatches were battened down a second time, and the consequence was, that 300 more of the slaves perished from the same cause, and a 100 of the remaining 300 died on the passage to Mozambique harbour."

Peel then informed his audience that the commander of the ship, unperturbed by this terrible loss of life, had immediately set about finding another 'cargo' of slaves! His audience were clearly moved by this, but Sir Robert continued, making the point that until this country rescued Christianity and the character of the white people from the grievous infamy of these sins, it would never succeed in the great object to which those

Peel then informed his audience that the commander of the ship, unperturbed by this terrible loss of life, had immediately set about finding another 'cargo' of slaves! His audience were clearly moved by this, but Sir Robert continued, making the point that until this country rescued Christianity and the character of the white people from the grievous infamy of these sins, it would never succeed in the great object to which those present desired. Britain would never be able to convince the black population of Africa of the moral superiority of their European fellow men, and we would not be able to convince them of the truths of Christianity, which continued to tolerate such monstrous sins.

The Bishop of Chichester then rose, and made the point that when Fox and Pitt had debated the issue, it was stated that 80,000 slaves were annually transported across the Atlantic, but it now appeared that 150,000 were annually exported to Spanish and Portuguese colonies. No less than 400,000 persons were annually sacrificed, to enable this importation to exist. They were destroyed by war, by ill treatment, and by disease. Thus 500,000 slaves might be said to be sacrificed every year.

The Bishop then drew the attention of the meeting to the fact that it was pleasing to know that the commander of the proposed expedition was a man that all could have confidence in. Captain Trotter had been the commander of H.M.S. *Curlew*, one of the vessels employed in the anti-slavery squadron. Four or five years previously Captain Trotter, when on patrol, had found a vessel that had been plundered by the crew of a vessel half pirate, half slaver. The pirates had secured the crew beneath the hatches, and had prepared to blow them up, when a Spanish vessel had fortunately come to their rescue. When Captain Trotter heard about this matter he obtained more information from an American Consul, and pursued them for fifteen months, and at last captured them, and had them sent to America, where they were brought to justice.

The great meeting continued for some time, with speaker after speaker recording their support for the work of the Society, and the pending expedition to Africa, under the leadership of Captain Trotter. From the outset the Church Missionary Society was in close contact with the Government, and the organisers of the great expedition. Buxton being anxious to see that Christians missions played a part in the 'redemption' of Africa. The Mission Society's view being that the Niger must be claimed as a ' highway for the Gospel.' - Missions, as well as government posts and trading stations, would have to be opened along the great river. The Society was allowed to send representatives with the expedition, and they chose two men, then in Sierra Leone. One being the Rev. J. F. Schon, a missionary with eight years experience; the other a remarkable young African lay teacher, Samuel Adjai Crowther.

The great Samuel Crowther, a man who was destined to influence the development of Africa, came from Oshogun, a town with a population of about 12,000 people, far away in the vast forests of the Yaruba Country, in the Lagos hinterland. One morning, in the early spring of 1821, when Crowther was still a young child, Raiders launched a surprise raid on the town. The place was surrounded by a deep moat, and defensive walls of earth and palisades, four miles in circumference, and despite the fact that they rapidly mustered 3,000 defenders, who seized their weapons, and rushed to the walls, they were not enough to hold so long a line of defence. The Attackers soon took an undefended gate and entered the town.

Fierce hand-to-hand fighting in the streets followed, with women and children attempting to flee to the forests. Soon though the battle was over, and the people of Oshogun were captives, victims of one of the Yoruba inter-tribal wars. The town was put to the torch, and the survivors led away, to be sold as slaves. Adjai eventually found himself in Lagos, where he was sold, with others, to a Portuguese slave dealer, who chained them together by their necks and put them on board a slaver. As luck would have it they had only been a few hours at sea when H.M.S. *Myrmidon* and *Iphigenia* hove in sight. Crowther, with his fellow slaves were rescued. He eventually ended up in Sierra Leone, where he was placed in a Church Missionary School, and his great intelligence soon caught the attention of the missionaries. In 1825 he was baptised Samuel, but kept his African name Adjai. He was then sent to the Parochial School in Liverpool Street, Islington, in London. He then took the name Crowther from a distinguished member of the Church Missionary Society. Crowther and Schon were to be charged with the new policy of 'Bible and Plough' on the expedition.

The expedition vessels were launched at the Laird shipyard, Birkenhead, in 1840. The *Soudan* in July, the *Albert* in September, and lastly the *Wilberforce* on the 10 October. They were then taken into the Trafalgar Dock, Liverpool, to have their rigging and engines fitted. The Soudan sailed for the Thames on 28 December; the *Albert* followed on 11 January,1841; and on Wednesday, 17 February, the *Wilberforce* sailed from Liverpool, bound for Kingston Harbour; Commander Allen having permission to visit Dublin in order to consult with Professor Lloyd on the use of a newly-invented magnetic instrument!

Great care and attention had been given to the construction of these vessels, which had roomy and airy accommodation for their officers and crews. To actually get these iron built, flat bottomed river vessels safely down the Atlantic, to the Niger, each had been fitted with a sliding keel, to keep them from being blown to leeward. To guard against the rather likely consequences of the ships striking rocks in the river and sinking, each was divided into compartments, by strong iron partitions, making water-tight divisions. Although this made the vessels much safer, it also made the circulation of air difficult. To remedy this problem a Doctor Reid devised a

156

system of ventilation by fanners, worked by the engines, which diffused air through tubes, to all parts of the vessels. This form of air-conditioning, devised by Reid, and engineered by John Laird, obviously being well ahead of its time. As they still imagined that tropical fevers were caused by 'deleterious gases,' the air, before being fanned round the ships, was made to pass through large iron chests, designed to remove its noxious properties.

Although the mission was essentially one of peace and goodwill, it was nevertheless considered right and proper that it should have an imposing appearance. Each of the larger vessels was therefore armed with one long brass twelve-pounder gun, two twelve pounder howitzers, four one-pound swivels, as well as musketoons and small arms, the smaller *Soudan* having just one howitzer, two swivels and small arms.

The *Wilberforce* left Kingston harbour on the 27th February, and arrived at Woolwich on 4 March, joining the other two expedition ships already waiting there. Preparations for the expeditions continued, and as the expedition had received much publicity, thousands came to visit the ships. On 23 March, H.R.H. Prince Albert came down to the dock, on a tour of inspection, and, as a gesture of support and goodwill, presented a handsome gold chronometer to each of the three Captains. Trials were then conducted on the Thames, and all was found to be satisfactory.

As these small river steamers could clearly not carry sufficient fuel for the long Atlantic voyage, coals were sent out to the Cape de Verde Islands, Sierra Leone, and Cape Coast Castle. A fast sailing transport was also hired to take further supplies and coals out to the mouth of the Niger, and also relieve them of all items that would not be required on the river, and which could be stored at Fernando Po. The crews were composed mainly of officers, petty officers, and artificers, with very few able seamen and marines. All were volunteers; and such was the danger from fever and malaria that double pay was granted from the time of sailing. Besides the complement of officers, several scientists, appointed by the African Civilization Society, accompanied the expedition, these being Dr. Vogel, botanist; Dr. Stranger, geologist and explorer; Mr Roscher, miner and minerologist; Mr Frazer from the Zoological Society, London; and John Ansell, collector of plants. When all was ready the ships made their way to Devonport, where they waited for final orders.

Meanwhile, back in London, Macgregor Laird, and many others, continued to oppose the whole project. A great farewell meeting was held in Exeter Hall; Macgregor attended it, resolved to protest to the last, against the expedition in which his elder brother John was so heavily involved. He was convinced that the venture would end in the loss of many valuable lives. His over-riding fear being that failure, and loss of life, on a grand scale, would so upset the British public with the very name of the Niger, that all subsequent, and reasonable plans for further exploration and development would be stopped, for at least a generation.

With commendable courage Macgregor stood up at the meeting, and said what he sincerely felt had to be said, but he was hooted and howled down, although he persevered until he lost his voice. Some of the promoters then had the audacity to sneer at Macgregor's earlier pioneering expedition, adding that a mere commercial venture had no relevance to an expedition inspired by the highest religious motives, and which would clearly sail under the special protection of the Almighty! Demoralised by the lack of respect the meeting had shown him, he made his way back to his home in Blackheath. At his knock Ellen came down to the locked hall door, but hesitated to open it, as Macgregor's voice had been reduced to a feeble squeak, with which he implored her to open the door and let him in. Unable to recognize her husband's voice, she hesitated to open the door; but he repeated "Nelly its me - let me in..." several times, which eventually induced her to open the door. On hearing what had happened, Ellen was full of sympathy for him, and furious when she heard how those at the meeting had treated him - the only man in the hall who had actually been to the Niger, and knew what he was talking about! Sadly though, he was fighting a lost cause.

At 6.50 p.m. on 12 May, 1841, the *Albert* and *Wilberforce* sailed from Devonport. As they passed the great men-o-war, anchored in Plymouth sound, they all honoured the expedition ships, each in turn manning their rigging, and giving them three cheers, thus giving the men who were about to sail into the interior of Africa a memorable send-off. Some ten weeks later they reached Sierra Leone, the people of Freetown, in 1841, being almost entirely composed of freed slaves. News about the proposed expedition, dedicated to the abolition of slavery, had got around, so as soon as the expected squadron cast anchor in the river there was a great deal of excitement, and a warm welcome.

Crowther and Schon helped to secure interpreters for the expedition from the freed slaves, taking care to choose men who had originally come from those parts of the Niger region that they intended to visit, specifically selecting men of the Ibo, Eggarra, Laruba, Kakanda, Yaruba, Hausa, Bornoa, and Fula tribes. Schon had some knowledge of Ibo and Hausa, and Crowther's own tongue was Yaruba. Many of the local people were eager to accompany the expedition as labourers or seamen, and a number were chosen. Special Services were then held in the main churches, the leaders of the expedition attending, and speaking to the attentive congregations. On 2 July they set sail for the Niger.

On 15 August the expedition ships crossed the bar of the River Nun, the main mouth of the Niger, the pilots were taken on board, and final preparations made. They weighed anchor on 20 August, and made their way slowly up river. The time had been well chosen, for the river was in flood, and there was a good depth of water, which made progress much safer. They passed mangrove swamps, and then came to more attractive forest areas, and the occasional village, with cultivated patches of yams and sugar cane. Occasionally they stopped and tried to get into conversation with the people, but they were obviously frightened, not so much by the strange ships, but because the only white men known in these parts were Portuguese slave traders. There was in fact much evidence that a large traffic in slaves was being carried on. Schon had a conversation with one Chief, who assured him that he had been praying to God to send a white man's ship, which pleased him, until it dawned on him that he had actually been praying for a slaver to arrive!

In accordance with their agreed plans they soon found themselves conducting negotiations with one of the most powerful Chiefs of the Niger, King Obi Asai, who had sent a message off to Captain Trotter, advising him that he would come to the *Albert* in order to discuss matters relative to trade, anti-slavery agreements etc., which he had been told constituted the object of the expedition. Very soon the state-canoe appeared, urged on at a rapid rate by forty 'pullaboys' of various sizes, most of them completely naked, but all appearing to be in good humour, and full of curiosity.

After much ceremony Obi Asai came on board, accompanied by his judge, or 'King's Mouth,' Amorama, and several of the magnates of the land. With interest Captain Trotter noted that he was dressed in a serjeant-major's coat, given to him by Lander, and a loose pair of scarlet trousers presented to him at the same occasion. To complete the picture, a black velvet cap was stuck on his head at a jaunty angle. As a gesture of goodwill Obi Asai brought with him some most acceptable presents, these being two hundred and fifty yams, and two small buffaloes. The King and his party were then taken to the quarter-deck, and they all got down to business.

Captain Trotter explained to the King that the expedition had been sent out to Africa by the Queen of Great Britain, in order to enter into treaties with African Chiefs, for the abolition of the trade in human beings, which Her Majesty, and all the British nation considered to be an injustice to their fellow-creatures, and repugnant to the laws of God. Through his interpreter Obi made it clear that he appreciated the implications of what was being said. It was then pointed out to him that selling slaves was injurious to himself and his people, as once a slave had been sold he had deprived himself of their services for ever, whereas if these slaves were kept at home they could be employed for years, producing palm-oil, and other items, that would provide a permanent source of revenue. Obai Asai replied that he would indeed be willing to stop trading in slaves - provided another trade could be developed to replace it.

The Palaver continued, during which Obi Asai assured the Commissioners that in any event, as a man of great integrity, he would not even consider selling slaves from his own domains. He *only* acquired slaves to sell from

Slave Market at Igbegbe

other tribes, during the course of a local war. These wars, it would seem, being rather frequent! On the question of future business arrangements, the King then indicated that he, and his people, would be interested in trading for cowries, cloth, muskets, powder, coral beads, hats, and in fact any produce of the white man's country would please. In return the Commissioners assured Obi Asai that they would be willing to trade for raw cotton, indigo, ivory, camwood, and other local produce.

More pressure was then put on the King to stop selling slaves, which he somewhat reluctantly agreed to. However, when advised that he could not sell slaves because the British had many war ships at the mouth of the river, and the Spaniards were therefore afraid to come and buy there, he became highly amused. The expedition leaders suspected that his amusement arose from Obi Asai knowing that slaves were shipped from scores of places on the coast, most of which he knew were not watched by the British fleet. The great abundance of Brazilian rum in Aboh providing ample evidence that he was doing a great trade with nations heavily engaged in the slave trade, Spain and Portugal being the obvious suspects. However, negotiations continued, which culminated in a treaty being signed, under which both sides agreed to trade, on condition that Obi Asai stopped dealing in slaves.

From the area controlled by King Obi Asai they made their way up the Niger to Idda, the country of the Atta of the Egarra. This great leader was invited to come on board the *Albert* to hear the message from the Queen of England. Though friendly, he was not able to accept such an offer. He then went on to explain, via his representatives, that a King never puts his foot into a canoe, such a thing being beneath the dignity of a person of high status. He also made it clear that the gifts sent to him were not sufficient for his rank, adding that as he was like a God, the presents should reflect this fact. However, if the leaders of the expedition wished to speak to him, they could come ashore and do so - but he would not go to them. To make amends, it was agreed that the Commissioners, with several officers, and Mr Schon, would go ashore to visit the great man, and they were to be accompanied by a guard of honour. This consisted of six marines, led by John Duncan, master-at-arms of the *Albert*, wearing the full dress uniform of the Life Guards, and carrying a very large Union Jack. Clearly impressed , the Atta made them most welcome, and the Palaver began.

Firstly, British opposition to the slave trade was made known to him through the interpreters, and he gave every indication that he fully understood the issue. When the question of human sacrifice came up he wanted to know how a prohibition would work in practice, should, for example, he be compelled to make war, or his country was invaded by another tribe. However, agreement was eventually reached on these secondary issues, and the treaty was signed by the King. Now more relaxed, he brought the conversation round to the age-old issue of Further Education, for ones sons and heirs, the King asking Schon if he could arrange to have two of his sons educated in England. Schon and Crowther then raised the issue of religious education with him, and to their delight the Atta asked them to leave a teacher with him. It was now becoming clear that the Niger Chiefs were just as prepared to listen to black teachers as to white men, which fact they found most encouraging. One very definite step was also gained from this King, he agreed to sell to the Commissioners a strip of land on the banks of the Niger, for an English Settlement and the proposed model farm. The location of the project being some six miles up river, by the mountains known as Etse and Erroo, and immediately opposite the confluence with the Tschadda. For the purchase of this land Captain Trotter agreed to pay seven hundred thousand cowries - about £45. Mr Kingdom, a school master, and others, being left to look after the settlement, whilst the steamers proceeded up river.

However, as with the Laird expedition of 1832, men now started to go down with fever and malaria. Soon after leaving Ida there were fifty-six on the sick list. Six died in the course of a couple of days, and were buried on the land just purchased for the model farm. The importance of drinking water that had been boiled and filtered was unknown, and no one yet saw a link between the mosquito and malaria. The *Wilberforce* now began to look more like a hospital than an expedition ship, with quarter-deck, forecastle, and cabins full of the sick and dying. The medical officers did all they could, but things only got worse. Captain William Allen, and Captain Cork then fell seriously ill; and things got so bad that it was decided to send the *Soudan* down river, and back to the sea, with the sick men. She began her sad journey down stream on 19 September, and two days later the *Wilberforce* had to follow her, so great was the number of sick. Despite everything, it was then agreed that Captain Trotter, with Captain Bird Allen, and the missionaries Crowther and Schon, would continue the voyage up river, in the *Albert*. The decision to continue actually being welcomed by the survivors.

The *Albert* weighed anchor, and headed up river, but before nightfall Captain Allen and several of the crew fell sick, then, day by day, others were added to the sick list; but they pressed on, until they reached the large town of Egga, in the Nupe Country. Here they found a slave market, and in one shed saw fifteen tragic human being exposed for sale. Egga was actually in an area that was dominated by Islam, and where slavery was an inter-tribal system, almost entirely without connection with the Spanish and Portuguese traders, far away in the Bight of Benin. Schon could speak in Hausa, so he immediately addressed the people around him, on the sinfulness of slavery in the sight of God.

The river was now starting to fall, making navigation hazardous, but Captain Trotter pressed on, anxious to reach Rabba, the final objective of the

162

expedition. Sickness among the crew was increasing, and then he himself went down with fever, leaving just one officer on duty. The brave commander then had to face the fact that they could not continue, and the anchor was dropped. He then wrote a message to the King of Rabba, advising him of the purpose of the expedition, which, accompanied by a gift of a handsome Arabic Bible, was sent on to him by messenger.

On 4 October, 1841, Captain Trotter gave the order to return, but there were few fit enough to act on the instruction. The stokers and the engineers were all sick, and no one knew how to get the engine started. Dr. Stranger, one of the scientists, was still well, who studied a book on engineering, to discover what had to be done. One of the engineers then began to recover, who offered some advice, and at last Stranger managed to get the engine working. The inexperienced scientist then had the unenviable task of steering the vessel down the Niger, past the shoals and sandbanks which presented a real peril to the small steamer. Meanwhile, more men were falling sick, Crowther and Schon looking after them, and ministering to the dying. On the sixth day after leaving Egga they reached the model farm that had been purchased with such high hopes just a month before.

Here they found that Mr Kingdom, the gardener, and Ansell, had been struck by fever. They were taken on board the *Albert*, and others left in their place. Interestingly, the men left as replacements were of African origin, one being Ralph Moore, an American emigrant, who had joined the expedition at Liberia, and Neezer, a negro printer from Sierra Leone, who was to act as storeman, and otherwise assist Moore in the management of the project; the work force consisting of twenty African men, women and children, all of them from Sierra Leone. A whole day was set aside for taking provisions ashore, in fact enough to keep the group going for about nine months. Moore was then left with the above people, plus forty local workers to help work the place. Eleven acres of ground were cleared, and cotton was planted within a few days, and from the nature of the soil, all anticipated good crops. The best thing about the project being the fact that the local people seemed to be on very friendly terms with all the settlers, and, importantly, willing to work on the farm for the equivalent, in cowries, of three pence per day!

It was agreed that the *Albert* would leave the settlers to their fate on Sunday, 10 October. The morning broke beautifully, after heavy rains during the night. At 6 a.m. Captain Allen, and another officer, Carr, walked to the summit of Stirling Hill, to take a last look at the magnificent view over the nearby confluence of the Niger and Tchadda. Deeply impressed with the scene, and also thankful that they had not been struck down by the fever, they returned to the settlement, and made final preparations to leave. Carr though soon fell sick (but was to recover later at Fernando Po.) They weighed anchor once more and headed down the river. Soon only one white sailor

163

remained in good health, who, with Dr. McWilliam, managed to keep the vessel moving. They were still a hundred miles from the mouth of the Niger, and there they would be faced with the difficult task of crossing the bar.

Help was on the way though, for a ship soon came into sight. It was the *Ethiope* coming to the rescue. Two days later the *Albert* crossed the bar in safety, and they headed for Fernando Po. Here the three ships of the expedition fleet were soon moored alongside each other. Sadly though, Captain Bird Allen and several other officers and men died soon after their arrival. Thus the expedition which had set out with such high hopes and ideals, with the blessings of the British Queen, her Government and people, ended in tragedy.

Though Captain William Allen could not be blamed for any of the numerous misfortunes of this expedition, he was, on his return, placed on half-pay, but was to retire from the service as a Rear Admiral in 1862. From many points of view the Niger expedition of 1841 was a great failure, and it certainly marked the end of large scale exploration in West Africa. The Church Missionary Society though considered that valuable experience had been gained, and though obviously discouraged, they, and the promoters of the expedition, believed that the failure was not final, and they had no thought of giving up the effort. Reports they received from Crowther and Schon indicated that the great Chiefs were ready to listen to British Missionaries, but they were also willing to be taught by black men. The C.M.S. recognising this new factor, strengthened their obligation to train more Africans as religious teachers of their countrymen.

Added to this, there was the fact that, in Sierra Leone, the Christian Missions already had a very strong base. Here many thousands of liberated slaves, who owed their freedom to the vigilance of the British West Africa Squadron, were settling down to a new way of life; but naturally their thoughts kept turning to their home lands, many being natives of the Niger Country, and thus familiar with one or more of the languages of the area. In view of this Sierra Leone was considered by the Church Missionary Society the best place to train Africans for the task of advancing the Christian religion. It was therefore from the 1841 expedition that missions to the Niger Country became a definite policy of the Church Missionary Society. These missions, would have much to do, apart from preaching the Gospel, and opposing slavery, for, among other things human sacrifice, often associated with the death of a chief, was still widespread. Such an occasion being a signal for large scale sacrifice of many innocent lives. Twin murder was still practiced; and widows were often forced to remain in total seclusion, without washing for many years. In 1850 a Society for the Suppression of Human Sacrifices in Calabar was established, and, in 1858, when King Eyo Honesty died, not one man was sacrificed. Progress was being made.

CHAPTER EIGHT   EIGHTEEN FORTY ONE TO EIGHTEEN FIFTY ONE

The decade following the Niger Expedition had much in store for the Laird family, which would culminate in a maritime development of historic proportions for the Niger Country. Other developments were also to occur during this period that were to have a direct bearing on all matters concerning the West Coast of Africa. Meanwhile, back in August, 1841, Macgregor Laird made his way to Birkenhead. Here he found the men in the family shipyard were working on the construction of a 270 ton sailing barque, named after his brother, the *John Laird*. Ellen was disappointed that this journey north was preventing Macgregor and herself from spending 1 August together, the fourth anniversary of their wedding; but this visit could not be postponed, for letters received indicated that his father, William, was not well.

The family doctor was consulted, who suggested that he would probably benefit from a trip abroad. The actual destination finally agreed on being Aix Lex Bains. The plan was that his daughter, and niece Mary Macgregor, were to go with him, whilst his wife was to remain at Blackheath with Macgregor. Eventually William Laird and his party reached Havre, but he must have been more ill than was suspected, for he then stated that he could go no further. Perhaps sensing that the end was near, he expressed a strong desire to see his favourite son, Macgregor, once more. A letter was sent to Blackheath, urging Macgregor to come and see his father without delay.

Immediately the letter was received Macgregor hurried off to Southampton, to be there to receive his father on arrival. But as fate would have it, this was not to be - his daughter subsequently stating that the dying William Laird struggled to live until the boat came into port, on which it was expected that Macgregor would arrive. When it became clear that his son would not be coming, William gave up the fight to live - unable to find the strength to hold on until the next tide. Macgregor arrived a few hours later, gave comfort to those present, and then made arrangements to accompany his father's body back to Birkenhead.

In a letter written to his mother at this time Macgregor makes a few short references to the Niger Expedition, which remind us that he publicly opposed the expedition, whilst his brother John built the ships for it. This must have led to some rather bitter arguments, but the following extract from this letter indicates that Macgregor regretted the fact that their differenced over this issue had clearly caused some ill feeling to be generated:-

"The account from the Niger Expedition renews in my mind the feelings which used to rise in it, when thinking far away of yours and his anxiety

Liverpool in 1837

respecting me; I often then resolved never to vex his affectionate nature or your tenderness by again giving you pain or anxiety on my account, but I fear it has been too frequently the case since my return and frequently to him must have seemed so, when not intended on my part. It is hard to realize that it is impossible to make up for our short-comings as his children now, and all we can do is to endeavour to do our duty to you and to each other."

It was at this time that Macgregor took the decision not to continue working directly with his brother in the Birkenhead shipbuilding business. Whilst it is clear that there was much that held the family together, it is equally clear that there were strong differences in outlook, and perhaps because of this, Macgregor acted as he did - in the interests of family peace; he set himself up in business in London.

In a letter written to his mother the following year - 1842 - Macgregor makes a further reference to the Niger Expedition. It would seem from this note that the naval officers in London were not great admirers of this expedition, and in particular its leader, Captain Trotter, who they had decided to "Blackball" at the Navy Club. They did not approve of the fact that he had 'left' the expedition, but as we have seen he hardly had any option but to call the venture off, and was himself suffering from fever. On the injustice of their stance, and their inability to take this last factor into account, Macgregor observed " but none of them I dare say have had the African Fever."

The failure of this expedition had put the spotlight on all matters relating to the West Coast of Africa, and in particular the Slave Trade. And, as mentioned in passing, a Select Committee was set up to examine these issues, and Macgregor Laird was called to give evidence. He also put in some papers on the Slave Trade, charting its sad history from earliest times, and his own views on how it could be stopped. The Committee met in June, 1842, and the line he pursued at the hearing was that it would benefit and protect the negroes on the West Coast if they could be brought into contact with the Europeans in the West Indies, then returned to Africa, under a scheme managed by the British Government - not private merchants. These people would then act as a catalyst in Africa, breaking down the old slave based society, and the slave trade, and helping them to break with reactionary forms of religion, and superstitions founded on fetish worship, sacrifices etc. He was then asked : " Would you propose that provision should be made for bringing back those negroes to the coast of Africa?" He replied -

"Certainly; I think it is an essential feature in allowing them to be taken from the coast at all; I think it very unfair to the negro to take him from his own coast without giving him afterwards the option of returning to it: we take them, I suppose, to benefit ourselves by their coming to the West Indies; and I say also, to do the men good, to civilise them at the same time. The great benefit that I would expect in this emigration from Africa would be in

167

the return of those people to Africa with improved civilisation; so that I would make it a *sine qua non* that they should be allowed to return after a certain time, at the public cost, to the place from whence they came."

Macgregor then made it clear that the whole scheme hinged on it being compulsory on the colony to find a free passage back to he emigrant, after say three years, and that it was vital that wages offered to the labourers were not allowed to fall below a fair level. He was not optimistic about 'civilising' the labourers in Africa, " because you cannot bring them into contact with any large mass of European society, or a regulated form of government, or anything of that sort. The government of Sierra Leone is a very fair one in its way; but when the Governor dies on the average of every two years, it is impossible that you can have a good regular Government there."

Although it is clear that Macgregor Laird was very much opposed to slavery, and his proposal was given with the best of intentions, the whole plan bore a remarkable resemblance to proposals then being advanced by some West Indian Planters; anxious to find labour to work their estates, following emancipation. There can be no doubt that, consciously, or unconsciously, some of these ideas had influenced his own thinking on the issue.

When Africa was closed to the British West Indies Planters, as a source of labour, many of them looked to India. This gave rise to the ' Indian Coolie Labour Trade' as it was commonly called. Full coverage of this trade being given in an official report on 'Emigration from India to the Crown Colonies and Protectorates.' produced by a committee set up by Lord Sanderson in 1909. From this report it is clear Mr John Gladstone, Liverpool Merchant, Plantation Owner, and father of the great statesman, William Ewart Gladstone, was one of the first promoters of this trade.

On 4 January, 1836, John Gladstone, wrote to a Calcutta firm, with which his family did business, indicating that the emancipation of their negro slave labour had created problems, and they wanted to obtain labour from other quarters. He then gave a glowing account of the West Indies, indicating that any labour that they could recruit for them would have light labour, comfortable dwellings, abundance of good food, schools and religious instruction. The Calcutta firm replied, stating that they had already sent several hundred men from India to Mauritius, and would have no problem sending more to the West Indies. Large consignments of Indian Labourers were then shipped out for Gladstone, who obtained an Order in Council sanctioning labour contracts for five years. In January, 1838, the public became aware of this, when it was denounced in the Anti-Slavery Society paper " The Emancipator" as giving birth to a new form of slavery.

The Secretary of the Anti-Slavery Society then visited British Guiana, where many of the Indian Labourers had been sent. Here, not surprisingly, he found that conditions were not as described by John Gladstone, there was in

168

fact a high death rate, sickness, bad housing, a lack of good food, many runaways, and no legal provisions for taking these people back to India. All this being subsequently confirmed by a Government Enquiry into Gladstone's own estate in that country!

The report, which was tabled in 1840, showed that terrible abuses existed. However, Sir J.P. Grant recommended that emigration to Mauritius was resumed, under certain safeguards. In 1844 it was permitted to Jamaica, British Guiana and Trinidad, and to other colonies at later dates. Regulations were tightened up, mainly as it related to conditions on the ships carrying them, but, in 1856, the report notes the efforts planters were making to retain their hold on the 'Coolies' after the expiry of their period of indenture:

"The Planters and the colonial governments, in which the planting interest is generally powerful, did not at first appreciate the fact that Indians make excellent settlers, and that it was to the advantage of the colony to encourage them to settle down as free citizens and to contribute to the general prosperity. The aim of the planters, who had suffered so severely from the discontinuance of slave labour, was too often to acquire complete control over the labour market by means of regulations and administrative measures which aimed at compelling the coolie to re-engage himself on the expiry of his indenture, rather than encouraging free settlers."

Another observation from Natal was:-

" Wages were paid only every two months and were subject to severe reductions in the shape of fines for absence. After the expiry of the indenture, immigrants were expected to re-indenture. If they did not do so and worked for wages, they came under an ordinance applicable to native African labour, under which a servant was liable to whipping for neglect of work."

Conditions on the ships actually taking the emigrants to the colonies did improve, under stringent regulations, but the report for 1907-8, regarding British Guiana, noted that the estate managers there still had an extraordinary tendency to use the courts. In that year the indentured population stood at 9,784 persons, with no less than 3,835 charges being preferred against the 'coolies' under labour laws. Most of the charges being for 'idleness' or alleged idleness, and trumped up charges such as 'insulting conduct or words or gestures.' Added to this the 'right of return' was not always assured, for in some colonies workers found that they were expected to pay one-third of the fare for his women relatives, and half of his own.

But to be fair to Macgregor Laird, in 1842 these abuses lay in the future, and one can assume that he would have been shocked, when the harsh reality of such schemes, in actual operation, emerged. On putting down the slave trade from the coast of Africa, he was asked his views on this later in the hearing. He pointed out that the West Africa Squadron had been in operation since 1819. The existence of these patrol ships had made the slave trade a smuggling concern. The cruelties of the trade remained, and the number of slaves exported from the coast had not appreciably diminished. He then made it clear that he supported the principle of the patrol, but was saddened by the fact that the commanders of these ships could not be given more effective powers, which would make them a stronger force in the struggle to end the slave trade.

He was then asked if he was aware of the nature of Britain's latest treaties with other powers for the suppression of the slave trade. He assured the hearing that he was, but then stated that they were altogether wrong in principle, as there was no powers in these treaties which would allow the British Government to punish the crews of Captured slavers. The Chairman then asked Macgregor if he agreed with the recommendations that had been made to the committee, that the crews of slave vessels should be conveyed to the countries to which they belonged, handed over to the authorities there, and tried as criminals. Macgregor's response to this is worth noting:-

"The authorities of those countries are the parties who at present carry on the slave trade: they connive at it. The government of Spain and the government of Portugal, there is no doubt, have connived at the carrying on of the slave trade under the respective flags in Africa. I do not think it would be productive of any good consequence handing over to those very powers that have been breaking treaties for so many years, the crews of the slavers for punishment; I think the disposition to punish is wanting. I do not think anything will do, unless you give the British Government, who are the only honest parties in this, the power of dealing with the crews of those slave vessels, under whatever flag they sail."

On the huge extent of the problem Macgregor pointed out that 25% of the Royal Navy were then employed in efforts to suppress the slave trade, and that if Britain was to put every man-o-war it had off the coast, the trade would still go on, and with perhaps more cruelty, if the demand on the other side of the Atlantic continued. Slaves, he informed the Committee, could be obtained from all the ports from Morocco, where one could openly purchase them, to San Benguela; a stretch of coast some 4,000 miles in extent. He then put before the Committee figures which, he felt, showed that since the establishment of the Mixed Commission Court and the African Squadron, the slave trade had apparently increased - slavers putting out from the port of Havannah playing a significant role in this increase.

Macgregor continued, stating that he recognised that the Spanish flag had been replaced by the Portuguese, but felt that the trade had not abated. Portuguese papers were readily procurable at the Cape de Verds and Princes Islands for a few dollars by Spanish vessels. The trade was merely changing its colours. The great irony of the situation was that despite all efforts by the British, the slave trade, he felt, was increasing, and that when the trade was a legal one larger vessels were employed, since it had been made illegal, more slaves were being crammed into smaller, fast vessels, with the result that mortality had actually increased alarmingly.

The actual situation with Spain and Portugal at this time is interesting; the "Equipment Article Treaty" had been signed by Britain and Spain in 1835, which gave both nations the mutual right to search ships suspected of being slavers. If the equipment of slavery was found on board a vessel the Courts of Mixed Commission at Sierra Leone then adjudicated. At first the Portuguese refused to sign a similar treaty, and it was this that led to the Spanish traders sailing under Portuguese colours, as correctly reported by Macgregor Laird. However, before the close of 1842, the Portuguese Government at last agreed to sign an "Equipment" treaty. The slave traders responded to this move by sailing *to* the West Coast under the American flag, and *from* the Coast under Spanish, Brazilian, or Portuguese colours, the potential profits still making the risks worth while.

The British Government had responded to popular demands to increase the strength of the West Africa Squadron, for by 1842 the fleet contained five steamers. These early steamers though were made of wood, but during the first part of the 19th century all naval steamers only used their engines as auxiliary power. Their full sets of sails providing most of the motive power required. Iron steamers were soon to replace those made of wood, but to the end of its days, the West Africa Squadron never acquired one! In the 'forties other nations were persuaded to co-operate by Britain, who then sent out their own anti-slavery squadrons. This decade also saw the introduction of more positive tactics. The Royal Navy took steps to cut off the supply of slaves. It did this by moving into the creeks and rivers along the West Coast, and destroying the bases where the slaves were held awaiting shipment. Naval Commanders were given powers to offer salaries to African Chiefs, provided they signed treaties agreeing to abandon the slave trade. This was the 'carrot' - the 'stick' being to advise the Chiefs that if they did not abandon the trade the Navy would stop all European goods reaching them, and, in addition to this, would come ashore and release all slaves, held prisoner, awaiting shipment. This tactic began to work, for within two decades a complete network of these treaties were in place.

Whilst the failure of the great expedition of 1841 had set back the promotion of commercial enterprise by a decade, from an African perspective it had succeeded in a remarkable manner. At this time the Church Missionary Society was debating the issue of the Niger Mission. There was only one bishop in West Africa in the 'forties, this being the Bishop of Sierra Leone, nearly 2,000 miles way from the Niger, making it totally unrealistic for him to assume responsibility for this area. The expedition had apparently shown that Europeans could not survive on the Niger, and certainly proved that black Africans, on the Niger, were willing to learn from those of African origin, who had been educated by Europeans.

Henry Venn was at this time secretary of the West African field of he Church Missionary Society, and it was he who put all his faith in the Yoruba ex-slave, Samuel Adjai Crowther. The Niger mission would be pioneered, staffed and directed by men of Negro race, and this would be done under the guidance of an African bishop, Crowther! Venn met with some opposition, but he won the approval of the Archbishop of Canterbury, who in turn secured Government support, and in due course the Royal License was issued for the consecration of Samuel Adjai Crowther, clerk in Holy Orders, Bishop of the Church of England in West Africa.

Venn then set to work to obtain for the bishop-elect a degree, to add to his prestige., and on his recommendation the University of Oxford conferred upon him the Honorary Degree of Doctor of Divinity. Crowther had, nevertheless, worked for this - as he had already produced an English - Yoruba Dictionary, worked on Yoruba Grammar, and translated many parts of the Bible into his native language. Crowther was destined to make a further historic voyage up the Niger, on a Laird built exploration vessel, and following that be honoured at a great ceremony in Canterbury Cathedral, in 1864. All of this though might not have happened, had Captain Trotter realized that he had carried with him, on his ill-fated expedition, the medication that was to make life possible for Europeans in West Africa. His ships had ample supplies of the one thing that could have cured them: quinine. But they did not appreciate its real value, and consequently only used it when a patient showed signs of recovery! Writing in 1930, Deaville Walker describes the moving scene, in 1864, when Samuel Crowther was formally consecrated Bishop of the Niger Territories:-

"On St. Peters Day (June 29), 1864, in Canterbury Cathedral, Crowther, the ex-slave boy, was solemnly consecrated Bishop of the Niger Territories. Close by, dressed in full naval uniform, sat Admiral Sir H. Leeke who, forty-two years before, had rescued him from the stinking hold of the slave ship in Lagos lagoon. And not far away sat an old lady, widow of Bishop Weeks of Sierra Leone, who quietly remarked to an officious sidesman who challenged her right to be there: "I think I have the right to this seat, for I taught Mr Crowther his alphabet."

Crowther was the first man of colour to be advanced to a bishopric in modern times."

Other important developments were also in hand in 1842, of crucial importance to West Africa. In 1841 a new treaty had been negotiated with King Pepple to abolish the slave trade, but it was never ratified. However, the West Africa Squadron continued to patrol Bonny waters, but Pepple responded by diverting his trade in slaves to the state of Brass, from which enclave large numbers of slaves were exported to Cuba and Brazil. Palmerston, the then British Prime Minister, responded in 1842 by trying to regain the settlement at Fernando Po, which had been abandoned. This so that the island could be used as a base by the Squadron, for monitoring slave-trading activity at all ports on the Oil Rivers, as this region now came to be known. Between 1830 and 1850 the value of legitimate trade was to grow by 87 per cent; and, due to the continuing activity of the West Africa Squadron, slave-trading was soon to be virtually eliminated at Old Calabar, with Lagos remaining as the main place of concern.

Development were also in hand at this time between Britain and the United Sates, which would strengthen the hand of the Squadron. One of the first actions of Lord Aberdeen, when he became Foreign Secretary in 1841, was to try and settle outstanding differences between the two nations. Lord Ashburton was sent to Washington to negotiate with Daniel Webster, the United States Secretary of State. The treaty signed at the close of the revolution had left in question a large territory of about twelve thousand square miles. The Webster-Ashburton treaty of 1842, which was the result of their meetings, resolved the matter, thus putting relations between the two powers on a much better footing. Following ratification of the treaty the United States accepted a British invitation to send an American anti-slavery squadron to the West-Coast, this notwithstanding the fact that many of the states in the Union, were still economically and socially bound to slavery. From this a system of joint cruising emerged, but the United States Government did not dare go so far as to grant the Royal Navy the right to board and search American ships.

Meanwhile, Macgregor Laird, the man who would soon be playing the leading role in the commercial development of the Niger, moved back to Birkenhead with his family, taking up residence in a small house in Clifton Park. He had decided to rejoin the family shipbuilding enterprise. At the yard John and his men had just seen the launch of the 800 ton *Guadaloupe*, which had been built to the order of the Mexican Government. A two-masted paddle frigate, she had the heaviest armaments carried by any ship of that class, and she created considerable interest at the Admiralty.

In the town itself much was happening, the first sod of Birkenhead's famous park being cut in 1844. On 30 June the following year the Act for the construction of the great dock system at Birkenhead received the Royal Assent, work on this gigantic scheme starting soon after this date. The Birkenhead Dock Company was then set up, with Macgregor Laird acting as Company Secretary. The vast amount of capital required to fund this extensive new system being largely provided by the principal promoters and subscribers to the Dock Company, which included William Potter, who subscribed £100,000; Sir J. Goldsmith, £30,000; William Jackson, £80,000;

173

and the Laird Brothers; John subscribing £80,000, and Macgregor £35,700. They were now heavily committed to the future development and prosperity of the town.

Unfortunately, the year of 1846 marked the beginning of troubled times for Birkenhead, contracts for the dock works had to be withdrawn from a Mr Tomkinson, because of his inability to cope with such a vast project. In the summer all the masons and bricklayers went on strike, causing the suspension of all major developments. All of this coincided with the horrors of the Irish Potato Famine, with countless thousands of starving Irish emigrants pouring into Merseyside each month. The density of population in Liverpool at this time being over 138,000 per square mile, many being forced to live in damp cellars. In Birkenhead things were little better. J. Hunter Robinson M.D. reporting at this time that small apartments in the town were crammed with eight to ten people, and cellars not fit for dogs, were full of poor local and emigrant workers. Epidemics of cholera and typhus began to occur.

A general recession then set in but work on the great dock system continued, until they were completed and formally opened on 6 April, 1847. The Laird brothers being among the prominent guests at the great celebration held to mark the occasion. One of the speakers at this celebration being Lord Monteagle, who praised the way the town was being developed, men striving for their just and legitimate gain, and the career of noble enterprising commerce! In fact the harsh reality of the situation was that Birkenhead was in decline, and most of the inhabitants were merely struggling to stay alive.

On the 15 October Sir Robert Peel paid a visit to the town, he was shocked by what he saw, and was nearly killed by a worker who ran at him clutching a spade. Birkenhead, at this point in time, was little more than a splendid ruin. The population of the town dropped by 50 per cent, leaving many streets completely empty, and to add to the troubles, the docks project then ran into severe financial problems. The Laird family fortunes declined with the worsening situation.

For Macgregor Laird and his family, things moved from bad to worse. Ellen was reduced to telling the children to take care of their clothes as there was no money to buy any more. They remained in Birkenhead until the spring of 1848, at which time it was decided to move back to London. There were Bills before Parliament relating to Birkenhead, and on 1 April Macgregor once more gave evidence before a Select Committee on the Slave Trade, at which he put forward his ideas on how best to end the trade. Soon after this he brought his family back to Birkenhead. The family were split up, and to cover debts everything in their old house was put up for auction. If things were bad for the destitute labourers in the town, things were clearly now not much better for those who had recently put up vast sums of capital to develop the port.

Macgregor and Ellen Laird then moved to Chester, staying at a lodging house overlooking the river. The auction had produced enough to pay pressing debts, and leave something in hand. Macgregor then decided to take his family to France, via Jersey, so they could live with Colonel and Mrs Nicolls, until things improved; the Nicolls family having moved to Avranches, Normandy, in 1845. They set sail at the end of May. It was a seemingly inappropriate time for a middle-class English business man to take his family to the continent, for France, and indeed most of Europe, was then in a state of revolutioary upheaval. It was though a case of any port in a storm, here at least they could live cheaply with their relatives.

It would seem that some time during the early forties' Colonel Nicolls had been invited to become a Director of a railway company, which promptly led to financial problems. It was this which led to the decision to move to France. He rented a large country house, and settled down, taking up gardening and pig keeping as hobbies. During the summer of 1848, when his daughter, son-in-law and children arrived to live with him, the French revolution of 1848 continued unabated; Paris going up in flames once more on 23 June, but all remaining peaceful in Normandy. But surprisingly, it was in 1848 that laws were to be passed in France for the Abolition of Slavery in French possessions. However, a good deal of the credit for this has to be given to successive British Governments, urged on by the Anti-Slavery movement in this country; although much credit also has to be given to the work of the French Anti-Slavery Society. This development would have pleased both Macgregor Laird, and Colonel Nicolls, despite their preoccupation with pressing personal problems.

Macgregor Laird then came back to Birkenhead, leaving his wife and family in France, but things went from bad to worse, with all his hopes of coming to some private arrangements with his creditors being doomed to failure. He spent the winter of 1848-49 with his family in Avranches, but was formally declared bankrupt later in 1849, although he subsequently managed to clear all his debts, and even those that he felt he was not really legally liable for. In the summer of the same year Macgregor and his family came back to England, taking modest lodgings in Great Russell Square, near the British Museum, before moving to Queens Road, Bayswater.

Never a man to let things get him down, Macgregor Laird now occupied himself by designing a sectional boat, for use in Africa by his old friend John Beecroft, who had just been appointed Consul, by Lord Palmerston, for the Bight of Biafra and Benin. The idea seemed a good one, but his daughter, Eleanor, recalled him saying that he never really made much money out of it, but it had been worth a good deal to him, as it had given him hope, and occupied his mind until things got better. In the same year he met with more success, when he patented improvements on the design of metallic ships, material for coating ship's bottoms, and steering gear. It was also about this time that he manged to set himself up as a merchant trading from 3 Mincing Lane London.

Meanwhile, back in Africa, interesting and far-reaching developments were taking place, centred on Beecroft. It had been the desire to stabilize the condition of the delta trade, and put an end to the slave trade, that had led, in 1849, to the initiation of British consular jurisdiction over the area, backed by the Royal Navy - with John Beecroft being appointed to the post. And it was Beecroft who was destined to lay the foundations of British power in Nigeria.

Beecroft began his truly remarkable career in West Africa in 1827, at Fernando Po, when the island was occupied by the British, and being used as a base for the suppression of the Slave Trade by the West Africa Squadron. The British then left the island, but Beecroft remained there, looking after the interests of the many freed slaves who had settled on the island. In 1843 Spain appointed him Governor of the colony, and he then built up a very detailed knowledge of the West Coast. It is also interesting to note that in 1835, just after the Laird - Lander expedition, he had managed to travel up the Niger until he reached Idah, with all the Europeans on this modest expedition surviving. He then mounted further expeditions to the Benin and Cross Rivers.

During the second half of the 1840's he was employed on various political and diplomatic missions by the British Government, all of which led to him becoming the obvious choice as the first British Consul for the Bights of Benin and Biafra. During his six years as consul he was to become extremely powerful and influential, and at the same time win the respect of the Coastal Chiefs. He had disputes with King William Pepple, over his persecution of British merchants, some of whom had actually been murdered on the New Calabar River in 1848. He was active in all moves to end slavery, but at the same time worked to promote British trading and political interests on the Coast. In 1852 a development of tremendous importance was to take place, which was to increasingly occupy the attention of John Beecroft, and lead to the development of modern Nigeria. It was the introduction of a small fleet of steamers on the Niger, by the recently bankrupt Macgregor Laird!

Another historically important expedition to the Niger Country was also mounted in 1850, which was later to influence the plans of Macgregor Laird. This expedition was backed by the British Government, and was led by a deeply religious supporter of the Anti Slavery Society, James Richardson. Travelling with him was the German explorer, Dr. Heinrich Barth, and another of the same nationality, Dr. Adolph Overweg. They set out from Tripoli, heading south across the Sahara, their intention being to explore the eastern territory of what was later to become Northern Nigeria. After being robbed, blackmailed, and insulted they reached the Western Sudan. They then split up. Richardson died in Nigeria, whilst Dr, Overweg lasted long enough to carry out a survey of lake Chad in a collapsible boat, but by August, 1852, Barth was alone. For the next few years he explored, with true German thoroughness, the country between Bornu and Timbuktoo - later writing a celebrated account of his travels, which ran to five volumes of six hundred pages each!   From his vast experience, Barth was later to advise the British Government that the Benue be utilised for trading with the interior.

The continued existence of Barth was known in Britain, which led to relief expeditions being planned.   In 1854 he met in the Sudan Dr. Alfred Vogel, a German who had been sent out to help him, who was accompanied by two British soldiers, Corporal Church, and Private Macguire. Dr. Vogel and Private Macguire set out to explore the country towards the Nile, but were murdered.   Barth and Church made off in another direction. The necessity for relieving Barth was later to provide the British Government with an opportunity to make one further river exploration of the Niger, but not along the lines of the one led by Captain Trotter in 1841.   This one was to be organised by Macgregor Laird,   with the proposed leader being John Beecroft, one of the pioneers of this type of river work. Unfortunately though he died before the expedition started.

Back in London, during the summer of 1850, all attention was focused on the Great Exhibition, which was to be held the following year. Eleanor Laird remembering that she walked over the ground were it was to be built, with her father, Macgregor, and Mr. - afterwards Sir Charles Fox, whose firm were the main contractors for the project. Towards the end of the year things must have been getting a little better for the Laird family, for they decided to move out of lodgings. They did much house-hunting, at Blackheath and Greenwich, but it was still hard to find a house they could afford to take, and that would hold them all. At last they managed to find one, at the foot of Grange Hill, Greenwich, which they moved into in October.

The house was a large old-fashioned one, very sparsely furnished, but it did at least mean that the family could be brought together again. Three of the children were brought over from France, and for the first time in several years they enjoyed a happy Christmas together.   However, their stay in this house left something to be desired, as the children became sick, and they ultimately reached the conclusion that the drains were defective, and they were being poisoned by them!   Fortunately though their financial situation improved again, and so, before the close of 1851, they were able to move to a better furnished house at Lee, which was taken for a period of six months.

At last things were starting to look somewhat brighter for Macgregor Laird, but matters relating to his future were to improve dramatically within a short period of time. By 1850 the registered tonnage of sailing ships employed in the growing trade between Britain and West Africa amounted to just over 40,000 tons, freight charges, on average, being about £3.50 per ton. Much of this work being in the carriage of Palm oil. Macgregor Laird saw an opening, and moved in. He was of the opinion that the trade would increase, and this, with the freight rates being obtained, justified the creation of a *subsidised* steamship line to the West Coast.

Macgregor Laird was ever mindful of the fact that Samuel Cunard had contributed to the downfall of his British and American Steam Navigation Company, by securing a monopoly mail subsidy on the trans-Atlantic run. With this thought uppermost in his mind he approached the Government, and, after prolonged negotiations, managed to secure a ten-year mail contract, with generous subsidies amounting to over £20,000 per annum, for himself, on the West Coast run! The fact that his brother would be able to build the required ships for this service no doubt influencing this turn of events. He then issued a prospectus, in order to obtain financial support for this new venture.

Macgregor Laird had almost lost his life on the Niger expedition, and been with Junius Smith when the British and American Steam Navigation Company had folded. He had poured funds into the development of Birkenhead, and become bankrupt as a result this investment. Despite these monumental setbacks, he had now bounced back, and was setting up a company that would succeed - and in doing so be instrumental in shaping the future of West Africa.

CHAPTER NINE. THE AFRICAN STEAMSHIP COMPANY, AND THE VOYAGE OF THE *PLEIAD*

The Royal Charter Granted to the African Steamship Company in 1852 held the directors responsible for forming a company for " the purpose of establishing and maintaining a postal and other communication, by means of steam navigation, between Great Britain and Ireland and the West Coast of Africa and elsewhere." It also noted that the directors had agreed to pay the sum of about £83,000 to acquire certain steam vessels. The main purpose of the venture being the conveyance of Government Mails. The directors named in the Charter being Macgregor Laird, of Fenchurch Street, shipowner, John Foster, of New City Chambers, merchant, and William Law Ogilby, of Ingram Court, ship and Insurance Broker. The capital of the Company, in the first instance, to be the £250,000, held in 12,500 shares of £20 each, which amount though included the sum already expended on buying the required ships.

The Charter also stipulated that the company could carry goods and passengers, and had the power, on any outward or homeward voyage from the West Coast, to call at any port of Portugal, or any port of France or Spain - not eastwards of the Straights of Gibraltar. Interestingly, the Company was also allowed to establish a line of communication between the West Coast of Africa and the British West Indies. However, although the Charter gave the Company the right to build, or take possession of wharfs, docks, offices, and houses, in order to conduct their business, it specifically stated that they must not operate as traders. The actual prospectus of the company, as published in the "Times," 13 July, 1852, was as follows:-

"This company is formed to carry out a contract with H.M. Government for the monthly conveyance of the mails to Madeira, Teneriffe, and the principal ports and places on the West Coast of Africa, viz., Goree, Bathurst, Sierra Leone, Liberia, Cape Coast Castle, Accra, Whydah, Badagry, Lagos, Bonny, Old Calabar, Cameroons and Fernando Po; and to establish a line of steam communication between Sierra Leone and the British West Indies as soon as satisfactory arrangements are made with the Government.The contract for the mails was taken by Mr. Macgregor Laird in December last, and is for a term of ten years from 1st September next. The annual payment by the Government commences at £23,250, and diminishes at the rate of £500 yearly during the continuance of the contract, making an average payment of £21,500 per annum. Five iron screw steamships for this service are in the course of construction by Mr John Laird, of Birkenhead, with engines by Messrs George Forrester & Co., and Fawcett, Preston & Co., of

The *"Pleiad"* exploring vessel, built by Messrs. Laird

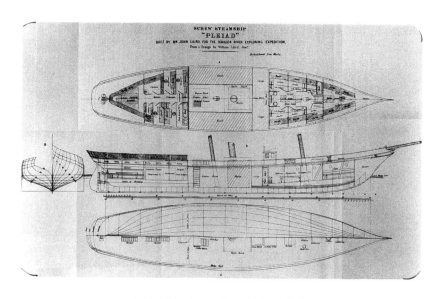

Plan of the Screw Steamship *Pleiad*

Liverpool. The first of these vessels is to be launched on 3rd July, and will be ready to commence the mail service in accordance with the terms of the contract on 1st September. Two of them have the capacity for 700, two of them for 1,000, and one for 250 tons of cargo, with excellent accommodations for first class passengers. The company are also to have Mr Laird's services as Managing Director. A negotiation is going on with the Portuguese Government for an extension of the line from Fernando Po, the valuable African possession. Plymouth will be the first port of arrival, and the last port of departure for the company's vessels, but he voyage will terminate and commence from London."

The prospects of the company looked good, and as the firm also had limited liabilities, which was unusual at the time, the shares were soon taken up. The first directors of the Company then became - Sir John Campbell, K.C.H. (Chairman), James Hartley, Esq. (Director of the P. and O. Co.), John Black, Esq., Henry William Currie, Esq., William Law Ogilby, Esq., and Charles William Gregory, Esq. Bankers, Messrs Currie & Co., Cornhill.

John Laird, and his team of skilled workers, now had to produce the required vessels for the service. The 381 ton *Forerunner* being launched at Birkenhead in July, 1852, when the prospectus was published. This was followed by the launch of the 894 ton *Faith* in October, 1852, and a ship of identical size, the *Hope* in January, 1853, and the 1077 ton *Charity*, on 23 May, 1853. All these screw-steamers being built to the order of the African Steamship Company. John Laird then built the 518 ton screw-steamer *Bachante*, to the order of his brother, Macgregor, which was placed on charter to the African Steamship Company.

John laird had in fact not delivered the *Faith* and *Hope* on time, and in accordance with his contract. This unexpected delay meant that Macgregor had to charter other vessels, in order to meet the terms of his contract. This resulted in a loss to the company, for the compensation received from John Laird did not offset the cost of chartering other vessels. The belated arrival of the ships put the company back in the black, when the first half-year results showed a net profit of almost £2,000. However, the onset of the Crimean War had engendered an increase in wages, coal, oil, and provisions, which soon destroyed any hope of making a profit on the operation.

On the solicitations of Messrs Fletcher and Parr, of Liverpool, the firm were subsequently induced to start operating from Liverpool to the West Coast, and as this was to prove successful, Liverpool later became the home base for the fleet. The first voyage for the Company was made by the *Forerunner*, which left London, bound for the West Coast, on 24 September, 1852. When homeward bound she ran into a storm, losing her funnel, main and fore masts, and was thus obliged to put into Gibraltar for repairs. She made six more voyages for the firm, without incident, but in October, 1854, she was wrecked off the coast of Madeira A subsequent enquiry considered that her master, Captain Thomas Johnstone, had been negligent, as he had run the ship onto a well known rock, 200 yards from the cliff at Fora, when visibility was excellent! (Lost with the ship were Dr. Livingstone's African Journals!)

Two other ships were to be built for the African Steamship Company by John Laird, The first of these being the 660 ton iron screw schooner *Candace*, which was launched on 27 May, 1854. She remained in service a little longer than the *Forerunner* before being lost; going to the bottom of the ocean on 4 May, 1858, when she was in collision with a Dutch vessel, and sank within fifteen minutes. The second was a similar vessel, launched two months later, the *Ethiope*, which remained in service until 1867, when she was sold, but chartered back to the company. Among other vessels which were to sail for the firm were the *Armenian, Niger, Macgregor Laird, Calabar, Margaret, Biafra, Athenian* - and the *Cleopatra*, which was to be lost in 1862.

Whilst Macgregor Laird was re-emerging as a pioneer steamship owner, Junius Smith, his old partner in the British and American Steam Navigation Company venture, was suffering a sad fate, and unable to appreciate what was happening to his ex-partner. Back home in the States, in 1847, he had made an unsuccessful bid for a mail contract. Failing in this he then turned his energy to an experiment in the growing of tea in South Carolina, then a slave state. Smith, like Laird, was a strong opponent of slavery, which did not go down well with the pro-slavery elements in the Deep South. In the winter of 1851 thugs broke into his home, and he was beaten up. Pro-slavery "Patrollers" were suspected of the crime, but never caught. Smith never recovered from this attack, dying in an asylum in 1853.

Meanwhile, back in Britain, the pending conflict in the Crimea prompted the Government to take advantage of the small print in the African Steamship Company's Contract, which obliged the directors to make their ships available to the Government in time of need. The *Hope* and *Faith* were thus put on charter to the Commissariat Service, which is why John Laird had been called upon to replace them, with the *Candace* and *Ethiope*. On April 27, 1854, exactly one month before the *Candace* was launched, John Laird launched the Niger exploration vessel *Pleiad*, built to the order of his brother - Macgregor. Not only was Macgregor Laird back in business - he was back in the business of exploring Africa!

Matters relating to the building of the *Pleiad* are of great historic interest, and directly related to the aforementioned explorer Doctor Heinrich Barth, whose written accounts of his travels set a standard of observation and accuracy seldom, if ever, equalled. Barth first began his explorations in 1845 from Tangier, visiting and traversing Tunis, Tripoli, and Barca. By 1849 he was an experienced traveller, who now carried a Bedouin bullet in his leg, a constant, and painful reminder of a fight in Egypt, in 1846, from which he had been exceptionally lucky to escape with his life.

The disaster of the Government sponsored expedition of 1841, which Macgregor Laird had so strongly opposed, had made the government wary of backing other similar, large scale ventures. However, they did remain determined to explore the Niger Country, and it was this that had led them to back the small expedition led by Richardson. and accompanied by Barth. The news that Barth was still alive, and had crossed the Benue, was received in England in 1852, and it was then considered essential to mount a rescue expedition, prove that this was the same river that had been explored by the Laird-Lander expedition in 1833, and establish the navigability of the stream. Accordingly, a contract was drawn up between the Lords of the Admiralty and Macgregor Laird, that he should build the required steamer, and pay all the expenses of the voyage for the sum of £5,000.

The Laird built exploration vessel *Pleiad* was a small screw-steamer of just 71 tons register, a hundred and five feet in length, with a twenty-four foot beam, she had an engine of just forty horse-power. She was the first exploring vessel ever to be fitted with a screw-propeller; and having been built to the design of the famous yacht *America,* displacement was obtained by breadth, not length. With her propeller lifted she became a fast sailing schooner; but when required she could steam at 10 knots.

Internally the ship was very well fitted, there being five state rooms for the officers, with a steward's pantry, and a bath. Ventilation was obtained by means of moveable 'jalousies' and the after cabin was 'elegantly fitted up' with mahogany tables - a green leather sofa - a bronzed chandelier - marble sideboards - and mirrors on either side of the entrance. The ship also carried a large library, and was exceptionally well armed.

On hearing about the proposed expedition Consul John Beecroft offered to lead it, and the Secretary of State for Foreign Affairs accepted, and granted him permission to be absent from his Consulate. Macgregor Laird asked the Church Missionary Society to allow Samuel Crowther to accompany the expedition, offering him a free passage on the *Pleiad.* Crowther was eager to go, and the C.M.S. was only too glad to seize the opportunity. Dr. William Balfour Baikie was appointed Medical Officer and naturalist, with John T. Dalton acting as a Zoological Assistant. Captain Thomas C. Taylor was appointed to command the ship. In all just 12 Europeans were assigned to go on the expedition, 54 Africans to provide all other assistance required. Admiralty Instructions were then sent to John Beecroft on 23 May, 1854.

It was explained to him that the expedition had two main objectives; the first being to explore the river Chadda, or Benueh, the eastern branch of the Kawara from Dagbo, the highest point reached by Oldfield and Allen in 1833, to the country of Adamau, a distance of about 400 miles, where the

Map of Nigeria and Gold Coast, 1856

river was crossed by Doctor Barth, in 1851; and if possible to push on up-river to the furthest point possible. The other being to try and meet Dr. Barth, and, if found, to offer him all assistance required. The same applying to Dr. Vogel, who had left England in 1853, and it was then thought might have reached the banks of the Chadda.

In carrying out these objectives he was also advised to take advantage of every opportunity for opening up trade with the Africans, and was provided with one hundred pounds worth of presents, and samples of goods that could subsequently be supplied. He was also ordered to make enquiries as to the political power of the respective Chiefs, and, if they were engaged in the slave trade, see if they would consent to put an end to it, if lawful trade could be ensured, and markets opened up for ivory, and other local products; whilst Mr Crowther would naturally enquire into their willingness to receive religious or secular instruction. The commander of the ship, he was informed, had been engaged to comply with his requirements, a copy of his instructions from the owner, Macgregor Laird, being attached for his attention.

Beecroft was then given details of the armaments carried by the *Pleiad*, which were a 12-pounder pivot gun, four swivels, Minie rifles and double-barrelled guns for the officers, and muskets for the crew. At the same time though he was instructed to use the greatest forbearance towards the local people, and on no account let any member of the expedition ill-treat, insult or cheat the Africans. He was told that divine services should be held each Sunday, and that only essential work should be done on that day; but he should observe the spirit rather than the letter of the law, and must not allow the vessel to be put at risk, merely because it was the Sabbath.

John Beecroft was told that he was to give top priority to the health of the party, but should fever break out, "and assume a threatening appearance" he was to remember that he was not called on to persevere in the ascent of the river, as the first care was the safety of his people. When he got back to Fernando Po he was to resume his consular duties, whilst Dr. Baikie would return to England, bringing with him the journals, plans, and collections connected with the expedition, and report himself to the Admiralty on his arrival.

Macgregor Laird's instructions to Captain Taylor were sent from 3 Mincing Lane, London, on 8 May, in which he was told that all trading operations were subsidiary to the main designs of the voyage, and that he must treat Captain Beecroft, and Dr. Baikie as first-class passengers, affording every facility to them, by stopping, proceeding, or delaying the voyage as they required, and supplying them with whatever they required for their scientific pursuits. " In case of any difference of opinion you will require an order in writing from the senior present, and that order you will obey. These gentlemen to join the *Pleiad* at Fernando Po."

Macgregor Laird

He was to conform to the customs of the country, giving presents to the Chiefs as required, and enforce strict disciple with his officers and crew, making sure that no one insulted or cheated the Africans, and, in particular, he was not to permit women to remain on board on any pretence. So far as his armaments were concerned, he was told that the natives were, as a rule, well disposed, but in the lower parts of the river they could not resist the temptation to plunder - if they thought they could get away with it, but once above Ebo there would be no danger. Particular instructions were given to Captain Taylor regarding Samuel Crowther:-

"The Rev. Mr. Crowther, to whom I have offered a passage on the *Pleiad*, will join at Fernando Po from Lagos. It is my desire that he has every opportunity given to him of seeing the country and the people. His position on board is that of my guest, and you will see that he is treated with deference and respect."

Captain Taylor was advised that the mail-packet *Bacchante* had taken out, on the 25 April, to Fernando Po, the cargo, provisions and stores for the *Pleiad*, and two iron sectional boats, 50 long by 8 ft beam; and by the mail-packet of the 24 May, three interpreters selected from the liberated Africans at Sierra Leone by Mr Oldfield, who would join him at Fernando Po. These being men of the Ebo, Hausa, and Yariba tribes. On arrival at Fernando Po, he was to assume command of the *Pleiad*, which would be brought out from England by Captain Johnston.

He was to depart from Fernando Po as soon after 1 July as possible, and if he lost the vessel on any of the numerous rocks and banks of the rivers, he was to get his party down-river in the trade boats. Macgregor adding, that he would move the Lords of the Admiralty to order the mail-packet to call off the river on every voyage. When he got back to Fernando Po he was to take passage, with his Government passengers, in the first contract packet for England, and send the *Pleiad* home under canvas, with a suitable officer in command.

The *Pleiad*, having made a very satisfactory trial trip across the Irish Sea, finally took her departure from Dublin on 20 May, 1854. Dr. William Balfour Baikie leaving Plymouth by the *Forerunner* four days later, and with moderate weather, and a fair wind they soon reached the Bay of Biscay. They continued until they reached Madeira, and in the afternoon after leaving the island they sighted Teneriffe, anchoring off Santa Cruz at eleven at night. Four days after leaving this port they got their first sight of the African continent, Cape de Verde appearing in sight. They touched at the island of Goree, and then set sail for Sierra Leone, which they reached at night.

Here they found the anchorage full of trading vessels from various nations, the town itself being full of activity, with porters, boatmen, labourers, and traders hurrying along the principal streets. Close to the river

S.S. *"Faith"* (1852) – African Steamship Co.

S.S. *"Abossa"* (1912) – African Steamship Co.

Dr William Balfour Baikie

they saw many large stores and buildings, barracks, and the great tower of St. George's Cathedral standing out above all the other lesser buildings; whilst to the left of the town they could see the Church Missionary College at Fourah Bay. Baikie experienced a great deal of hospitality from the merchant residents - in particular from Mr Oldfield, Macgregor Laird's old colleague, from the first Niger steamship expedition. As arranged, Oldfield had selected a group of well-qualified interpreters for the expedition.

On the morning of the 13 June, a small steamer made her appearance, and on anchoring near the *Forerunner* they were pleased to discover that she was the *Pleiad* from Madeira, where she had called in to coal, and to ship some seamen. The *Forerunner* left the same afternoon, the *Pleiad* making arrangements to leave the following day. They touched at Monrovia, Cape Coast Castle, and then got under steam for Akra, at which place they anchored, and where they heard the sad news that John Beecroft had died ten days previously. They pressed on until they reached Lagos, where they were joined by Samuel Crowther, who had come from Abbeokuta to join the expedition. They called at several other places, then, thirty-two days after leaving Plymouth, they reached Fernando Po. Dr. Baikie noting that whilst the *Forerunner* was not a very comfortable vessel, under the able command of Captain Barnwell, was very quick.

At Clarence the sad news of John Beecroft's death was confirmed. From their anchorage they could see his isolated grave, under a wide-spreading silk-cotton tree, on Point William. In the town they soon found that many people were still grieving over the loss of the man they respected, as a kind-hearted friend and protector. Dr. Baikie then examined the Admiralty Instructions, but found that no actual provision had been made in the event of Beecroft's death! However, after consideration, and being next to him in seniority, Baikie resolved to continue the expedition, as the preparations were so far advanced, feeling it would be wrong not to proceed. The Acting Governor and British Consul, Mr Lynslager, then endorsed this proposal. Soon after these matters had been resolved the *Pleiad* arrived at Clarence.

Dr. Baikie then set about preparing the *Pleiad* for the expedition, making sure that the coals, stores etc. were all got on board, and in the correct order. Although he had nothing to do directly with these arrangements, they being under the management of Captain T.C. Taylor, it was then that he realized that this officer was not really suited for the work he had been engaged for. The stores seemed to go aboard in a very haphazard manner, and all seemed confusion, with little real progress being made. Captain Miller of the support ship *Crane* noted the situation, and came to the rescue by sending a party of his men over each day to help sort things out. The *Crane* sailed on 7 July, and the next afternoon the *Pleiad* made ready to start.

On the afternoon of the 8th Samuel Crowther came on board the *Pleiad*, and at about 9 p.m. they weighed for the Nun, with the two large iron canoes, laden with coal in tow. The engine then broke down, causing the ship to drift to the eastward, but it was eventually repaired. On the 10 of July they came to the mouth of the Bonny River, reaching the Brass River the following day. At about 12 p.m. on 12 July the little vessel crossed over the bar at the mouth of the Nun branch of the Niger. She was piloted by Thomas Richards, a Yoruba man, who had made many voyages up the Niger with John Beecroft, and consequently had an excellent knowledge of the river and coast line.

Their first objective was to reach the town of Abo, where the Obi had been very co-operative, and had signed a treaty with Captain Trotter, but they found that he was dead, and there was a dispute in progress as to who would succeed him, their hope then being that whoever it was would have the same attitude. At the appropriate moment Crowther introduced the subject of a Missionary establishment among them, pointing out that these had already been put into operation at Badagry, Lagos, Abbeokuta, Calabar, and the Cameroons. The Chief expressed a willingness to go along with this offer, saying that he would find a place to meet their requirements. So far as trade was concerned, the Chief pointed out that it was the English who had not fulfilled their promise to get things moving, they were willing to do business at any time, and were glad they had now arrived in the *Pleiad.*

As the ship slowly proceeded up river there were increasing signs of warfare among the tribes themselves. There was also the constant threat of a greater danger, this being from organised raids by the Fulani, the Moslem conquerors from the Sudan, who had imposed their rule on the Hausa nation, whose country lay to the north of the Niger and the Tshadda, a region then known as the central Sudan. They were then notorious for their slave-raiding activities, constantly attacking the tribes of the Niger Country, and, also sowing dissension among them - setting up one tribe against another, so that they could later benefit from the troubles they had created.

On the forenoon of 16 August the *Pleiad* ran aground - once more - but was got off after the usual delays. Since entering the river Captain Taylor had never once been out of the ship, but after this grounding he announced his intention of going out in the gig himself to take soundings. From what Baikie could see though he appeared to be looking for shallow, rather than deep water. The following day he requested an interview with Dr. Baikie, when he stated that it was *impossible* for the ship to go any further up the river. Baikie told him that he completely differed from him, and would therefore relieve him of his command, and attempt to take the vessel up himself. Taylor then tried to modify his line, but Baikie stuck to his guns, kept control of the ship, and they pressed on. By 18 August they had ascended to Dagbo, the furthest point reached by the *Alburkah* in 1833. From this point onwards navigational problems increased dramatically. At the break of day Baikie

191

sent the African pilot Richards ahead in the gig to take soundings. By 7 a.m. the *Pleiad* was moving ahead under full power, threading her way along very circuitous channels. The following morning Mr Richards was sent ahead again, after which they proceeded with great care through ever-decreasing waters, until at last the river was only a fathom and a half deep. However, they pushed on at half speed until they eventually reached a better channel. Soon though they encountered numerous shoals and sandbank, making progress extremely hazardous, and causing them to move continually from one side of the river to the other, in attempts to remain in the deepest waters.

On 5 September they made an early start from their anchorage, which was close to Mount Ethiope. The scenery here being very attractive. They passed several small farms and fishing villages, but did not stop, pushing on towards Wukari. From Ojogo to Anyisha they made more contact with the villagers, noting that they were far less timid than other people they had met. Crowther attributed this to the fact that the ship had anchored off Ojogo for some days, and people had got to know and trust them. His view being that villagers did want to make contact with them, and would have done so more frequently, but the *Pleiad* would not wait long enough for them. About the ship itself, Crowther noted at this time:- "The *Pleiad* was well adapted for the navigation of the river, and even when she went at half-speed, neither her own boat, nor the canoes of the river, though well manned, could keep up with her in stemming the current, which runs from one and a half to three knots per hour. "

Two days later they went ashore to have an interview with another local Chief. Conversation though was difficult, because everything said in English had to be interpreted into Hausa, and the Hausa again into Filani or Djuka. They asked about Dr. Barth, but were told that they had not heard of him. Importantly though, they stated they would be very willing to trade with them, adding that if there was no trade their country would not prosper. Crowther and Baikie were then given permission to walk about the town. They also visited a local village called Gandiko, where they saw some Arabian horses in very good condition, which were kept exclusively for catching slaves! Other points of interest at this place being dress - or rather the complete lack of it. Crowther, the ex-slave later writing - " I saw two females in the town whose only clothing consisted of a few leaves, and who seemed quite unconcerned about their condition." They returned to the ship at 2 p.m., finding the Krumen busy wooding the *Pleiad.* Some ivory was then brought on board, which was purchased.

On 8 September they anchored off the town of Zhibu, which was about a mile from the bank of the river. A messenger was sent ahead to inform the Chief of their arrival, and soon after this Dr. Baikie and the Rev. Crowther were in discussion with Chief Zumbade, the head king of the Zhibu district.

He seemed to be about forty years of age, and, according to Crowther, had a rather surly countenance. After the usual polite exchanges, Dr. Baikie advised him of the purpose of their visit; namely to enquire after Dr. Barth, and to enter into trade with people of the Niger Country. They were told that no intelligence of Dr. Barth had reached them, but the ship need proceed no further, as they could do all the trading they liked - but with them!

On 24 September the expedition was at the town of Hamaruwa, a place that is beautifully situated on a hill, on the south side of the Muri Mountains, which is to the east of the Benue. Here they did some trading, Dr. Baikie buying a pair of brass leglets weighing five pounds, for which the owner asked 45,000 cowries, the local going rate for a slave, but after much haggling settled for less. They found that traders from Kano and Katshina regularly visited this town, in large caravans, and sometimes passed onward with other parties to Adamawa, where they would buy slaves and ivory, the former carrying the latter, both then being sold to the Moors in Kano or Bornu.

They then established that there was a man at Katshina, who was trading for an Arab dealer in slaves and ivory. This man had just given the local King a suit of silk dresses and some carpets, in exchange for fifty slaves. There was in fact a huge trade here in ivory and slaves, tons of ivory being carried away each year by the slaves from the banks of the Benue, leaving the country depopulated by the slave-dealing Filanis. Sometimes these slaves would find their way to the west of the Kowara, and thence to the coast. Another route the slaves would be forced to travel was around the Fumbina mountains, suffering greatly on the way.

On 29 September they started to make their way back down the river. They soon came to 'Mount Laird' and 'Pleiad' Island, passing quickly along the northern shore of the latter and by 4 p.m. they reached Bandawa, and by 5 p.m. Lau; off both villages being met by numerous canoes. They continued down the river the following day and several times ran aground, and only after great efforts were they able to get the ship afloat again. On 13 October a great many people came on board to trade in provisions and various other items, whilst the crew took the opportunity to put a good stock of wood on board the ship. They then continued down river. The *Pleiad* anchored off the town of Igbebe, on 20 October, where they were welcomed by the crew of the canoe which they had met when heading up river some seven weeks previously. Eight days later they anchored off Adamugu, where they landed. This being the place where Macgregor Laird had buried thirteen of the crew of the *Quorra*, and two of the *Alburkah*, but no one at this place had any recollection of this sad event.

They pressed on, and on 4 November dropped down to Angiama, to visit the Chief, and at the same time purchase some wood. They found that the place was completely swamped, and was in such a bad state that it prompted Crowther to wonder how people manage to live there. Dr. Baikie went on shore and presented the Chief with a sheep, yams, and cocoa-nuts. He then impressed upon him the necessity of maintaining friendship with the white men, that trade might be carried on with him, and Chiefs in the interior, and on the river. It will be remembered that this was the place where Richard Lander was mortally wounded. Having completed their business at Angiama, they left at about 9 a.m. and were in sight of salt water again at 2 p.m. - just 16 weeks since they had left this place on the way up-river. All had returned safely, both Europeans and Africans, without losing a single person, either from sickness or accident; this in itself being a major achievement. The *Pleiad* lay at anchor on Sunday 5 November, preparations being made to cross the bar on the following day.

On Monday 6 November they got up steam before Daylight. The tide was not yet suitable, the flood running strongly, but at length they weighed anchor, and moved the ship down to Palm Point. There was no swell, no sound of rushing breakers, and by this time it was slack water. They pushed ahead at full spead, and at 6.45 a.m. crossed the bar, without having encountered a single roller, and never having less than three fathoms of water. They had come out by the eastern passage, which required them to keep close by the shore for two miles, and it was whilst on this coast line that they came across the schooner *Mary* of Fernando Po, riding at anchor. The master of this ship, Captain Roberts, came on board the *Pleiad*, and gave them a newspaper, which was much appreciated, even though it was three months' old, and from it they gained some information about the start of the Russian War, which was, amongst other things, having a profound influence on the affairs of the African Steamship Company.

On the afternoon of the following day they were near Cape Bullen, at which point they decorated the ship, as best they could, and steered into Clarence Cove. As they came into the port the *Pleiad* fired a salute, which was returned by Governor Lynslagers huge battery. They anchored at 5.40 p.m. - their long voyage at a successful conclusion. Dr. Baikie then made his way to the Governor, who was also acting as agent for Macgregor Laird, and requested him to take the required steps to hand the ship back to her master Captain Taylor - or whoever he thought proper. What Captain Taylor thought about all this being left to the imagination, incompetent or not though, he was certainly out-ranked, and had no power to influence these developments.

The African Steamship Company vessel *Bacchante*, under the command of Captain Dring, arrived at Clarence on the evening of the 26 November, bringing fresh supplies of letters and news. All the effects of the expedition members were put on board, and they left Clarence, bound for England on the night of the 28th. (The *Pleiad* was to follow the next day, under the charge of the chief mate of the *Bacchante* who was put on board for that purpose!) At Lagos they parted with Samuel Crowther, who then returned to his duties at Abbeokuta. Other incidents on the way home were few, apart from meeting the huge ship *Great Britain*, and one dark night being almost run into by a large brig. They passed the impressive snow-covered peak of Teneriffe, then continued northwards, until they touched at Madeira, which place they left on 24 January. The *Bacchante* reached Plymouth sound on the night of 3 February, 1855, after a voyage from Fernando Po, of 67 days. The following day Baikie left by train for London, in order to report to the Admiralty.

From every point of view the expedition had been a great success. There had, as stated been no loss of life, and they had found that for 600 miles the Niger and Tshadda were navigable, and the people were, on the whole, friendly and eager to establish trade relations with the British. The Church Missionary Society were also pleased with the progress made, and particularly gratified to learn that Crowther had done a great deal of preparatory work on the Niger languages. In presenting his full report to the Society he urged the immediate undertaking of a River Mission. The commercial results of this expedition were also considered satisfactory by Macgregor Laird, but he also felt that it was essential that the Government continued to give support until the trade could become self-supporting. This policy eventually being agreed by both sides.

As noted, Dr. Baikie had returned to England, in February, 1855, on the Macgregor Laird ship *Bacchante*, which had now, it would appear, become an integral part of the African Steamship Company Fleet. The *Forerunner,* which had taken Dr. Baikie out to the West Coast in May, 1854, having subsequently been wrecked on the coast of Madeira, now had to be replaced; the ship selected to fill this gap being the 321 ton *Retriever*, a screw steamer which was built at Dunbarton in 1854. The close of the Crimean war left the African Steamship Company with just six vessels. The recently acquired *Retriever* which, with the Laird built vessels *Candace* and *Ethiope*, maintained the service to West Africa. In the future these vessels would be supported by the *Niger* and *Gambia*, then, at a later date, the *Calabar* and the *Macgregor Laird* would be added to the fleet. This was the fleet, but one is left wondering who the passengers would be, on a typical voyage, and what life at sea was like, for those who set sail for the West Coast of Africa, on these small steamers. Fortunately, two written accounts of voyages in these ships remain, the first being by the author Captain J.F. Napier Hewitt F.R.G.S. - the other by a fellow member of the Royal Geographical Society, the great explorer and orientalist, Sir Richard Francis Burton.

In the spring of 1854, duty dictated that Captain Hewett had to make his way out to the West Coast of Africa. He reluctantly packed his bags and made his way to Plymouth, where he soon found himself on board the African mail steamer *Forerunner*. Moments later the signal gun was fired, and the sailors started to roar out a chanty, as they laboured to haul in the anchor. A parting toast of "God speed you" was drunk by the passenger's friends and the port authorities, and they put to sea - and as the little craft was tossed about by the sea they watched the sun sink behind Mount Edgecumbe. Many knew they would not be returning, for they were bound for a place that still bore the ominous and uninviting appellation of the "White Man's Grave!"

Meditating on his doubtful prospects, Hewett then took a stroll around the deck, and to his astonishment found "countenances contorted with laughter; and I heard, in lieu of lamentations, uproarious mirth mingled with the vivacious explosion of champagne corks!" Leading these "bacchanalian revellers" was a short fat man, bald, but with a massive beard, and a comical expression - his general appearance being that of a stage comedian. He, and the rest of his party, Hewett subsequently discovered, had previously met on "The Coast," and were, he assumed, making the most of life, whilst they had the chance! The remaining passengers, he found, were people unacquainted with "The Coast," and as they did not appear that night he assumed they were "bewailing their fate in the solitude of their cabins."

Hewett then introduced himself to his fellow-passengers, the first one being a friend of the jovial comedian, who was, by profession, a "Palm Oil Doctor!" From this character Hewitt gleaned some information of what life was like for these palm-oil agents, who had to live in total isolation on board their receiving hulk, moored amongst the mangrove swamps of the Niger delta. He was told that the climate was so deadly that the agents seldom ventured ashore, and consequently the only excitement they ever had was to watch alligators floating along the stream. During the long hot days they would anxiously watch the shore, and when a canoe laden with palm oil pushed off, speculate whether it was heading for their hulk, or a rival vessel.

When they felt like some company they would visit other hulks at night, usually scrambling through the cabin windows, then pulling the occupant out of his berth, urging him to get the beer and spirits out, so that they could forget their troubles, by drinking the night away together. Most of these men got very depressed, and Hewett was amazed that such people could be found. The bait was the prospect of acquiring a small fortune in three years - the usual term of office. However, few of them managed to live through the term, and those that did would, more often than not, return home, moderately rich, but completely broken in health.

It was pointed out to Hewett that the greatest enemy of the palm oil agents was the slave-dealer, who paid for their miserable freight in hard cash; and as the Chiefs were money-mad, and little trouble was involved in seizing and selling their own people, they upheld the trade. On the other hand, more work went into producing oil, for less money, so that when a slaver was in the vicinity the canoes carrying the palm oil out to the hulks tended to disappear, and business would cease. This particular "Palm Oil Doctor" must have been one of the fortunate few, who had survived one term of office, and was now returning, either to make another small fortune, or find a grave among the dreary mangrove swamps of the Niger Delta.

Among the other passengers on this trip were a black "gentleman of Fortune" - a German Church Missionary - a Baptist Preacher - and Dr. Baikie, with a German colleague, both of whom where travelling out to join the *Pleiad* - on the third, but their first, exploring expedition up the Niger! Also on board on this notable voyage was an ex-naval officer, who had married a young lady that his relatives had considered inferior to him in fortune and social position. He had been promptly disinherited by his parents, and from lack of means had to leave the service. He had then collected his small capital together, and was making his way, with his bride, to establish himself as a merchant on the West Coast. One wonders if they survived, but can reasonably assume that many such people, in similar circumstances, made their way out to Africa at this time - in the hope of increasing their capital.

Sir Richard Burton has much more to tell us about the actual conditions on vessels of the African Steamship Company. Burton, it will be remembered, had first served as a subaltern in Bombay, and, on his return to England, had published several books on India. In 1853 he set out on his famous journey to Mecca and Medina, disguised as a Moslem; his accounts of these exploits causing a sensation when they were published in 1855. In 1854 he undertook an even more dangerous expedition into Somaliland, which he accomplished successfully, even though he was in constant danger. Two years later he was sent by the British Government to search for the source of the Nile and, accompanied by Speke, discovered Lake Tanganyika. In 1861 he entered the permanent service of the Foreign Office, and was appointed Consul at Fernando Po in the same year. To take up this post he booked a passage on the African Steamship Company vessel *Blacklands* (?) which sailed from the Mersey on 24 August, 1861.

At 12.15 p.m. the steam-tender conveyed Burton, and his fellow-passengers, from the North Landing to the *Blacklands*, Captain English, commanding. At 1.45 p.m. thirty-five huge mail bags were put on the ship, the last passengers came aboard, and they weighed anchor and steamed down the Long Reach " past the five miles of dock - the pride of the Liver - past New Brighton - not yet *L'pool sur mer*, but treeless, barren, horrid, hideous, past the North Fort and the South Fort, fine gingerbread-work for Mersey's mouth against Armstrongs, Whitworths, Blakeleys, Dahngrens, Parrots, and canon rayes - past unpicturesque Waterloo, most like a modern barracks, over a bar breaking, to starboard and port, heavily as the Grand Bonny's, past a bit

197

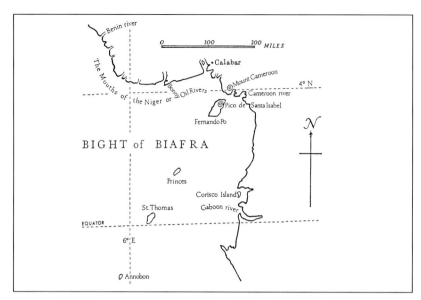

Sketch map of the Bight of Biafra and Fernando Po in the 1890's

Fernando Po in the 1850's

198

of sandland reminding me of Araby the accursed, and - tantalizing contradiction! - forth into the open sea, heading straight for the North Pole whilst bound for Tropical Africa." Burton was even less impressed with the steamer!

On the first night out he records that he, and his older companions, slept in the main cabin, whilst the 'juveniles' preferred the little bunks, five feet by two feet, with flimsy cushions of compressed horse-hair, 'between back and board' which proved to be most uncomfortable. The lack of space above the bunks also came in for some scathing observations, Burton stating that this 'chanced broken heads' - and the lack of air engendered nightmares! All these problems were soon over though, for the policy of the A.S.C. was to wake all passengers at 6 a.m. sharp - with a shout of "coffee up." Burton then dragged himself onto the deck, smoked his morning cigarette, and watched Tuskar Lighthouse, as they steamed past. They then went down to breakfast, which experience Burton considered justified the inclusion of the following poem -

> "Hurrah, the bell for breakfast!
> Hark to the mingled din
> Of knife and fork and hissing chops
> Stewards are bringing in.
> The fiery skipper's pricking fast
> His fork into the dish,
> Despatching quickly his repast
> Of coffee, eggs and fish.
> In burst the guests and on they rush
> Around the jolly tar,
> Who calls on semi-seasick folks
> To Prosecute the war."

He then went on to explain that all A.S.C. vessels were built for cargo, not for passengers, and whilst their 'Intercolonial' boat could carry eleven, there were only berths for four! " A stewardess is impossible, also a doctor. There is no bath but under the hose" and passengers could only reach the conveniences by pushing through a crowd of seamen. Burton considered that a tour of the oil rivers in the 'Intercolonial' craft would be certain death to a sick man. On the other hand, he felt the feeding was good, on their larger ships, without too much preserves, and the beer and stout were tolerable, but in rather short supply. His further, somewhat ruthless observations, about the catering arrangements, the Company, and the ship, are worth noting!

"But the wine is dear, and what is worse, execrable: the African Steam Ship Company makes little by it, so we have to pay dear for simple carelessness touching our comforts. The claret is black strap, the hock is sourish, the champagne all syrup, the Burgundy is like the house Burgundy of the Reform Club - meat as well as drink; the Moselle *sent son perruquier;* the sherry is a mine of bile; and of the port - the less said the better of such "strong military ditto." The coffee and tea are not naturally bad, but artificially; and to distinguish between them requires a very superior nose. Finally, our berths are, it is true, uncrowded, but they are capable of containing more than one, which should never be allowed on board. I have heard of four and even five human beings stuffed into one of these loose boxes, and it is not to be wondered at if ladies who have never suffered in Africa, have been poisoned by their cabins when going home. Why should not the passengers be allowed legally to claim what is allowed to the denizens of every hospital, so many square feet of vital air? "

Burton noted that the average rate the ship moved at was eight knots an hour, and the company 'device' (Logo) was a Negress who presents to Britannia ("off the bare leg") a little heap of potatoes and some pumpkins! A contract passage out to Africa cost £45.00, and he considered it ridiculous that there was no difference in the cost of a passage between Liverpool and the Benin River, and Liverpool and Fernando Po. An enthusiastic supporter of free competition, he thought the Liverpool merchants would soon provide the African Steamship Company with a rival and, " The More the Merrier." He considered that this would lead to freight rates dropping by half, and exports being trebled.

However, Burton did feel that the line was beneficial to the West Coast of Africa, particularly as it would encourage the "tin-pot trader," - this being Oil-River-Slang that meant a small trader that could not afford a ship of his own. " It may fairly be recommended to the public as one of the great civilising agents of the Benighted continent." Also on the plus side, he felt the line was then offering a regular service to invalids, who were unfortunate enough to be "banished to Madeira."

Writing about the A.S.C. fleet in 1861, Burton stated that the *Faith, Hope,* and the *Charity,* had been large, and slow, and that because of this they had all been sold, which was true. The next batch, he continued, were unlucky, the *Candace*, being run into by a Dutchman, near Gibraltar - when all the watch were asleep. The accident did actually take place on 4 May, 1858, when she was homeward bound, and she sank in 15 minutes, the master and four members of the crew losing their lives in the tragedy. The *Niger,* he correctly stated, had been wrecked by hugging the iron-bound coast of Teneriffe, and the *Forerunner*, which had been carrying Dr. Livingstone's African Journals, was lost on 25 October, 1854, which again was correct, but interestingly, he pointed out - "as a hint to divers" - that her gold was still on board, and that all attempts to date had failed to recover it. He added that the *Gambia* had been sold, which again was correct, this actually being to Moss

200

& Company in 1859.

In 1861 the A.S.C. Fleet consisted of the *Cleopatra*, which had been built in 1852, and acquired by the line in 1859. She was a vessel of 1,400 tons, and was then commanded by Captain Croft. The *Armenian* , a vessel of 1000 tons had been bought by the company in 1857, and in 1861 was commanded by Captain Wylde. The *Athenian* was then in service, and commanded by Captain Lowry, and the Laird built *Ethiope* was then under the command of Captain French, whilst the *Retriever* was in service under Captain Delmonte. The *Macgregor Laird* was added to the fleet in December, 1861, some 11 months after Macgregor Laird had died, and the Dunbarton built *Cleopatra*, Captain Delmonte, was lost on 19 August, 1862, this being at the mouth of the Sherbro River, when 40 miles out of her course. An engineer and five Krumen were drowned. The crew escaped on rafts; and the passengers who, though two days on board, managed to escape in a remaining small boat, three others having been lost. Mr Hanson, Her Majesty's Consular Agent, Sherbro River, was drowned, with his boat's crew, as he came to the assistance of the stricken vessel.

The establishment of this small fleet of steamers by the African Steamship Company was an event of momentous importance in the history of West Africa. Prior to the creation of this company trade on the West Coast had been dominated by a handful of wealthy and monopolistic Liverpool Houses. Small traders could not engage in the trade, as they, individually, lacked the capital to own ships. Macgregor Laird ended this unsatisfactory state of affairs, for the creation of the line enabled almost 200 firms to start operating in the Niger area, which remarkable influx was achieved by the year 1856. Not surprisingly, this did not make Macgregor Laird very popular with the old-established Liverpool merchants, who had previously monopolised the trade. It did, however, make him very popular with many Africans, opening their eyes to the outrageous profits these old firms had been making out of them for many years, and the poor quality of the goods they had been supplying to them.

In October, 1855, Macgregor Laird stood down as Managing Director of the company, although he remained on the Board of Directors. He re-established himself as a broker on Merseyside, using John Laird's home and business address for this purpose. John Laird, it should be noted, at this time lived at 60 Hamilton Square, his shipbuilding yards being at 18 Canning Street, Birkenhead, and 24 Sefton Street, Liverpool, the latter yard having been acquired from Vernon & Company in 1852. William & Hamilton Laird, sons of John Laird, were also in business at this time, on their own account, as shipbrokers, wharfingers, and coal merchants, with offices in Fenwick Street, Liverpool, and coal yards at Crown Street and Lightbody Street, Liverpool, and Commercial Street, Birkenhead.

From July, 1856, Messrs William & Hamilton Laird assumed practical day-to-day management of the African Steamship Company, by acting as main agents for the firm. The Board of Directors accepted their recommendation that sailings should be from and to the Mersey, on a trial basis, which arrangement later became a permanent one. These agents later became Laird & Fletcher, then Fletcher & Parr. To the staff of these agents two young men were appointed, Alexander Elder, and John Dempster, whose names were subsequently to be given to the Elder Dempster Company. Macgregor Laird had indeed laid the foundations of one of the greatest shipping enterprises in the world. Soon though he was to be organising yet another exploration venture to the Niger, and designing a small river steamer for the legendary 19th century explorer, Dr. David Livingstone.

Lieut. John Hawley Glover, R.N.

CHAPTER TEN   THE CENTRAL AFRICAN COMPANY - AND THE VOYAGE OF THE *DAYSPRING*

Until the voyage of the *Pleiad* in 1854, trade, for Europeans, had been restricted to the West Coast. Trade with the interior being run exclusively by African middlemen, with no effective trade links of any type existing with the lands beyond the Niger and the Benue. This Laird backed expedition had been responsible for changing this situation; for it had established that Europeans, with care, could survive in the interior, and trade directly with people far from the Delta. Unfortunately though Macgregor Laird had lost so much money on this venture that he was in no position to back further exploration voyages. However, the Church Missionary Society was most anxious to establish a mission on the Niger. The main obstacle being access, for there was no regular steamship service plying up-river, beyond the Niger Delta.

The British Government was preoccupied with the Crimean War, there was little public interest, and even the Liverpool Merchants were apathetic. The C.M.S. decided to make the first move. Soon after the Treaty of Paris had ended the conflict, the Committee put a proposal to Lord Palmerston, and this resulted in a contract between the Government and Macgregor Laird to maintain a steamer on the Niger for five years. A subsidy of £8,000 was offered for the first year, which dropped annually by £500. This led to the establishment of yet another Africa related business; the Central Africa Company, and, once again, John Laird was to build the ships his younger brother required for the conquest of the Niger.

Central to the whole venture was the exploration vessel *Dayspring*, a 77 ton screw-steamer that was to be launched at Birkenhead on 25 April,1857, the much larger screw-steamer *Sunbeam*, launched on 3 October, 1857, and the small 161 ton paddle-steamer *Rainbow*, launched on 26 May, 1858. Also related to African exploration at this time, the Laird brothers were to build a small 23 ton steam river-boat, the *Ma Robert*, to the order of Doctor David Livingstone, this being launched on 15 February, 1858.   This was a busy time for Macgregor Laird, he was establishing a new enterprise, whilst at the same time remaining highly active in the affairs of the African Steamship Company, even though he had stood down as Managing Director.

The original contract for the *Dayspring* stipulated that she should not be less than 160 tons burthen, 80 feet long, 22 beam, draught not more than 5 feet loaded, and must make 10 knots. She also had to be supplied with machinery, engines, apparel, furniture, stores, tackles, boats, fuel, oil, tallow, provisions, anchors, charts, chronometers etc. etc. Other specifications included engine power of 30 horse-power, and coal for twenty days of 12 hours steaming. The ship that was actually produced only had a registered measurement of 77 tons gross, 71 nett, but in other respects she was as specified. The plan was that after her voyage of exploration up the Niger, she would become the first regular steamer on the river. A support ship was required, the one chosen being the *George*; which the *Dayspring* was to tow up to the confluence, and leave there as a trading and depot ship. In fact factories or trading posts were to be established at Aboh, Onitsha and Lairdstown - later to become Lokoja - on the confluence of the Benue and Niger.

The hulks to be moored at these sites were to act as stores, pending the arrival of the regular steamers. They had the advantage of being very mobile, and more practical to defend if subjected to an attack. Long strings of cowrie shells were, at this time, the only currency on the upper reaches of the Niger, which contributed to accounting - and storage problems. The ever-resourceful Macgregor Laird overcame this problem by issuing his own small copper coin, to the value of one-eighth of a penny, but when Queen Victoria heard about it she was not amused, as its issue was held to be an infringement of the royal prerogative, and it had to be withdrawn.

The Liverpool supercargoes and the African middlemen were even less amused by the activities of Macgregor Laird! His attempts to deal directly with the people of the interior being seen as a direct threat to their livelihood, and they were, in the near future to combine in attempts to wreck his commercial ventures. Soon these forces were to have huge guns placed at strategic points on the river, and Laird steamers were frequently to come under heavy fire, and even be stopped and boarded. However, back in the spring of 1857, all these interesting developments lay in the future, when the Laird workers were putting the finishing touches to the *Dayspring*, whose figure head was that of a dove bearing the olive branch of peace!

Apart from trade and missionary considerations there still a great deal of general exploration work to complete. Nothing, perhaps, was more important to begin with than the sounding and accurate charting of the river channels and an examination of its course, to determine how far up-river light-draught ships, such as the *Dayspring, Sunbeam,* and *Rainbow* could safely go. It was on this information that the value of the Niger, as a trade route in to the interior, would be determined. The Royal Geographical Society were aware of this, and gave their considerable backing to the expedition. Clearly, the expedition would have to embrace the varied interests put forward. Lord Clarendon, at the Foreign Office, endorsed the joint proposals, and it was then that the machinery of official organisation began cumbrously to move.

Dr. Baike was made leader of the expedition, and to make the required survey of the river, Lieutenant John Glover, of the Royal Navy, was selected by the Admiralty, and seconded to the expedition - but, it should be noted, on half-pay! He had made a reputation for himself both in hydrography and gallantry at that time. He was the son of Frederick Glover, soldier, author of works on Egyptology, cleric and inventor. He was the grandson of Admiral Broughton. At the age of twelve he joined the *Queens*, as a first-class volunteer, he soon distinguished himself and, in 1850, he was serving on the West African coast in the *Penelope*, and was made a lieutenant in the following year. He then served in the Burmese war, on the *Rosamund* in the Baltic, and with the British Foreign Legion at Heligoland. He was later to be knighted, and become the Governor of Lagos. In the Ashanti Campaign of 1872-3 he raised the Haussa Force. The history of this war being written in the *Life of Sir John Hawley Glover.*

The other official members of the expedition were Surgeon Davis, seconded from H.M.S. *Hecla* then on the West Coast, for service as medical officer (presumably on half-pay!); Barter, as botanist, Dalton, zoologist, and D.J. May, who had been with Baikie on his previous venture up the Niger, and was to act as assistant to Glover in the survey work. Messrs Crowther and Taylor, African Missionaries, together with Baikie and Davis were to join the expedition at Fernando Po. To work the *Dayspring* out to Fernando Po there was a captain and a crew of ten. Captain Alexander Grant was selected to command the ship, and, when on the Niger, take charge of trading operations. Grant seems to have been an odd choice for this pioneering venture, which clearly required a man with some diplomatic skills, apart from the ability to trade. He had at one time served in the American Navy, which was a rough school, and afterwards had worked on the West Coast of Africa with a certain Captain Jackson, who was a notorious character, as Baikie subsequently reported. The second in command was John P. MacIntosh; George Berwick was the ship's doctor; Rees was the mate, Heward was the purser, there were two engineers, and four other ratings, seamen and supercargoes. A full crew of African Krumen were to be recruited when they reached the West Coast, for service up river.

The central plan was therefore to survey and chart the Niger, explore the region, make trade and anti-slavery treaties with the African Chiefs, extend missionary work, and generally further British interests. They were to follow the main stream of the Niger to Rabba, from whence Baikie and Crowther were to travel overland to Sokoto, the capital of the powerful Fulani Empire, and visit the great Fula Sultan, then thought to be the most powerful in all West Central Africa. To further good relations with the then Sultan of Sokoto, Alieu, Queen Victoria caused a letter to be written, explaining the reasons for the expedition and requesting the friendly attitude of the Sultan towards the members of it. This was accompanied by a firman from Constantinople obtained as a religious introduction. Apart from this diplomatic mission Glover also wanted, if possible, to push north, into what later became the

French Sudan. Destiny though had other plans in store for them.

The establishment of the Niger Mission by Crowther was the main objective required by the Church Missionary Society, and in this work he was to be helped by the Rev. J.C. Taylor, a son of slave parents of the Ibo tribe. Simon Jonas, who had been on the previous expedition was to go with them, with a few other catechists from Freetown. The intention was to station these people at Abo, Idda, the farm, and elsewhere. But Crowther's purview also extended to the great Moslem areas of the Sudan, Rabba, Bida, Kano, and Sokoto. No convert from Islam was available for this great Christian Crusade, so Crowther selected a liberated Yoruba slave, still a Moslem, who was a teacher of Arabic, and at the same time full of gratitude to both the British Government, and the Church Missionary Society for all they had done for him. Crowther shrewdly considered that such a man could do much to promote Christianity, *provided* they did not start their missionary work in areas under Mohammedan control by entering into heated disputes about the truth or falsehood of one religion or another; " but we should aim at toleration, to be permitted to teach their heathen subjects the religion we profess."

On 8 May, 1857, the *Dayspring* was at sea, and with wings outspread, and her figure-head clutching an Olive Branch, she sped gallantly on her way to Fernando Po, in the Bight of Benin. All went well until about 4 p.m. on Wednesday, 13 May, when there was a violent shock, followed by screams. On gaining the deck Glover found there was a large Prussian barque under the bows of the *Dayspring*. The barque passed on, having knocked away the bowsprit, jibboom, and, sadly, the beautiful Figure Head of the Dove with the Olive Branch. A sad omen perhaps, but all on board thanked God that the damage was no worse, and the carelessness of the crew of this ship, from Gastia in the Baltic, had not caused them to turn back. They arrived at Madeira on 23 May, when the circumstances of the accident were reported to the Consul, sailing from the island the following day.

On the 26 May the high Peak of Tenerife was in sight, and as there was no wind the engines were started, and they steamed past the island. In all it took them three full days to reach and pass this sub-tropical island, then, with the coming of a breeze, the fires were drawn, and they sailed on - leaving the towering peak behind, looking like a small blue-grey triangle, hanging mystically in mid-air, above a ring of snow-white clouds. Eventually it was lost from sight as night fell, and on a tranquil sea, beneath a sinking moon, the *Dayspring* glided on like a dream-ship towards the coast of Africa.

The mainland was soon reached, and on Friday 12 June, they anchored between Grande Sestos and Cape Palmas, where they engaged their crew for the river voyage. These transactions took three full days, the fathers of those who were to man the ship coming on board to negotiate the appropriate rates.

Top: The *"Dayspring"*
Bottom: Accommodation at the Court of Fundah

Their demands were higher than normal, this because they felt that the young men were not being engaged to load palm-oil, as usual, but were being taken to the "War Country." Those who were eventually engaged received 2 months' pay in advance, that is 2 pieces of cotton cloth, each piece containing 14 yards, and worth just five shillings! The affectionate fathers would keep the cloth for themselves, and as soon as the bargain was completed make sure that their sons were locked up below, until the canoes had gone, or the ship had sailed - otherwise the youngsters would jump overboard and be off. Once away they had no option other than to remain with the ship, for if they ran away whilst on the Niger the people there would promptly have made slaves of them!

On Saturday, 20 June, they sighted Cape Formosa, but because of light winds they could not overhaul it quickly. They sailed on, and on Monday 22, June, after a 47 day passage, they were at Clarence Cove, Fernando Po. Dr. Baikie came out to meet the ship, then Glover and the other officers went on shore to dine with the 'Spanish' Governor, the Dutchman, Lynslager. They were then introduced to the African Missionaries, the Rev. Crowther, and Dr. Taylor, who were to go up the Niger with them. The main ocean voyage had ended, as from the island they only had a short run over to the Brass River on the mainland. They were to spend a week ashore, dining with the Governor each day, and learning much about the island, the late Governor, Beecroft, and Lynslager himself.

These two remarkable men had both come to the island at about the same time, in 1829 - Beecroft then being the master of a sailing vessel, who had remained there until his death in 1854. He had become H.B.M.'s Consul and eventually Governor of the island under a Spanish Commission. At least old records gave him that title, but Glover suspected that his real position had been Agent for the Spanish Government.

Beecroft, they were told, had gone up the Niger in 1840, and done much to start legitimate trade in the Bight. It was during his time that the first palm-oil ship had started trading in Bonny, which until that time had only exported slaves. Beecroft had then concluded treaties with every slave export port in the Bight, and explored the Calabar River. Dedicated to duty, he had died a poor man - although in those days, 1830-1850, fortunes were made, without much trouble, in the slave, then the oil trade.

Lynslager, who succeeded him as the 'Spanish' Governor, was generally considered to be a Dutchman, but was thought by others to be English! What we do know for sure is that this remarkable man arrived at Fernando Po, when he was just 17 years old, as a poor sailor boy. For a time he made a living by mending and making sails, but then became a successful trader, prior to becoming British Consul, and Spanish Governor of the island. A truly remarkable rise! Spain did not actually pay him a salary for his services, but under a somewhat bizarre arrangement allowed him to take the import and export duties as a personal income! However, as he was the main trader on the island, he paid most of the dues himself, and was thus, in the main, collecting dues from himself, to put back into his own account! "Daddy" Jim Lynslager, as he was affectionately known, was a popular, but autocratic man. In 1858 he was superseded by a Spaniard as Governor, and it was then that the island became a dumping ground for political exiles from Cuba. Lynslager was to remain on the island until he died there in 1864.

After a pleasant week spent in Fernando Po the *Dayspring*, with the trading schooner *George*, started for the Niger, the two ships sailing out of Clarence Cove on the evening of 29 June. On Sunday 5 July they sighted Cape Formosa, and, after running along the land for about 5 miles eastward, anchored for the night outside the bar of the Rio Bento, known by the English traders as the Brass River. After breakfast the following day the *Dayspring* weighed, surmounted the heavy surf, and with a fair wind, and flowing tide, entered the Brass River mouth of the Niger. At the harbour they found five English ships loading palm oil, and noted much activity around the English Cask Houses on the otherwise deserted shore. The ships remained here until Wednesday 8th, giving John Glover time to survey the creek they were going to pass through into the main stream of the Niger, and also wait until the *George* could get across the bar and join them. He completed a chart to send back to Macgregor Laird, for the benefit of the vessel that he was due to send out to them in September; and tried hard to complete another one for Lord Clarendon, but ran out of time.

The *George* eventually managed to join them, and she was then lashed alongside the *Dayspring*. In the afternoon of 20 July they weighed and started to head up-river, entering a large lagoon just as it was getting dark. From here they had to pass through a narrow winding creek, about a mile in length, with just sufficient breadth to allow the two vessels to pass through, before finding a clear channel and broad water. Surrounding them on all sides were the vast Mangrove swamps, the trees with fantastic stems and roots, their branches and many creepers hanging down into the stream. Flying overheard were innumerable brightly coloured screeching parrots, whilst on the mud-flats long-legged cranes, and graceful white egrets attempted to fish, in spite of the disturbance created by the *Dayspring*.

The great Niger, as we now know, flows for 2,600 miles to this delta, which covers an area of coast line 270 miles long, and 120 in depth - 32,400 square miles in all; thus exceeding the total land area of Scotland by 2,604 square miles. Its two main mouths are considered to be the Nun and the Forcadas, but the Brass, Benin, Bonny, and Opobo streams all help to increase the area of swamp land. The sea fringe, where the slimy rooted mangroves thrive, covers a belt of land 30 miles in depth. Behind this, in the forest swamp, stretching back for 90 miles, there is a seasonal rise and fall on the river of no less than 45 feet. The entire swamp and forest area being a haven for thousands of crocodiles, mudfish, water-snakes, and millions of winged and crawling insects. Up the numerous creeks were villages peopled by Africans, living in miserable conditions, their houses being damp and waterlogged for nine months of the year.

It took the *Dayspring*, with the *George* lashed to her side, twelve long days to make her way through the Akassa creek, into the Nun branch of the Niger, and up the latter to the town of Abo, which stands above the fork in the river. Here they anchored , and in about two hours were honoured by a visit from Chief Aje, who was impressively dressed for the occasion in a scarlet coat and multi-coloured trousers, the whole surmounted by a Cardinal's hat. With him was his favourite wife, a young girl of about 16, who sat at his feet and fanned him, and when he spat over her, which he did rather frequently, she dutifully wiped the deck clean. He was one of the more important Chiefs on the Niger, but he had deteriorated into a greedy and rapacious ruffian. Not surprisingly, the Rev. Crowther found him stony ground for Christian seed, and therefore, although it had been his plan to leave Simon Jonas at Abo, to carry on the work he had begun in 1841 and 1845, he thought it wiser not to leave this poor Christian soldier to the tender mercies of Aje. However, they did manage to get some fresh supplies from the town, and the *Dayspring*, now burning wood for fuel, continued up-river, towards the confluence of the Benue and the Niger, where Lairdstown lay.

The *Dayspring* and the *George* reached the junction of the two great rivers in the middle of August, where they remained for three weeks. At Onitsha, on the eastern side of the Niger, the outlook for the Christian Missionaries seemed more promising. Baikie and Glover visited the Chief, Akazura, and he, and his councillors, gave their visitors a very cordial welcome, and readily gave them sites for a mission - and a trading station. Because of this reception Crowther founded the Niger Mission at this place. Dwellings were obtained, and Taylor was left, with Simon Jonas, and three young Christians from Sierra Leone, to get things started. Thus the famous Niger Mission was established and staffed entirely by Africans. After his first night ashore, Simon Jonas came running back to the *Dayspring* to inform Crowther that a human sacrifice was just about to be offered, the victim being a female slave, Crowther came ashore, denounced those responsible, and succeeded in saving her life. For one African at least, the Christians could not have arrived at a more propitious moment.

When they arrived at Lairdstown, near the confluence, the steamer anchored under a 300 foot high column, known as the Bird's Rock, and it was whilst they were here that the Europeans began to suffer from Malaria - despite the regular use of quinine. Glover, Baikie, Davis, the mate, and one of the engineers, going down with the fever.

However, as soon as Glover recovered he did a great deal of survey work among the hills behind what is now Lokoja. From Mount Patte he would have had a wonderful view of the two great rivers, winding in from north and east, to unite in one vast stream. Here he also established the site of the new mission and the trading station.

Baikie then had more troubles to contend with. May, the second master, refused to work with Glover, saying that the latter had usurped his place. Baikie eventually reporting him to the Foreign Office asking for his suspension. The African crews, recruited less than willingly on the West Coast, were now constantly hovering on the verge of mutiny. They complained bitterly about the behaviour of Captain Grant, and Berwick, the surgeon of the *Dayspring*. Baikie made this problem the subject of a further letter to the Foreign Office, in which he pointed out that the conduct of these two, towards the Africans, and the Government party on the ships, was unacceptable. The Foreign Office though was thousands of miles away, and the issues clearly required Baikie to take control of the situation, there and then, which he obviously failed to do. Fortunately, Captain Grant was under standing instructions to take the *George* up the Benue to trade, but Berwick was left on the *Dayspring,* and he continued to damage the unity of the expedition. MacIntosh was left in charge of the *Dayspring,* but he appears to have been taking his orders from Grant, not Baikie, the former leaving Mackintosh with instructions that were very prejudicial to maintaining good relations with the African Missionaries and crews.

On the 9 September the *Dayspring* reached the confluence of the Niger and Kaduna, and as this river seemed navigable, and appeared to lead towards the centre of the Fulani Empire, they decided to explore it. For a day the ship steamed cautiously up-river, until at sunset she reached the ruins of Gbara, the ancient capital of the great Nupe kingdom. Like many other places it had been destroyed by the Fulani. By chance, one of the interpreters on the ship recognised the place as the home he had been kidnapped from forty-five years before. He told those on the ship about the invasion, and the desolation it had caused, explaining first how prosperous the place had been until the Fulani attacked:-

"But then came the Fulani into the land. Our young men were sold into slavery. Our women were dragged to their camps. Nothing but grass was grown on the farms. The apes stole the last ears of maze. The looms fell to pieces. The towns were wasted with fire. Foreign thieves (i.e.the Fulani) built their nests in the farmsteads. The Fulbi slaughtered our beeves. They struck of the heads of our kings and set them on boards in the markets. Our smiths were only allowed to make handcuffs for the wrists of our fathers when they were driven away."

Baikie, Crowther, and their fellow travellers, must have listened to many such tales about the Fulanis, and for that reason, they were anxious to meet the great Fula King, Sumo Zaki, and his half-brother, Dasabo, in their stronghold at Bida. Baikie wanted to establish diplomatic relations with them, on behalf of the British Government, whilst Crowther felt that he required promises of security for his missions, from such powerful rulers. They sent messengers ahead to announce their approach, and with true Moslem courtesy the King sent horses for the use of his distinguished guests.

Baikie and Crowther arrived at Bida early in the morning, where they found a great number of Moslem warriors at prayer. In striking contrast to this scene of pious worship, Crowther then made for the market place, where he found a great number of slaves being offered for sale. As he arrived, a mother and child were being sold for the equivalent of about £7.00.

After a great deal of ceremony Baikie, representing the interests of Britain, and Crowther representing the interests of the Christian Religion, met with the powerful Moslem leader, who had been responsible for killing thousands, and devastating hundreds of square miles of country. Sumo Zaki received them with kindness and respect, declaring that he owed the favour of their visit to God's mercy. However, in dealing with such a man Crowther was well aware that the first step was to establish friendly feelings, and his policy of having with him a Moslem interpreter more than justified itself on this crucial occasion. The king and his chiefs were surprised that a Moslem had come to them in the company of Christians, and they questioned him closely about his experiences. Crowther then proved his worth as a skilled diplomat. Knowing that it would have been counter-productive to ask this great Moslem leader for permission to preach Christianity, he presented himself as a teacher, sent by Britain to instruct African people in the religion of Anasara (Jesus) and also establish trade relations. This line went down very well, the King agreed, and even offered to give them a site for a station at Rabba, a little higher up the Niger.

On the completion of their mission the *Dayspring* made her way back down the Kaduma, and continued up the Niger to Rabba. Here Dasaba, the King's half-brother, thought the concept of the mission was a huge joke, roared with laughter, and, with tears streaming down his face, rolled about on the floor, completely overcome with amusement. Kola nuts were then brought in, and eaten together, as a symbol of friendship, but Crowther felt suspicious and uneasy. He was well aware that a mere change of mood could lead to people being set against his Christians, by these ruthless Moslem leaders.

At the close of their visit, the party, including Baikie, Glover, Davis, Dalton, and Barter, rode back to Wuya and got on board the *Dayspring*. They then found that more people had gone down with fever, and another death had taken place. All members of the expedition had lost faith in Dr. Berwick, who, rightly or wrongly, was held responsible for the sad state of affairs. People were frightened and demoralised, and the engineer, who was sick, begged to be taken back down-river to the confluence. But on 6 October Baikie decided to go further up-river, to examine the rocks at Boussa, to see if a passage was possible, and then to return to the confluence, in about six weeks time, when they were due to meet the *Sunbeam*.

Whilst at Rabba Crowther had spoken to men who were able to throw light on the death of Mungo Park and his companions, fifty years before, when their small boat, the *Joliba*, had been wrecked among the rocks at Boussa. They steamed on, not realising that a similar fate awaited the *Dayspring*. Glover was still sick, although he continued to work on his charts for Lord Clarendon, but when they came near to the rocks the anchor was dropped, and he went ahead with a small party to examine the channel.

When Glover and his men arrived at the dangerous stretch of river they found they could make headway against the current, in their five-oared gig, and wrongly concluded from this that the *Dayspring*'s engines could face the current, strong as it was, between the two immense rocks. They reported back to Baikie, and the fateful decision was made. The steamer moved forward slowly, and then steered safely through the narrow channel beside Jebba Island; until they saw the great rocks looming, ominously, above them. The *Dayspring* soon found she was struggling hard to remain in a safe position in the stream when suddenly, a swirl of water hit her bow. She swung round rapidly, and crashed against a rock. The ship settled, then started to fill. According to Glover, the Captain was promptly sick, and the chief engineer went to look for his dog, whilst other members of the crew concentrated on trying to save their personal possessions. Thankfully though, Lieutenant John Hawley Glover R.N. was made of sterner stuff - " Somehow I found myself in possession of a naked sword, driving overboard the wretches that would save their rags instead of getting sails and provisions on shore!" He continued, "However, by dark three tents were pitched and most of the things on shore. That night we enjoyed the cooling pleasure of a tornado."

According to F.D. Walker, the people of the neighbourhood were quite convinced that the disaster had occurred because the great spirit that dwelt in the rock was taking revenge on the white men, who had dared to invade his dominions; and he was probably even more offended by the colour of the clothes they were wearing! But, unlike the *Joliba*, the doomed *Dayspring* was not surrounded by enemies. If the local spirit was offended, the local people were not. Dug-out canoes swiftly came out to the stricken vessel, and it was due to their help, to a considerable extent, rather than Glover's antics with his sword, that the whole ship's company, (wretches included!) managed to reach the bank in safety - together with a fair amount of equipment. These all-important facts being omitted from Glover's account of the tragic incident.

The survivors, twelve Europeans, and thirty-eight Africans, huddled on a sandbank all through that long night, lashed by the tornado. Weeks later, when the news reached Lagos, Consul Campbell, who was stationed there, wrote home, suggesting that the cause of the disaster in the strong current was that the ship had a screw, rather than two paddles, which, he believed would have kept her straight against the stream. This convenient theory seems to have been accepted back in London, and no blame whatsoever attached to Dr. Baikie, or the socially well-connected Lieutenant John Hawley Glover, for any error of judgement, in attempting such a hazardous passage. One wonders though, had the unpopular Captain Grant made the decision to take the *Dayspring* through this stretch of water, would a less forgiving version of events have entered the pages of history?

Stranded in the interior, they then had to make the best of things. Glover and Mr Barter, the naturalist, went on a three week cruise in a canoe, their objective being to reach the Rocks of Yauri, whilst Crowther concentrated on spreading the Gospel. With the permission of the Chiefs, he obtained a piece of land on which to build five traditional style conical huts to serve as a base for his mission. He then purchased a large canoe, which he fitted out with seats for six passengers, and began to sow the seeds of Christian truth in darkest Africa. Meanwhile, the other survivors were left with a variety of problems to deal with. After making themselves as comfortable as possible, by building thatched huts on the bank, sickness struck, many going down with fever. A few days later the engineers became unruly, and refused to obey orders. The Krumen came to the verge of mutiny, and were only quelled by Baikie, and others, taking a strong stand. It was felt that Berwick was the instigator of the trouble, so he, with an engineer and Fisher, were sent down stream in two canoes to Lairdstown, to await the coming of the relief ship *Sunbeam.* Mr. May, whose conduct had improved, was sent with Abdul Kadar to Abeokuta, by land, in order to facilitate the carrying of mail to the coast. Glover and Barter then set out to make their way up the Niger to chart and inspect the river, leaving Baikie, Davis and Dalton - all very sick men - with Mackintosh, an engineer, and Richard Heward, the purser, to recuperate.

After various adventures, which included close encounters with some elephants, and being shot at with arrows from a tree capped ridge, Glover, Barter, and their party, obtained some horses, and continued on their way until they entered the Kingdom of Boussa, on Tuesday 22 December, 1857. A messenger then went on ahead to announce their arrival to the King. They were well received by his Majesty, who, at first, treated them with respect, but later they were allocated a very dirty corner of a yard to sleep in. Glover

215

Machinery of the *"Dayspring"* salved, and erected as a memorial
at Lagos railway station.

would not accept this, stood his ground, and met with the King once more. Things were eventually smoothed over, and they were then given four of his best huts! Early in the morning breakfast arrived, which consisted of three dishes of fufu, six bowls of fresh milk, some yams, and a live bullock! Glover promptly had the bullock killed, and, as was the custom, sent part of it back to the King, and the chief men of the town. He also saved a portion of his ration, to serve as Christmas dinner - the following day. Meanwhile, back on the banks of the Niger, the rest of the party had been preparing to make the best of their Christmas Day.

Whilst Glover and Barter were away the main party had managed to establish excellent relations with the local people, and were soon engaged in lively bartering, trading what they had been able to save from the wreck for food and other items. When one of the Chiefs produced a couple of fowls, the ship's purser, Richard Heward, began to fatten them up for Christmas Day, and obtain other items for the feast. His detailed account of that memorable Christmas meal makes fascinating reading:-

"We turned our attention to dinner and I must say that the spread and manner of cooking would not have disgraced an English table' viz:- soup, roast haunch of mutton, boiled fowls, roast fowls, boiled tongue, yams, fried plantains, plum pudding, native beer and palm wine, and a small drop of brandy each from the medical stores - just to aid digestion. For desert we had ground nuts, and ripe plantains, and to the surprise of some I introduced two bottles of champagne. Our first toast was " A merry Christmas to each and all of us, followed by health, happiness and a merry Christmas to all at home: success to the Niger expedition."

Glover and his men eventually got back to the main party on 5 January, 1858, after being away fifty-two days, only to find they were still waiting for news of the relief ship, *Sunbeam*, which should have been out to them with a fresh supply of provisions and trade goods. Nothing had been heard of her and they began to doubt if she had been sent at all. There was no news either from the men who had been sent down to the confluence to meet her, and general demoralisation was starting to set in. However, their monotony was relieved one day, when, to the amazement of all, an American Baptist Missionary, the Rev. M. Clark arrived, having travelled overland from Abeokuta. He brought with him news of the Indian Mutiny, which had broken out at Meerut on 10 May, 1857, and, more importantly, was able to give the party some coffee, sugar, and tea, which was much appreciated. Although Crowther was also separated from his wife and family, albeit, not by as many miles as the Europeans in the party, he did not let the situation get him down. He never wasted a moment, seeing the delay merely as a splendid opportunity to study the Nupe language - and make a start on converting some of the local Moslems to the Christian faith.

At long last, in October, 1858, the somewhat overdue *Sunbeam* made her way up the Niger, the thankful survivors embarked and travelled down the great river - they were on the way home at last. Crowther though decided to leave the vessel when it reached Onitsha, in order to spend some time with Mr Taylor and his group. To his delight he found that they had already managed to win a small group of people over to Christianity. Crowther then started to preach in the market place, sometimes with as many as a thousand people listening to him. Amazingly, he then decided to continue his work by going back up the river in a small canoe. Inspired by the arrival of the American Missionary by the overland route, and the sending of his own messenger to Abeokuta, he then resolved to try the overland route for himself.

The exposure and worry of the long canoe journey back up-river to Rabba undermined Crowther's health, and he suffered from a severe attack of dysentery, but it was when he had completed some work, and was a little better, that he set out on the three hundred mile journey. He pushed steadily on through the Nupe Country, then through the forests of his Yoruba homeland, until he reached Abeokuta. To his surprise he found that the Bishop of Sierre Leone had just arrived, and with him Dr. Baikie, having just come up the Ogun from Lagos. Crowther himself promptly made his way to Lagos, to meet his wife and family whom he had left there two years ago.

Crowther did not remain in Lagos long, for he had taken the decision to spend the rest of his working life on the Niger. In the summer of 1859 he once more made his way up-river, this time on the *Rainbow*, another vessel sent out to trade by Macgregor Laird. He visited his workers at Onitsha, and intended to go on to Rabba, but a message from Dr. Baikie, who had gone overland from Abeokuta, advised him that it would not be safe to go there. Sumo Zaki had died, and Dasaba, the infamous Moslem slave-raider, who had laughed so uproariously at the idea of Christian Missionaries, had become King of Nupe. Quite understandably *he* had no use for Christian Missionaries! Unfortunately, this Laird organised voyage also ended in tragedy. As the *Rainbow* was passing through the dense Mangrove swamps of the Delta, shots rang out from the bank, and two of her crew were killed. This incident again delayed the establishment of a regular steamship service on the Niger, and the river was closed for two years. In August, 1862, Crowther was back, with a party of 33 African workers, but this time he was taken up by the gun-boat, H.M.S. *Investigator.*

At Gbede, at the mouth of the Tshadda, Crowther found that there were a company of people waiting to be baptised. One September morning, in the presence of two hundred people in the small mud chapel, he baptised eight adults and one child. Crowther then wrote: " Is not this an anticipation of the immense field opened to the Church to occupy for Christ?" At a more mundane level, with his new workers, he was now able to begin industrial

Samuel Crowther, Bishop of the Niger

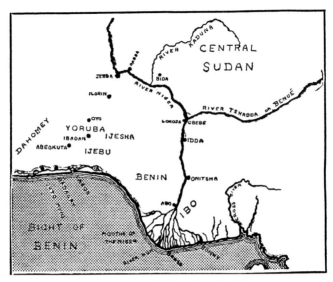

Sketch map showing Bishop Crowther's journeys

work for the purpose of preparing and packing cotton for export to England. It was at this time that the Church Missionary Society was facing a very profound issue with regards to the Niger Mission. There was only one Bishop in the whole of West Africa, the Bishop of Sierra Leone, nearly two thousand miles away. It was then that Henry Venn, Secretary for the West Africa Field of the C.M.S. put forward the solution. The Niger Mission had begun as a purely African enterprise - let it continue so under the guidance of an African Bishop - and Crowther was the obvious choice for this post. It was this decision that led to the already mentioned consecration of Crowther, as the Bishop of the Niger, in June, 1864.

The African Traveller, Dr. William Balfour Baikie was also to spend the rest of his life in Africa. A further expedition to the Niger was planned, involving Baikie, but for some reason the Government withdrew backing at the last moment, but at this point in time, Baikie, already on the Niger, had entered into binding arrangements with the African Chiefs, and therefore considered it prudent to await further orders before he quit his post:

"My supplies being limited," he wrote from Lokoja, September, 1861, "and my horses have all died, I was prevented from making any lengthened journey; but as I could not be idle, I tried to take advantage of a seeming favourable state of affairs, and accordingly made a settlement at this spot (Lokoja). The King of Nupe, the most powerful next to the Sultan of Sokoto, being desirous of seeing a market for European produce here, entered into relations with us, and undertook to open various roads for the passage of caravans, traders and canoes to this place, which promise has been faithfully performed: I, on my part, giving him to understand that it was the desire of Her Majesty's Government to have a trading station here. I have started a regular market here, and have established the recognition of Sunday as a non-trading day, and the exclusion of slaves from our market. Already, traders come to us from Kabbi, Kano, and other parts of Hausa; and we hope ere long, to see caravans with ivory and other produce. The step I am taking is not lightly adopted. After a prolonged absence from England, to stay another season here without any Europeans, with only a faint prospect of speedy communications, and after all my experience of hunger and difficulty last year, is by no means an inviting prospect. But what I look to is the securing for England of a commanding position in Central Africa, and the necessity of making a commencement."

These powerful representations had the desired effect on the British Government, and support for Dr, Baikie's venture was assured. Within the next few years he was to be among those who opened up the navigation of the Niger. He supervised the construction of roads, and apart from work in developing trade, collected vocabularies of numerous African dialects, and translated parts of the Bible and Book of Common Prayer into Hausa. In October, 1863 he expressed a wish to return home to see his aged father whom he had not seen for seven years. The Foreign Office relieved him, and Baikie made his way to Lagos, on the first leg of his long journey home. Here

Eleanor Bristow Laird (left) and Anne Thomson Laird, daughters of Macgregor Laird

221

he fell sick, and on the 12 December, 1864, he died, aged 39. Like so many early African Travellers, his health had been undermined, by climate, and lack of resistance to local ills. William Balfour Baikie had been born at Kirkwall, Orkney, in August, 1825, being the eldest son of Captain John Baikie, R.N. A monument to his memory was later erected in the Cathedral of St. Magnus, Kirkwall, by the proud people of this isolated northern island.

Meanwhile, back in England, Macgregor Laird was shocked when he heard that his vessels were under attack, and wasted no time in calling for Government protection for his fleet. His request was granted, but due to a misunderstanding no escort vessel was made available until 1861. For the next decade an armed escort vessel was sent up the river, at least once a year, to protect the growing trade. Unfortunately though, Macgregor's health was now deteriorating rapidly. In March, 1860, Nell received a particularly sad letter from him, describing how ill he felt, and dwelling upon his anxieties about the Niger business. It was about this time that the family decided to leave Brighton, and move nearer to London, as this would avoid the stress of long-distance commuting by Macgregor. After much suffering he lost the hearing in one ear, and it was soon after this that the Rev. Henry Venn, the Church Missionary Society Secretary, responsible for the West African field, came down to see him. His daughter, Eleanor Bristow, later recording that it was partly a visit of friendship and partly of business connected with the Niger steamers; for Macgregor had always given free passages to any of the Church Missionary Society's Agents who wanted to pass up and down the river. Eleanor then wrote: " I remember feeling startled by something in Mr Venn's manner when he was going away; he had prayed beside my father's bed and was evidently much concerned about his continued illness."

By Christmas, 1860, Macgregor Laird was terminally ill. His friend Hudson suggested that a visit to Switzerland might help. Macgregor laughed and said he feared he would never get there now! On the 26 January there was a hard frost, and the ground was deep in snow, sparkling in the moonlight. His children, Eleanor, Edward, and Minnie, not appreciating just how sick he was, went to a dance at a relatives home. When they returned late at night they found he was much worse. His wife, Ellen, was standing by the fire, and his eldest daughter, Eleanor, was by the bedside. He reached up, kissed Eleanor, then lost consciousness. He breathed his last at noon on 27 January, 1861.

At the time of his death he was registered as a merchant, trading from offices at 3 Mincing Lane, London - his home address being 1 Surbiton Crescent, Surrey. He left a modest fortune of £25,000 - £10,700 less than the sum he had invested in the Birkenhead Dock Scheme in 1845! Macgregor Laird was buried at Nunhead Cemetery, with his eldest son.

The death of Macgregor Laird in 1861 had an immediate impact on trading operations on the Niger. His Executors, on winding up his estate, found that the accounts showed all was in order, but took the decision to close the various trading factories he had established on the river. This decision was no doubt prompted by the fact that there was a growing hostility throughout the Niger Country to the new style of trader that Macgregor Laird had been responsible for introducing; and this opposition was being orchestrated by the African Middlemen, and the Liverpool supercargoes, working together in an unholy alliance. Laird's trading posts had been attacked and destroyed. However, despite these problems with trade on the Niger, trade between the West Coast and Britain was increasing rapidly, and this justified some investment. The directors of the A.S.C. commissioned a new ship, which they named the *Macgregor Laird* and she came into service in 1862. The vessel was to be employed on the West Africa service until the 15 December, 1871, when she was totally wrecked on a rock in Corisco Bay, whilst rounding the land to the southward of Cape St. John to enter Elonby.

However, from 1862 to 1870 was a period of ever-increasing trade, and the ships of the African Steamship Company lacked the capacity to bring home all the goods that were being placed on the market. The Liverpool agents, who were paid on a tonnage commission basis, kept pushing the directors to provide more ships - as they had everything to gain, and nothing to lose by such an arrangement. On the other hand, the directors who had to provide the capital were not so keen to increase the size of the fleet, at least not rapidly, their reluctance being based on the general uncertainties of business in West Africa. Nevertheless, from a situation in 1862, when they had been operating a fleet of five ships, grossing just over 4,000 tons, they did increase the fleet steadily, until by 1870 they had seven ships, grossing more than 8,000 tons. A significant increase in capacity, but it was still not enough to cope with the trade.

The over-cautious policy of the African Steamship Company directors left an opening in the market, which led to the establishment of a rival company. This being the British & African Steam Navigation Company. The men behind this venture being a group of Glasgow businessmen, who then asked John Dempster to act as their agent in Liverpool. As he was an ex-employee of the Liverpool Agents for the African Steamship Company, this was a bitter pill to swallow for those concerned. Within decades this new agency was to develop into one of the greatest commercial enterprises in the world, and, among other things, eventually own the largest fleet of merchant steamships in Great Britain. Macgreor Laird had laid the foundations for this enterprise, but it was left to others to build on it.

The Rev. Henry Venn

CHAPTER ELEVEN ELDER DEMPSTER & COMPANY – AND THE LAIRD CENTENARY CELEBRATIONS, 1932

John Dempster was appointed Liverpool agent for the British & African Steam Navigation Company at the close of 1868. He soon felt he needed a reliable partner, and remembered his old colleague, Alexander Elder; who had been superintendent at the A.S.C. agency at Liverpool, but was then working for the Board of Trade. Elder accepted the offer, resigned from his public service position, and the firm of Elder Dempster & Company was born. The African Steamship Company's Liverpool agents had at first been Messrs William & Henry Laird - Macgregor Laird's younger brothers, which became Laird & Fletcher, and finally Fletcher & Parr. It was to the staff of the latter combination that the two young Scotsmen, Elder and Dempster, had brought their considerable business talents.

Alexander Elder was a substantial young man, no mere clerk, for his brother owned a shipyard at Fairfield, Glasgow, which later became the famous Fairfield Shipbuilding & Engineering Company - all of which explains why the firm became Elder Dempster, rather than Dempster & Elder! Elder's yard then produced three 1,300 gross ton vessels for the British & African Steam Navigation Company, to establish a monthly service between Britain and the West Coast. These ships were the *Bonny, Roquelle* and *Congo*. The plan was to serve Glasgow, Liverpool, and London, in the United Kingdom, and call at various ports on the West Coast. The first ship to come into service was the *Bonny*, the maiden voyage of this vessel taking place from Liverpool in January, 1869. The voyage was a success, as were the subsequent voyages of her sister ships. Business was booming, so the company ordered three more ships from Elder's yard, these being larger vessels, the *Liberia, Loanda,* and *Volta.*

The arrival of this new company on the scene immediately prompted a policy of price-cutting by the African Steam Navigation Company, and induced the directors to increase their fleet - in spite of the reduction in revenue that dropping their fares and freight rates had caused. Profits slumped. Something had to be done to correct this situation, and it would seem the directors of the rival company, also suffering by the policy of offering unrealistic rates, had come to the same conclusion. They agreed to meet, and they resolved the issue by agreeing to share sailings. This, at first uneasy truce, enabled the firms to build up their fleets, but more trouble lay in store for the African Steamship Company. In 1872 the directors discovered that the Company Secretary, Mr Duncan Campbell, had embezzled about £20,000! This disaster was followed by another, the loss of the mail contract. To survive they would clearly have to get rid of their old uneconomic vessels, and invest in better ones, which policy decision was soon acted on. On the plus side there now seemed to be a more harmonious relationship between Fletcher and Parr, and the British and African Company, for in 1873 a new agreement was concluded, by which each company would send a ship out each alternate week. They had come to the conclusion that they had better work together, prosper, and be in a financial position to keep out other competitors, rather than cut each others throats. Two years later, in 1875, the African Steamship Company directors asked their Liverpool agents to take a reduction in their rate of commission, which did not go down too well, relationships deteriorated, and the end result of all this was that the African Steamship Company directors held a meeting in London, in 1875, and advised Fletcher and Parr that they intended to open their own office in Liverpool. This move resulted in a greatly reduced work-load for the agency - and far less scope for a very able and ambitious young Welshman, then working in their office - Alfred Lewis Jones, later to be Sir Alfred Jones - the man who is said to have placed the banana on the British dining table.

Unlike Elder, Jones was not born with the proverbial 'silver spoon' in his mouth, he was the son of a poor man, and started with few material advantages - but he did have an exceptionally sharp mind. Born in Carmarthen in 1845, his father, Daniel Jones, was a currier by trade. Although the area had some industries Daniel considered his prospects would be better if he moved to Liverpool, and when Alfred was still very young he took his family to this bustling northern port. Alfred remained at school until he was fourteen years old, and obtained only a very poor education. With little influence, money, or education, Alfred Jones then had to decide how to survive. Like so many Liverpool youngster in the 1850's he frequented the docks, watched the clippers and steamers, and wondered what life at sea would be like. He had few prospects ashore, so he eventually decided to try and obtain a berth as a cabin boy. Finally, he managed to persuade the Captain of one of the African Steamship Company's ships to engage him, and he made one round voyage to the West Coast. Alfred and the Captain got on very well together, the latter being so impressed with the young lad that when they got back to Liverpool he persuaded Fletcher and Parr to engage Jones as a junior clerk. Mr Parr found he worked hard, took a liking to him, and consequently Jones was invited to spend much time at Parr's home, which had the effect of increasing his social skills. More importantly though, Parr encouraged him in his work, and then paid for him to attend evening classes at the Liverpool College, Shaw Street.

Jones soon rose to occupy a senior position in the firm, and was with the agency when Elder and Dempster started to operate as agents for the rival company. He then played a leading role in bringing the two firms together. When the agency lost the African Steamship Company business he was immediately aware that his own opportunities to rise would be strictly limited. Three of his former office colleagues had now struck out on their own, and done well, these being John Dempster, Alexander Elder, and John Holt - who had just laid the foundations of another shipping and trading enterprise in West Africa. Jones decided he was not going to be left behind, and promptly set himself up in business, chartered some small sailing vessels, and began to send out goods to West Africa. He did well, got more ambitious, and eventually decided to charter a steamer. Elder and Dempster watched this development with concern, for although Jones was only operating in a small way, they were well aware that he was capable - and managing his business efficiently. Fearing potential competition they offered him a junior partnership in their own company. Jones accepted the offer, and on 1 October, 1879, he became a junior partner with Elder Dempster & Company. The firm was then controlling twenty-one ships, of which the largest was 2,000 tons. The two senior partners were only to remain with the firm for another six years, both deciding to opt for early retirement in 1884, leaving control of the rapidly growing enterprise to the ex-cabin boy - Alfred Lewis Jones. A genuine rags-to-riches story!

Neither Elder or Dempster seem to have suffered unduly by this development, for the former later moved to Albert Road, Southport, where he died, aged 81, on 25 January, 1915, leaving a fortune of £309.000, whilst John Dempster bought a substantial house - *Tynron* - at Noctorum, on the Wirral, where he died, aged 78, on 19 July, 1914. Sir Alfred Jones - as he became - remained a bachelor, living at his beautiful home, *Oaklands*, Grassendale, Liverpool. The strain of remaining in office appears to have taken its toll, for he died long before his retired partners, in 1909, when he was just 64 years old.

When Elder and Dempster retired in 1884 the African Steamship Company had its head office in London, whilst the British and African Steam Navigation Company was controlled from Glasgow. Through a series of complex deals, which appear to indicate that Jones bought up many African Steamship Company shares, the firm was persuaded to close its Liverpool office in 1890, and appoint Elder Dempster and Company as its managing agents. Ships were then sold back to the African Steamship Company, under a capital re-structuring move. Jones now dominated the European West Africa trade, and to further strengthen his position he entered into a 'conference' (monopoly) arrangement with his sole remaining continental rival. The African Steamship Company, established by Macgregor Laird, retained its separate identity, under Elder Dempster Management, until 1932.

The History of the British and African Steam Navigation Company ran from 1868 - 1883, when it became a limited company, remaining in existence - under Elder Dempster Management, until 1932.

Jones was a man who had a colossal reserve of energy. In 1900 he was described by the Liverpool press as a 'Shipping Napoleon' who presided over the destinies of Africa House, Liverpool. At this point in time Elder Dempster & Company where managing five shipping enterprises, and would soon control many more. From this powerful position Jones was now in a position to influence the destinies of millions of people - notably in Africa, but also throughout the world. A measure of the wealth and power of the company, at the turn of the century, can be measured by an event without parallel in shipping history. In <u>one day</u> in 1900 three huge vessels were launched for the company, these being the *Montreal,* of 16,000 tons displacement; the *Delta,* a West African river boat, and the *Lake Champlain,* fitted for the Canadian trade.

At the turn of the century the company were managing 95 vessels, with a gross tonnage of over 300,000 tons. These lines were the British & African Steam Navigation Company Limited, (25 vessels), the African Steamship Company (33 vessels), the Cie Belge Maritime du Congo (4 vessels), Elder Dempster Shipping Limited (16 vessels), Elder Dempster & Company (10 vessels), and the Beaver Line (7 Vessels). Most of these steamers were connected with the West Africa trade, but Jones was then busy developing the Canadian trade, and with much success.

Almost half a century earlier the Macgregor Laird exploration vessel *Dayspring* had taken three days to cruise slowly past the snow capped peak of Teneriffe, hanging mystically in mid-air, above a ring of snow white clouds. It is certain that no one on board that vessel at the time could have appreciated the significance of their voyage, in the long and fascinating history of Teneriffe, and indeed all the Canary Islands.

Macgregor Laird's successor, the energetic Alfred Jones, had now turned his attention to the development of these islands, which lay directly on the route to West Africa. When he first visited the islands they were in a poor state economically, but he soon developed an enormous fruit industry there, paying particular attention to the introduction of the banana. He then promoted the islands as a holiday resort, his firm buying the great Metropole Hotel at Las Palmas, to give them a direct interest in this development. The Company then started issuing special holiday tickets, which included first-class passage, out and home, and a fortnight's board and accommodation at their hotel on Grand Canary, for £15.00. Passengers were also offered the option of returning via Barcelona or Genoa, by the steamers of "La Veloce Navigazione Italiana a Vapore" (The Italian Express Steam Navigation Company.) Jones owned his own coal mine in Glamorgan, which not only

228

Sir Alfred Jones, K.C.M.G.

supplied his ships, but also the Grand Canary Coaling Company, which controlled coaling stations at Las Palmas and Teneriffe, where nearly all the government vessels, and other ships, took on coal - and at rates that were not calculated to impoverish Alfred Lewis Jones!

At this time he also established a fleet of fast steamers of the "Jebba" type, which could reach Sekondi, then the centre of a new gold mining industry, in 15 days. They were specially constructed for the trade, and no expenses had been spared to make them comfortable for the passengers. The saloons were spacious, the staterooms lofty and well ventilated, while extensive promenade and bridge decks enabled the passengers to enjoy the sea breezes. A far cry indeed, since the time, 50 years previously, when Sir Richard Burton had made his epic voyage to the West Coast, on the hard boards of an early African Steamship Company vessel - with the prospect of sleeping 5 to a bunk!

About the man himself, Jones, in appearance, was described as "thick-set, smooth-featured, well-complexioned, iron-grey, and clean shaven, save for a small moustache. His expression was serious and kindly, his manner smart." He was also a very approachable man, and one that was, perhaps above all other things, dedicated to promoting bananas! The reporter for the Liverpool Review stating:- " Call at him in his office, and he will offer you a seat with the grace of a Talleyrand. Indeed, he will do more, he will give you the finest banana you ever tasted, and you will straightway fall to blessing the business that makes that splendid fruit so cheap. "Have a banana," he will say - the finest fruit in the world!" It is therefore not surprising that he then went on to develop the West Indies fruit trade in a similar manner.

Alfred Lewis Jones, the former cabin-boy, was now very much a part of the British Imperial establishment, and heavily involved in the affairs of Empire. In 1899 the Boer War had begun, and in one week in December, there were three British reverses - at Stormberg. Magersfonteign, and Colenso. Lord Roberts, with Lord Kitchener as his Chief of Staff, now took command. Troops were needed urgently at the Cape, and the Government came to Alfred Lewis Jones for assistance. Twenty of the firms ships were chartered by the Government as transports, for conveying troops to the conflict, with Alfred Jones being given the sole responsibility for conveying Strathcona's Horse from Canada to the Cape. Soon the Elder Dempster ships *Milwaukee* and *Lake Eyrie* were each taking 500 prisoners to St. Helena. Before May 1900, the *Monfort* was on its third voyage to the Cape with troops, and the *Monteagle* on its second.

Jones also held shares in hotels in Jamaica, and was a founder member of the Bank of West Africa. He owned barges and river craft on the West Coast, and at Liverpool he was operating engineering shops, and had controlling interests in portering, insurance, and ship's chandlery firms. He was also heavily involved in public works, his most notable and lasting contribution in this sphere being to give major support to the founding of the Liverpool School of Tropical Medicine, for which he was knighted. In the main though, the development of his business empire is what he lived for. His motto was: Work; his favourite maxim being - " A merchant that gains not, loseth." An interesting instance of Jones' business acumen was given by Sir Clement Jones, in his book Pioneer Shipowners:

"Once, during a shipping depression..... he saw and seized the opportunity of buying new ships cheaply, as orders were badly wanted by the large shipbuilding firms. In this way he became possessed of what in itself constituted a small fleet bought at the bottom of the market. His friends and rivals freely prophesied that he had overreached; that the shipping depression would last a long time; that he would be ruined. By the time, however, that the new ships were ready for delivery, the clouds of that particular depression rolled away, and the ships arrived in time to make money."

In 1901 the firm introduced a new class of steamer, with which to develop the aforementioned West Indies Fruit Trade. This service operated between Bristol and Jamaica, and Jones then employed his well-known publicity methods to advertise the Jamaican banana. The new service also carried the mails, for which the company received a subsidy of £40,000 per annum from the Government. Jones then floated a further company, this being Elders and Fyffes, Ltd., to handle this trade, which later became Fyffes, with its own fleet of banana ships, but with no continuing link with Elder Dempster & Company.

Other carefully considered business moves by Alfred Lewis Jones are worth noting. Firstly, he managed to secure a major share holding in the British and African Steam Navigation Company, after it was reorganised in 1900. Three years later he sold his Canadian fleet for £1,500,000. With some of this capital he steadily bought up the shares of the African Steamship Company, so that by 1909, the year of his death, he held 78% of the shares. On his death the Elder Dempster Fleets were acquired by Lord Kylsant, and a new limited liability company formed - Elder Dempster and Company Limited, but the respective fleets retained their identities. It was also at this point in time that Lever Brothers made an initial attempt to ship oil directly from the coast, by purchasing the firm of W.B. MacIver, who had some experience of chartering in this area. Levers then opened mills in Africa, but neither ventures met with success, and they were closed in 1914. After the war though the ending of the existing Conference allowed Lever Brothers to establish themselves on the coast once more. The combined Elder Dempster fleets consisted of 101 steamers when the 1914 war with Germany broke out. Of these 43 were lost during the war, the company ships being marked out for special attention by the enemy because their cargo of vegetable oils could be used in the manufacture of high explosives. 25 of the 43 losses occurred in 1917, when the U-boat war was at its peak. One instance of the service performed by Elder Dempster ships during this war should be noted.

The Mail Steamer *Ebani*, 4,862 gross tons, served as a hospital ship, during which time she steamed almost 200,000 miles and carried 50,000 sick and wounded men - and survived the conflict. At the end of the war the company were faced with the monumental task of building up the fleet again. Contact was made with the Clydeside yard of Barclay, Curle & Company, and it was established that they had a part-completed vessel on offer. She had not been designed for the West Africa trade, as she was being built in response to an order placed during the war by the Tsarist government of Russia, but before she was completed the revolution had taken place. However, before the close of 1918 work on this twin-screw motor ship of 7,937 gross tons was completed, she was bought, named the *Aba*, and thus became the first post-war addition to one of the Elder Dempster fleets. From this point on the fleets were soon built up again.

Lord Kylsant now had control of the organisation, and a 'Conference' was set up. Vessels under this arrangement managed to carry most of the raw materials required by Lever Brothers, until 1929, at which point Levers' purchased a rival company on the West Coast - the African and Eastern Trade Corporation, which evolved into the United Africa Company. They soon started to carry their own goods. This was a blow to the company, but worse was to come. The trade depression of the twenties set in, and it was found that the ships purchased during the immediate post-war years were heavily overvalued. This factor brought about the collapse of the Royal Mail group, in which Lord Kylsant had a large interest. The situation dictated that in 1932 his commercial empire had to be split up, during which development Elder Dempster Lines Limited was set up with a capital of £2,500,000. A head office was established at Liverpool, and the new company then took over most of the ships belonging to the old fleets. They then had to choose a house-flag. After due consideration they elected to use the flag of the old African Steamship Company - first used by Macgregor Laird, in 1852, which featured the Crown, that was permitted under this firm's original Royal Charter. The following year, 1933, all the former African Steamship Company vessels were re-registered at Liverpool. Three years later the Ocean Steamship Company Limited, (Alfred Holt & Company) became the managers of Elder Dempster Lines; but it clearly goes beyond the scope of this work to deal with the subsequent history of this vast enterprise.

The decision to use the old house flag of the African Steamship Company for the newly restructured Elder Dempster fleet was prompted by an article that was written in the Elder Dempster Magazine of June, 1927, about

Macgregor Laird - the founder of the original company, upon which all subsequent developments rested. It also prompted others to take action, and on 27 January, 1932, exactly 70 years after the death of Macgregor Laird, the following letter appeared in The Times:-

" To the Editor of The Times,

Sir, - The Royal Geographical Society and others interested in Africa - especially in its economic development - feel that the approaching centenary of the date on which the first expedition for the opening up of the interior, to legitimate trade, set out from Liverpool forms a fitting occasion to commemorate the efforts of its promoter, Macgregor Laird. They hope and believe that the coming year will bring a revival of the wonderful prosperity which has followed Laird's early initiative, and it is proposed to celebrate the anniversary on July 19th. On that day in the year 1832, two steamers, one of them the first iron vessel to make a sea voyage, left Liverpool and conveyed an expedition up the Niger to open up trade with the interior, and Laird was convinced that by this means only could an end be put to the slave trade. Only nine of forty-eight survived, and Laird's own health was shattered, but he remained undaunted and fitted out a second expedition two years later - this time without loss of life. This success induced the Government of the day to make contracts for annual voyages up the Niger.

"It is," said Sir Roderick Murchison, President of the Royal Geographical Society in 1861, " due to the memory of Mr Laird that he persevered in these undertakings with little or no prospect of personal advantage. Incidentally, he built the first vessel - the *Sirius* - to make the steam voyage across the Atlantic."

We have been asked by the organising committee to solicit your assistance by giving publicity to this proposal, with which the Royal Geographical Society is associated. Any communication may be addressed to Mr H.S. Goldsmith, C.M.G., "Batchelors" Ocham, Ripley, Surrey.

Yours faithfully,

W.E. Goodenough, President, R.G.S.

Lord Lugard

Lord Scarborough

Lord Selbourne "

The "West Africa Week" - arranged in honour of Macgregor Laird, took place, as planned, in Liverpool and London. At Liverpool the celebrations began at 3 p.m. on Sunday, 17 July, when a special service of commemoration was held in Liverpool Cathedral. Among those present at a special dinner in the evening, given by the Dean of Liverpool and associates of the Cathedral, to merchants and others interested in the development of Africa, were Lord Olivier, Sir John Maxwell, Sir F. Baddeley Sir Edward Sanders, Sir Ransford Slater, the Rev. J. McKay (formerly Archdeacon of

R.M.S. *Jebba* – African Steamship Company

Yoruba), Professor P.M. Roxby, and Mr R.D. Holt. The Bishop of Liverpool presided. At the dinner - attended mainly by capitalists - Lord Olivier made a notable speech - in which he warned of the dangers of too much capitalist involvement in Africa, which, no doubt, embarrassed some present!

"his 50 years experience of the Colonies of West Africa and the West Indies convinced him that we should never get a satisfactory solution of the problems raised by our contact with the native races if we gave way in West Africa to the demand for large concessions to capitalist interests and for any form of forced labour from the natives. Jamaica, the largest and most prosperous of British West Indian Colonies, had succeeded notwithstanding its heritage of slavery, because it now had 170,000 peasant proprietors side by side with large estates of European ownership. The Black people were therefore able to maintain themselves on their own land and work afterwards for the white man for wages if it pleased them to do so. In West Africa successive British Governments had constantly and successfully resisted the very tempting policy of economic development through large capitalist enterprises or through concessions of land."

With alarm bells ringing, Sir William Hinbury then stated that he doubted Lord Olivier's plea for the refusal of all concessions to traders and companies. He thought a moderate line on that question the better because the scientific capitalist development of some estates could teach the natives a great deal about the possibilities open to him and give him good models. Notwithstanding the fact that Olivier had clearly *not* called for the refusal of *all* concessions to traders, Sir Edgar Sanders then rose to defend the late Lord Leverhulme's work in opening up a section of the Belgian Congo industrially and said that he entirely disagreed with Lord Olivier on the concessions question. The Rev. J. McKay, for years a missionary in West Africa closed this interesting, and controversial symposium, with a warning of the dangers of destroying the black man's paganism without putting anything in its place! A generous, humble and far-sighted observation for a Christian Missionary to openly advance. A further commemorative service was held in Liverpool Cathedral on the morning of Monday, 18 July.

Several members of Macgregor Laird's family then attended the very grand London celebrations. There was a whole day affair on Tuesday 19th., beginning with a service in the morning at St. John's Westminster, followed by a garden-party in the afternoon at Lowther Lodge, the headquarters of the Royal Geographical Society, and in the evening there was a dinner at the Savoy Hotel. The later event being attended by the Prince of Wales and Mr Winston Churchill. The Prince of Wales, on rising to propose the toast "West Africa" was loudly cheered. He said:-

" It is a great pleasure to be present on the occasion of your centenary dinner to the memory of Macgregor Laird. It is certainly an historic anniversary in the history of the West Coast, for Laird's courageous expedition to the mouth of the river Niger marks a definite step in the real development of West Africa. He was not, of course, the first in the field, but he realised, perhaps better than anyone before, the possibilities of opening up the Niger delta to trade, and he was convinced that the establishment of legitimate commerce with the interior was the best, and indeed the only means of counteracting and eventually abolishing the slave trade......."

The Prince concluded his long speech by stating that it was his hope that the year 1932, which marked the centenary of Macgregor Laird's expedition to the Niger, would witness the beginning of a return to happier and more prosperous times, and see a great revival of world trade, in which Nigeria and her sister colonies would play an ever-increasing part. He then gave the toast of "West Africa."

Winston Churchill responded, saying that they were celebrating the epic of our West African Empire - "one might almost call it an empire with four great states. Britain's conquests there were not made over hostile armies of men. West Africa was defended by an insect!" ...... After praising British rule, and research that had conquered the mosquito, making life possible for the white man in Africa, he advanced the view that we now surveyed in West Africa vast and prosperous territories, where – the condition of the people was much better than it had ever been. He then went on to praise the Scotsman, Macgregor Laird, and all the other pioneers - and managed to amuse those present by saying that a West African dinner, in honour of Macgregor Laird, was a place where England should only be alluded to! Churchill then made it clear that he was also critical of the views advanced by the radical Lord Olivier:-

"Neither do I hold with Lord Olivier, that all private capitalist enterprise should necessarily be excluded from the Nigerias. I think cases should be judged on their merits, and that a competent and incorruptible Civil Service will not find it impossible to weave the powerful impetus of private capitalist enterprise into the life and development of the territories they administer."

During the evening a short message of loyalty was sent to the King, and Winston Churchill read the following message of support which was received in reply:-

"I sincerely thank you for the loyal message sent to me on behalf of those assembled at the West Africa Dinner. I am glad to learn that my son is taking part in these celebrations to do honour to the memory of Macgregor Laird, who did so much for the cause of freedom and commerce.

George R.I. "

Laird, Livingstone, Buxton, and indeed many Victorians had called for

Africa to be 'redeemed' by the "Three C's" - Commerce Christianity and Civilisation, and they wanted to see legitimate trade develop, to the mutual advantage of Africans and Europeans, replacing the horrors of the slave trade. Slavery was indeed defeated, but political and economic domination of Africa marched hand in hand with 'Legitimate Trade' - replacing one evil with another, a situation from which Africa has not yet recovered.

Before the days of Clapperton, Lander, Laird and Baikie, Africa was barely explored by European travellers, and even as late as 1880 most of the continent was still ruled by Africans At the close of the 19th century all of this had changed, five European Powers, and the over-ambitious king of Belgium - had annexed almost the whole continent, in what became known as the "Scramble for Africa" - but only a hint of this emerges from the speeches made at the 1932 Laird Celebrations. But those that led cannot be blamed for *all* the sins of those who followed, and in this context the words of Macgregor Laird, revealing his *own* sincere attitude to Africans should be noted:-

"I owe my life to the kindness and forbearance of the (African) race, so that I am constrained on every occasion, before any tribunal, to advocate their cause, if an opportunity offer of advancing their interests. Better, far better, for me to have left my bones to bleach on the banks of the Niger, than to have returned and shrunk from doing my duty to those poor people, because it might displease this or that party, or offend that or the other individual." - *(Letter of Macgregor Laird to the chairman of the 1842 expedition inquiry)*

In the special edition of the   "West Africa Review" of 23 July, 1932, produced to mark the occasion of the Macgregor Laird Centenary celebrations, there appeared a long article written by an African, Kobina Sekyl, who considered it would be worth the while of all who lived in Africa to read, and read again, Mr Leonard Woolf's "Empire and Commerce in Africa" - He then quoted from the last chapter of this work:-

" ...Only the sun, malaria, and sleeping sickness have saved and will continue to save the African from extermination at the hands of the white man.....

....The African will never obtain peace, prosperity, and progress until the European ceases to regard Africa as a place in which he may earn dividends, sell his cotton and his gin, obtain lead, rubber and metals, and buy cheap labour. The reader must answer for himself the question whether this change in the psychology of the European would require a greater change in human nature than that which appears to have converted a peculiarly savage variety of ape into a Plato, a Shakespeare and a Christ."

So far as the African Bishop Crowther is concerned, no one can doubt his sincerely, or that of the many other Christians who worked with him - even if they were, in one sense, used as tools of Empire. On the other hand Crowther also had the courage to stand up against the worst aspects of "civilisation" - and without much assistance from European missionaries. However, the

Niger mission was later strengthened by the arrival of some white men in 1890. Prominent among them came two from West Hartlepool, the vicar of St. James and his curate, the Rev. F.N. Eden, and the Rev. H.H. Dobinson, who soon joined with others to convert the 'Godless' Africans to the Christian religion.

History though has a habit of running full circle, a view which is endorsed by an article that appeared in "The Times" of 21 August, 1994. From this we learn that several hundred Missionaries are now working in Britain, a country they see as Godless and amoral! In a reversal of events a century ago, when Victorian Missionaries, such as Crowther, helped to build the empire, churches in Africa, are now asking missionaries to volunteer for service in Britain, to reverse Britain's religious decline. No doubt, much of what they have to say will fall on stony ground, as it is clear they face a harder task than Crowther did, working on the Niger in the 1860's. A Bishop, now retired from service in India, made the point that there are now more Anglicans in Nigeria than in Europe and North America! One African Missionary heading this way being a young Methodist - the Rev. Stephen Abakah, who had this to say:- "We in Africa are grateful to British Missionaries for bringing us Christianity, but now I think it is Britain that needs our help." He could well be right! However, if Macgregor Laird could read these words today one wonders how he would react, for one thing is certain - this was *not* an end result to his labours that he could possibly have envisaged, when he organised the first steamship expedition to the Niger in 1832!

The *Mary Kingsley* built in 1930

APPENDIX ONE

AIDE-MEMOIRE TO THE CONQUEST OF THE NIGER BY LAND AND SEA

484BC	Herodotus, African Traveller, born at Cappadocia
AD023	Gaius Plinius Secundus, writer on Africa born
AD127	Claudius Ptolemaeus (Ptolemy) writer on Africa born
AD900	Arab followers of Mohammed reach the Niger
1153	El Adrisa puts forward theory on the Niger
1349	Ibn Batuta, Arab traveller, sets out for Niger Country
1394	Prince Henry the Navigator born
1471	Gold trade opened up at Mina
1474	Las Casas, priest who started slave-trade born
1481	Portuguese reach the Gold Coast
1483	Pope John 11 declares himself to be the "Lord of Guinea."
1485	Portuguese explorer, Alfonso de Aviro, reaches Benin
1486	Prince Henry sends Batholomew Diaz on voyage to South Africa
1494	Leo Africanus, African Traveller, born
1497	Vasco Da Gama sets out for Africa
1511	Ferdinand V of Spain starts importation of Negro slaves into colonies
1553	English ships reach the Benin River
1554	English Expedition sets out for the West Coast of Africa
1557	Towrson's third voyage to the Coast
1618	The Company of the Adventurers of London Trading into Africa established
1620	Richard Jobson sails for the Gambia
1623	English start sending slaves to West Indies
1670	Royal African Company established
1713	The Assiento Company founded
1720	Society of Friends pass resolution condemning slavery
1736	Jonathon Hulls receives a patent for first steamboat
1752	Eighty-eight Liverpool vessels in 'Africa Trade'
1772	Granville Sharp argues against slavery in courts, wins Somerset case
1776	Motion put to the House that Slave-Trade was contrary to Laws of God
1783	Marquis de Jouffroy d'Abbans experiments with steam on River Doubs
1783	Fitch experiments with a steam boiler on the Delaware

1787	Society for the Abolition of the Slave Trade established
1788	The African Association established
1788	John Ledyard, African Traveller, reaches Cairo, and dies
1789	Lucas, African Traveller, arrives at Tripoli
1790	Captain Daniel Houghton, African Traveller, leaves England for The Gambia
1795	Mungo Park, African Traveller, sets out for Africa
1797	African Association send out another emmissary, Frederick Hornemann
1803	Symington builds steamboat *Charlotte Dundas*
1805	Mungo Park sets out on second expedition to Africa
1806	William Roscoe elected M.P.
1807	The Slave trade ended
1808	Henry Bell tries steamboat *Comet* on Clyde
1809	The *Accommodation*, first steamboat on the St. Lawrence
1816	Captain Tuckey sets out for the Congo
1816	Major Peddie reaches Kakondi, but fails to reach the Niger
1817	M. Bandia, African Traveller, reaches Panjikot, via Egypt
1817	The steam ferry boat *Etna* on the Mersey
1818	Ritchie and Lyon reach south-west border of Fezzan
1819	British West Africa Squadron starts anti-slavery patrols
1821	Steamship service established between Liverpool and Greenock
1821	Samuel Crowther, future Bishop of the Niger enslaved by raiders
1822	Clapperton, Oudney, and Denham, leave Murzak, bound for the Niger
1822	Denmark Vesey leads slave uprising in America
1825	Denham and Clapperton arrive back in England
1825	Clapperton starts again for the interior, with Richard Lemon Lander
1827	Clapperton dies at Changary, Lander continues with expedition
1827	Thomas Park sets out for Africa, to seach for information on his father
1828	Lander arrives back in England
1830	The Lander Brothers set out for Africa
1830	The Lander Brothers sail down the Niger, reaching the sea in December
1831	Richard and John Lander arrive back in England - acclaimed as heroes
1832	Laird - Lander Expedition leaves for the Niger, in *Quorra*, and *Alburkah*
1833	Macgregor Laird arrives back in England
1835	Great Western Railway Company plan to build the *Great Western*

1836	John Gladstone promotes 'Coolie Trade'
1838	The *Sirius* races the *Great Western* across the Atlantic, and wins
1838	Anti- Slavery Society opposes 'Coolie Trade'
1839	Buxton publishes 'The African Slave Trade and its Remedy'
1841	The steamship *President* lost without trace in Atlantic
1841	John Laird builds ships for the great Niger Expedition
1841	New Treaty negotiated with King Pepple to abolish slavery
1842	British West Africa squadron using five steamers for anti-slavery work
1844	Laird Brothers invest heavily in Birkenhead Dock Company
1849	John Beecroft lays the foundation of British rule in Nigeria
1850	Heinrich Barth, and Adolph Overweg, set out from Tripoli, bound for Niger
1852	Royal Charter granted to the African Steamship Company
1854	Barth meets Vogel in the Sudan
1854	Laird exploration vessel *Pleiad* leaves for the Niger
1855	Macgregor Laird stands down as Managing Director of A.S.Company
1856	William & Hamilton Laird managing the A.S. Company
1857	Macgregor Laird establishes the Central Africa Company
1857	The Laird exploration vessel *Dayspring* leaves for the Niger
1861	Macgregor Laird dies on 27 January
1861	Dr. Wm. Balfour Baike establishes a trading settlement at Lokoja
1862	Steamship *Macgregor Laird* launched
1864	Samuel Crowther consecrated Bishop of the Niger Territories
1868	John Dempster becomes agent for British & African Steam Navigation Co.
1875	African Steamship Company open own office in Liverpool
1879	Alfred Jones becomes junior partner in Elder Dempster & Company
1884	Elder and Dempster leave control of Company to Alfred Jones
1900	Alfred Jones described by Liverpool press as a 'Shipping Napoleon'
1900	Elder Dempster & Company move troops for Lord Kitchener
1901	Alfred Jones develops West Indies Fruit trade
1914	Elder Dempster & Company lose 43 ships in Great War
1932	Lord Kylsant's crash leads to re-structuring of Elder Dempster Fleets
1932	The Macgregor Laird Centenary Celebrations, at Liverpool and London, King George, The Prince of Wales, and Winston Churchill honour Laird

†APPENDIX TWO.

The Combined Elder Dempster Fleets, April, 1903

Abeokuta
Accra
Adansi
Akaba
Akassa
Albersville
Ancorra
Andoni
Anversville
Angola
Asaba
Ashanti
Axim
Kakana
Banana
Bathurst
Batanga
Bebguela
Benin
Biafra
Bida
Boma
Bonny
Bornu
Boulama
Baruta
Cabenda
Cameroon
Coomassie
Congo
Dahomey
Degama
Delta
Dodo
Egga
Egwana

Eko
Ekubo
Elmina
Ethiopia
Etolia
Fantee
Forcadas
Haussa
Iddo
Ilaro
Ilorin
Jebba
Kano
Kwarra
Lagoon
Lake Champlain
Lake Eyrie
Lake Manitoba
Lake Megantic
Lake Michigan
Lake Ontario
Lake Simcoe
Leon-Y-Castillio
Loanda
Loanga
Lycia
Llandulas
Madiera
Mandingo
Mayumba
Melville
Memmon
Milwaukee
Monmouth
Monrovia
Montauk

Monteagle
Montezuma
Montreal
Montrose
Monarch
Montcalm
Montenagro
Monterey
Montfort
Mount Royal
Mount Temple
Nigeria
Nyanga
Olenda
Oron
Perez Galdos
Philleville
Port Antonio
Port Maria
Port Morant
Port Royal
Prah
Roquelle
Sangara
Sansu
Sekondi
Sherbro
Sobo
Tarquah
Teneriffe
Viera-Y-Clavijo
Volta
Warri
Yola
Yoruba

APPENDIX THREE

The African Steamship Company Fleet, Prior to merger, 1932.
The British & African Steam Navigation Co. Fleet, Prior to merger,1932.

A.S.C.	B.& A.S.N.C.
Aba	*Abinsa*
Accra	*Achimota*
Alfred Jones	*Adda*
Apapa	*Barracoo*
Appam	*Bassa*
Badagry	*Bata*
Benguela	*Bathurst*
Boma	*Bereby*
Bompata	*Biafra*
Baruta	*Bodnant*
Calgary	*Boutry*
Calumet	*Cochrane*
Dagomba	*Deido*
Daru	*Eboe*
David Livingstone	*Egba*
Dixcove	*Egori*
Dunkwa	*Fantee*
Ebani	*Henry Stanley*
Edward Blyden	*Jebba*
Gaboon	*Macgregor Laird*
Gambia	*Mary Kingsley*
Jekri	*Mattawin*
Mary Slessor	*New Brighton*
Milverton	*New Brunswick*
New Brooklyn	*New Columbia*
New Georgia	*New Mexico*
New Texas	*William Wilberforce*
New Toronto	

SELECTIVE BIBLIOGRAPHY

General History

Akpofure, Rex, and Crowder, Michael, Nigeria. Faber and Faber, 1966

Baines, Thomas, History of Liverpool etc. Longman, Brown, Liverpool, 1825

Bindloss, Harold, In the Niger Country, Wm. Blackwood, London

Blower, B, The Mersey Ancient and Modern, E. Howell, Liverpool, 1878

Burdo, Adolphe, The Niger and the Benue, Richard Bentley, London, 1880

Burns, Sir Alan., History of Nigeria, Allen and Unwen, 1929

Burton, Richard (Anon. as F.R.G.S.) Wanderings in W. Africa, London, 1863

Crowder, Michael, The Story of Nigeria, Faber and Faber, 1962

Gentleman's Magazine, Nov. 1831, Re: Richard Lander and the Niger

Gores Directory, Annals of Liverpool, 1895

Hallett, Robin, Records of the African Association, Royal Geographical Society, 1964

Hewett, Capt. J.F.N., European Settlements on W. Coast of Africa, Hall, 1862

Hill, Christoper, Reformation to Industrial Revolution, Pelican Books, 1966

Howard, C, & J.H. Plumb, West African Explorers, Oxford University Press, 1951

Johnson, Sir Harry, Pioneers in West Africa, Blackie & Sons, London, 1912

Kingsley, Mary H., The Story of West Africa, Horace Marshall, London.

Pinnock, James, Benin, Journal of Commerce, Liverpool, 1897

Probate Register, 1861, Re: Will of Macgregor Laird, of Surbiton, Surrey

Probate Register, 1914, Re: Will of John Dempster, of Noctorum, Birkenhead

Probate Register, 1915, Re: Will of Alexander Elder, of Southport, Lancs.

Raphael, John R., Through Unknown Nigeria, Werner Laurie, London, 1914

Ridley, Jasper, Lord Palmerston, Constable, London, 1970

Smithers, Henry, Liverpool, its Commerce & Statistics, Thos. Kaye, Liverpool, 1825

Walker, F. Deaville, The Romance of the Black River, Church Missionary Soc., 1930

Wilson, Charles Morrow, Liberia, W. Sloane Associates, New York, 1947

Wilson, Rev. J. Leighton, Western Africa, Sampson Low & Co., London, 1856

General Shipping History

Birkenhead Docks' Bill, Sessions 1844, 1845, and 1847

Booth, E.C. Talbot, Ships of the British Merchant Navy, Melrose, London, 1932

Burn, Robert Scott, The Steam Engine, Ward, Locke & Bowden, N.Y., 1894

Chandler, George, Liverpool Shipping etc., Phoenix House, London

Hollett, David, Men of Iron, Story of Cammel Laird Shipbuilders, Countyvise, 1992

Holmes, Sir George, Ancient and Modern Ships, H.M. Stationery Office, 1906

Kennedy, John, History of Steam Navigation, C. Birchall, Liverpool, 1903

McIntyre, Birkenhead Yesterday & Today, Phillip Son & Nephew, 1948

Napier, James, Life of Robert Napier, Wm. Blackwood, London

Rose, J. Holland, Man and the Sea, Heffer & Sons, Cambridge

Smith, Capt. Edgar, Short History of Naval Engineering, Babcock & Wilcox, 1937

Tyler, David Budlong, Steam Conquers the Atlantic, Appleton Century, N.Y. 1939

White, L.G.W., Ships, Coolies and Rice, Sampson Low, Marston, London

Willox, John, The Steam Fleet of Liverpool, Journal of Commerce, 1865

Steamship Expeditions to the Niger

Allen, Capt.. Re: 1841 Exp., In Parliamentary Papers - Nov. 1847 - Vol. XX11

Baikie, Wm. Balfour, Exploring Voyage to Niger etc., John Murray, London, 1856

Crowther, Rev., Samuel, Expedition up the Niger & Tshadda, London, 1855

Hastings, A.C.G., The Voyage of the *Dayspring*, 1857, John Lane, 1926

Hutchinson, T.J., Narrative of Niger Exploration etc., Longman Brown, London, 1855

Laird, Macgregor, & Oldfield, R., Expedition into Interior of Africa, 1832 - 1834

Nautical Magazine, March, 1832, Re: Expedition to the Niger, 1832

Nautical Magazine, February, 1840, Re: 1832 Expedition.

Trotter, H. & Allen, H., Expedition to the Niger, 1841, Rch. Bently, London, 1848

Newspapers and Periodicals (in date order)

Gentleman Magazine, February, 1807, Re: Abolition of the Slave Trade

Gentleman Magazine, April, 1807, Re: Bill for Abolition of the Slave Trade

Liverpool Mercury, 12 October, 1821, Re: St. George Steam Packet Company

The Times, 14 May, 1832, Re: Anti-Slavery Meeting

Gentleman Magazine, September, 1834, Re: Richard Lander

Liverpool Albion, 28 December, 1835, Re: Laird v Dionysius Lardner on steam power

The Times, 2 June , 1840 - Re: Exeter Hall Anti-slavery Meeting

The Times, 24 March, 1841 - Re: Prince Albert's visit to Woolwich

The Times, 13 May, 1841, Re: Junius Smith and the ship *President*

The Globe, 26 June, 1844, Re: Birkenhead Docks' Bill

Greenock Advertiser, 23 May,1854 - Re: The Laird Family - Early History

Chambers Journal of Popular Literature, April, 1857, Re: Early Steamships
The Illustrated London News, 28 January, 1865, Re: Dr. Baikie
The Illustrated London News, 20 April, 1865, Re: The Town and Port of Liverpool
The Liverpool Review, 9 August, 1884 - Re: Slaveowning Liverpool
The Liverpool Review, 12 May, 1900, Re: Alfred Jones, and Elder Dempster & Co.
Journal of Commerce, July, 1913, Re: West Africa and Elder Dempster & Company
Elder Dempster Magazine, December, 1931, Re: Macgregor Laird
The Times, 27 January, 1932 Re: Macgregor Laird Expedition, 1832
Post and Mercury, 28 January, 1932, Re: Macgregor Laird Centenary
Liverpool Post & Mercury, 11 July, 1932 - Re: Macgregor Laird Centenary
The Times, 18 July, 1932, - Re: Macgregor Laird Centenary
Liverpool Post and Mercury, 18 July, 1932 - Re: Macgregor Laird Centenary
West African Review, 19 July, 1932, Re: Macgregor Laird Centenary
West Africa, 23 July, 1932, Re: Macgregor Laird Centenary
West African Review, August, 1932, Re: Macgregor Laird Centenary
West Africa Week, 23 July, 1932 Re: Niger Expedition
Journal of the African Society, October, 1932, Re: Niger and Maccgregor Laird
Mariners Mirror, Jan., 1937, (T. Sheppard, Hull), Re: The Steamship Sirious etc.
Sea Breezes, July - December, 1948, Re: Elder Dempster & Company
West African Review, December, 1951, Re: Macgregor Laird and the Niger
Journal of Commerce, 14 Nov. 1952, Re: City of Cork Steam Packet Company
Port of Liverpool News, Summer, 1966, Re: The Elder Dempster Story
Liverpool Daily Post, 13 December, 1991, Re: Slavery Haunts the Docks
The Times, 21 August, 1994, Re: African Missionaries fly to save Godless Britain
Dictionary of National Biography (Smith, Elder & Company, London, 1892)
Allan, William, (1793-1864) Naval Officer
Baikie, William Balfour, (1825-1864) Naturalist and Traveller
Banks, Sir Joseph, (1743-1820) President of Royal Society
Buxton, Sir Thomas Fowell, (1786-1865) Philanthropist
Clapperton, Hugh, (1788 - 1827) African Explorer
Denham, Dixon, (1786-1828) African Traveller
Laing, Alexander Gordon, (1793-1826) African Traveller
Laird, Macgregor, (1808-1861) African Explorer
Lander, John, (1807-1839) African Traveller

246

Lander, Richard Lemon, (1804-1834) African Traveller
Park, Mungo, (1771- 1806) African Explorer
Rathbone, William, (1757-1809) Merchant
Roscoe, William, (1753-1831) Historian
Wilberforce, William, (1759-1833) Philanthopist
Early African travellers
Africanus, Leo, History and Description of Africa (1600)
Baikie, Heinrich, Travels and Discoveries in North & Central Africa, London,
1857
Battuta, Ibn, Travels in Asia and Africa, 1325-1354, Routledge & Kegan Paul
Clapperton, Hugh, Journal of a second expedition, plus Lander, London, 1829
Denham, Clapperton & Oudney, Discoveries in Africa, 1822-1824, John
Murray
Lander, Richard & John, Expedition to Explore the Niger(1830) John
Murray,
Park, Mungo, Travels into the Interior of Africa in 1795 & 1797, London,
1799
Park, Mungo, Journal of a Mission to Africa etc., 1805, London, 1815
Slavery and Anti-Slavery
Buxton, Thomas Fowell, African Slave Trade & its Remedy, John Murray,
London
Crow, Captain Hugh, Memoirs of, Longman Rees, London. MDCCCXXX
Flannigan, Antigua and the Antiguans, Saunders and Otley, London, 1844
Goodell, Wm., Slavery and Anti-Slavery, Goodell, New York, 1853
Greg, W.R., Past & Present Efforts for ext. of African Slave Trade, London, 1840
Harris, John, A Century of Emancipation, Dent & Sons, London, 1933
Historic Society of Lancashire and Cheshire, 1853-4 , Gleanings from old
Newspapers
Journal of Negro History, V13
Liverpool and Slavery, Liverpool, 1884
Muir, Ramsay, A History of Liverpool, University Press, Liverpool, 1907
Parkinson, C. Northcote, The Rise of the Port of Liverpool.
Parliamentary Papers, Re: Slave Trade - V4 Sessions, 1847 (IUP)
Parliamentary Papers, Re: Macgregor Laird on Slave Trade, Colonies V2,
1842 (IUP)
Parliamentary Papers, Re: Macgregor Laird on Slave Trade, 1847-48 (IUP)
Parliamentary Papers, Select Committee on Slave Trade, 1849. V.5 (IUP)
Parliamentary Papers, Correspondence re: Slave Trade, 1845-59 Sessions.
(IUP)
Parliamentary Papers, Colonies, Africa, 1865 Sessions V.5 (IUP)
Picton, J. A. Memorials of Liverpool, G. Walmsley, Liverpool, 1903
Williams, Gomer, The Liverpool Privateers , Liverpool, 1897

Unpublished Material

Maude, John R., Family History, Re: Briggs, Surgeon of the 1832 Niger Expedition

Customs Registers, Liverpool, 1832, Re: Launch of exploration vessel Alburkah

Laird, Eleanor Bristow, Family Memoir - Laird Family, Central Library, Birkenhead

List of Ships Built by Laird Brothers - 1829 - 1943, Central Library, Birkenhead

The Jackson and Laird Families, (Bridget Jackson, 1990)

Origins of the Laird Family in Kilmalcolm, Williamson Museum, Birkenhead

INDEX

249

251

M'Lean, George, 83
Moffat, Robert, 151
Molieu, 51
Monfort, 230
Monrovia, 190
Monteagle, 230
Montreal, 228
Moorja, 42
Morocco, Sultan of, 15
Moss & Company, 200.201
Mozambique, 154
Muir, Professor Ramsay, 118
Mulet, 24
Murchison, Sir Roderick, 233
Muri Mountains, 193
Murray, Sir George, 63
Murzuk, 52
Myrmidon, 156

Napier, Robert, 144
Napoleon, 44.115.123
Napoleon, 135
Napoleonic Wars, 46.50
Nasamonians, 14
Nelson, 48
Netherlands West India Company, 28
New Brighton, 197
New Calabar River, 176
New Orleans, 129
New York, 146.147
New Zealand, 141.142
New Zealand Company, 141
Newcommen, Thomas, 127
Newport, Isle-of-Wight, 24
Nicholls, Henry, Explorer, 45
Nicolls, Colonel Edward, 91.96-100.
  123.131-133.175
Nicolls, Mrs., 131.132.139.175
Nicolls, Elanor Hestor (Laird), 93.131.
  139
*Niger,*182.192.200
Niger Mission, 211.220.238
Niger River (Throughout),
Nile River, 14.15.29.44.50
Norfolk, Duke of, 151
North American Squadron, 103
Nourse, James & Company, 103
Nun River, 77.83.84.100.158.210
Nupe, Kingdom of, 44.59.212. 217.218.
  220

Obie, King, 87.88.97
Ocean Steamship Company, 232

O'Connell, Daniel, M.P., 153.154
Ogilby, William Law, 179.181
Old Calabar, 100
Oldfield, R.A.K. 91.94-103.139.183.
  187
Olivier, Lord, 233-236
Onitsha, 205.211.218
Orange River, 16
Oudney, Walter, 52.54
Overweg, Doctor Adolph, 176.177

Paine's 'Rights of Man', 110
Palm-Oil-Trade, 77.196.197
Palmerston, Lord, 173.175.204
Panjikot, 51
Papin – Inventor, 127
Park, Mungo, 22.39-52.59.63.214
Park, Thomas, 48
Parliamentary Reform, 110
Parliamentary Select Committee on
  Slavery, 174
Parliamentary Select Committee on
  West Africa, 125
Parry, Admiral Sir William, 148.149
Pearce, Captain, 57
Peddie, Major, 50
Peel, Sir Robert, 151.154.155.174
Pepple, King William, 172.176
Perier, Jacques Constantin, 128
Pim, Joseph Robinson, 131.137.139
Pinteado, Anes, 23
Pisania, 46
Pitt, William, 109.112.113.155
Pleiad, 179-202.204
Po, Fernao do, 15
Polo, Marco, 15
Pope John II, 16
Pope Leo X, 21.29
Port Praya, 78.81
Porto Rico, 19.22.25
Portobello, 31
Portsmouth, 21.45
Portugal, 15-19.22.26.28.62.111.155.
  162.170.171
Potingar, 91
Potter, William, 173
President, 146.147
Prester John, 22
Prince of Wales, 235.236
Princes' Island, 170
Privateers – Liverpool, 115
Protector of the Indians, 20
Ptolemaeus, Claudius, 14

St. Helena, 230
Stranger, Doctor, 157.163
Strathcona's Horse, 230
Sunbeam, 204.205.214.217.218
Susan, 83.84
Swiftsure, 129
Symington, William, 128

Taura, Kaafa, 42
Taylor, James, 128
Taylor, Rev. J. C., 207.209.211.218
Taylor, Captain Thomas, 183-194
Tebu Desert, 56
Tenerife, 187.200.207.228.230
Thomas, 69-71
Tigris, 138
Timbuctoo (Timbuktu etc.), 14.21.33.41.
45.48.50.58
Tintam, John, 18
Torrens, Colonel, 141
Towrson, of Newport, 24
Trinity, 24
Tripoli, 37.56.58.63
Trotter, Captain H. D., 96.148.150.151.
155.159.162.163.167.172.177.191
Trueman, Hanbury & Company, 124
Truro, 58
Tuckey, Captain, 50
Tyger, 24
Tyson, Captain, 64

Unicorn, 24
United Africa Company, 232

Vasa, Gustavus, 120
Venn, Rev. Henry, 172.220.222
Vernon & Company, 201
Vesey, Denmark, 112
Victory, 25
Vogel, Doctor, 157.177
Volta, 225
Volta River, 18

Wakefield, E. G., 141.142
Wallasey, 76
Wangara, Sea of, 14
Warburton, Bishop, 29.107
Washington, George, 32
Waterloo, 129
Watt, James, 110
Webster, Daniel, 173
Weeks, Bishop, 172
Wellington, Duke of, 48

Wesley, John, 106
West Africa Review, 237
West Africa Squadron,
71.73.103.123.164.169-173.176
West Indies, 28.31.32.103.106.109.
121.124.168.235
West Indies Fruit Trade, 231
West Indies Squadron, 103
White Nile, 33
Wilberforce, 124.156.157.158.162
Wilberforce, Archdeacon, 154
Wilberforce, William, 31.104.105.109.
112.113.114.121.124
William III, King, 29.107
William, Duke of Gloucester, 29
William Harris, 72
Woolf, Leonard, 237
Worcester, 41
Wordsworth, William, 123
World War (1914-1918), 231
Wow Wow, 59
Wylde, Captain, 201
Wyndham, Captain Thomas, 23.24
Wyvill's Yorkshire Movement, 110

Ximes, Cardinal, 19.20

Yaruba Country, 187.218
Yella Rapids, 50
Yimmahah, 91
York, 135
York, Duke of, 29
Yorke, Sir John, 24
Yoruba, Kingdom of, 18.218

Zaki, King Sumo, 213.218
Zambesi River, 29
Zuma – Widow, 59